Colonizing Sex

*Sexology and Social Control
in Modern Japan*

Sabine Frühstück

UNIVERSITY OF CALIFORNIA PRESS
Berkeley · Los Angeles · London

University of California Press
Berkeley and Los Angeles, California

University of California Press, Ltd.
London, England

© 2003 by the Regents of the University of California

Library of Congress Cataloging-in-Publication Data

Frühstück, Sabine.
    Colonizing sex : sexology and social control in modern Japan / Sabine Frühstück.
        p.   cm. — (Colonialisms ; 4)
    Includes bibliographical references and index.
    ISBN 0-520-23547-9 (cloth : alk. paper)—
    ISBN 0-520-23548-7 (pbk. : alk. paper)
        1. Sexology—Japan.   2. Sex role—Japan.   3. Sex customs—Japan.   4. Sex in popular culture—Japan. 5. Body, Human—Social aspects—Japan.   6. Social control—Japan.   7. Japan—Social life and customs. 8. Japan—Foreign relations.   9. Japan—Politics and government.   I. Title.   II. Series.
HQ18.J3 F78   2003
306.7'0952—dc21   2003002461

Manufactured in the United States of America

12   11   10   09   08   07   06   05   04   03
10   9   8   7   6   5   4   3   2   1

The paper used in this publication is both acid-free and totally chlorine-free (TCF). It meets the minimum requirements of ANSI/NISO Z39.48–1992 (R 1997) (Permanence of Paper). ⊚

Colonizing Sex

COLONIALISMS

Jennifer Robertson, General Editor

Contents

Illustrations

Acknowledgments

I began research for this project with my dissertation (completed in 1996), under the guidance of Sepp Linhart and Helga Nowotny, then both at the University of Vienna. Sepp taught me to be an intrepid adventurer and to examine the road maps, that is, all sources, as carefully as possible before embarking on my scholarly journey. Helga helped me muster the courage it takes to think things through and the boldness it takes to write them down. I will always be grateful to them both.

I run every new idea and any little discovery by Thomas Ludwig first. I thank him for his continued enthusiasm and critical support, without which this book would not have been nearly as pleasurable and gratifying to research and write. I also owe heartfelt thanks to Jennifer Robertson, who has read numerous drafts of this book. Her interest in my work has encouraged me tremendously over the years. I regard it a great honor to have my book included in her Colonialisms series.

I also feel indebted to colleagues and friends, several of whom have read drafts of the entire manuscript or individual chapters, for their critiques, expertise, and the opportunities to exchange ideas: my thanks to Akagawa Manabu, Jim Bartholomew, Kasia Cwiertka, Elise Edwards, Tak Fujitani, Furukawa Makoto, Shel Garon, Allan Grapard, Ann Herring, Inoue Shōichi, Bill Johnston, Kawai Yū, Kawamura Kunimitsu, Tom Laqueur, Stewart Lone, Morris Low, Regine Mathias-Pauer, Matsubara Yōko, Muta Kazue, Nagai Yoshikazu, Nakajima Hideto, Sumiko

Otsubo, Greg Pflugfelder, Don Roden, Saitō Hikaru, Miriam Silverberg, Brigitte Steger, Takahashi Ichirō, and Ueno Chizuko. Laurie Monahan has helped me see images, including those in this book, in new ways.

The development of this book was greatly facilitated by the hospitality of Tominaga Shigeki and Yokoyama Toshio at the Institute of Research in Humanities, Kyoto University (1992–1994), Hirowatari Seigo at the Institute of Social Science, University of Tokyo (1998–1999 and 2001), Andrew Barshay at the Center for Japanese Studies, University of California at Berkeley (2001–2002), and Jean Oi at the Center for East Asian Studies, Stanford University (2001–2002). I thank them for providing me with the opportunity to pursue the research and writing for this book in their midst. I am also indebted to my colleagues at the Department for East Asian Languages and Cultural Studies at the University of California at Santa Barbara; they have been supportive in many ways, including graciously allowing me time to complete this book.

I also am grateful to Lisa Rosenblatt and Patricia Marby Harrison, who edited and polished the text before it met any reviewer's critical eye. Three anonymous readers for the University of California Press have made invaluable suggestions. At the press, I owe special thanks to my editor Sheila Levine for her encouragement and patience and to Jan Spauschus for meticulous copy editing. I am also grateful to Mary Severance, who has expertly ushered the book through the publication process.

My research and writing in Austria, Japan, and the United States were generously supported by the following institutions, fellowships, and grants: the Japanese Ministry of Education Postgraduate Fellowship (1992–1994); the Tamaki Foundation research grant (1995); the Japan Foundation Postdoctoral Fellowship (1998–1999); a postdoctoral grant from the Faculty of the Humanities and Social Sciences, University of Vienna (1999); and the University of California President's Fellowship in the Humanities (2001–2002).

Introduction

Modernity is an endeavour: the discovery and appropriation
of desire.

> Henri Lefebvre, *Introduction to Modernity*

Sexuality is not the most intractable element in power relations, but rather one of those endowed with the greatest
instrumentality: useful for the greatest number of maneuvers
and capable of serving as a point of support, as a linchpin,
for the most varied strategies.

> Michel Foucault, *The History of Sexuality*

This book is a history of sexual knowledge in modern Japan and the uses
made of that knowledge. It examines radical changes in the perception
and description as well as the colonization of sex and sexuality. It follows the close and complicated exchanges about sexual behavior among
governmental agencies, scholars and other intellectuals, social reformers, the media, and the wider public in order to reconstruct the processes
of normalization, medicalization, and pedagogization. In addition, the
book traces the countless modifications in the modes by which sexual
knowledge was circulated, valorized, attributed, and appropriated. The
underlying structure of this book is informed by various sites and the
connections among them—sites where normative ideas about sex were
created, examined, weighed, transformed, and translated into cultural
practices in an effort to "colonize" the sex and sexuality of the Japanese
populace.

As with other instances of colonization (Osterhammel 1999 [1995]:
41), the colonization I describe here was not carried out via swift attacks
on unsuspecting victims but came about gradually. It began with what
a geographer or military man would call the reconnaissance of the un-

known terrain, including the discovery by military surgeons of a high rate of venereal disease among members of the imperial army in the 1880s and the recognition by pediatricians of infantile sexual desire around 1900. Through several phases, the colonization of sex shifted toward the development of what a colonialist would consider a complete colonial ruling apparatus. For example, sex for soldiers was eventually provided within and restricted to "comfort stations" under military control; parents, school and factory physicians, teachers, and, later, officials in the Ministry of Education and the Ministry of Health and Social Welfare became entrusted with the informed guidance of children's sexuality; and ordinary women and men were expected to consult eugenic marriage offices in order to ensure that their sexual union would result in desirable offspring or birth control advice offices to prevent the birth of undesired children.

Perhaps the colonization of sex has never reached a state of completeness. At certain moments in the modern history of Japan, however, it seems as if the boundaries and the control of the new terrain of knowledge about sex and sexuality were firmly set, while places within this terrain were (re)named, once and for all.

My analysis centers on the strategies employed in the colonization of sex in Japan. I am interested in the techniques at work in the conflicts and negotiations that aimed at the creation of a normative Japanese sexuality. This sexuality was viewed as existing primarily between women and men, and it was documented in military data that reflected soldiers' health, in moral police registers that tracked prostitutes and their diseases, in sex education for youth, and in pronatalist and expansionist propaganda that sought to reduce frigidity in women and impotence in men. This normative sexuality was declared vital to the health, improvement, and future of the Japanese empire.

The colonization of sex in Japan involved complicated power relations marked by two distinct technologies, those of bodily discipline and mass regulation. Power, as Michel Foucault noted, works on the entire surface of the social field via a system of relays, connections, and transmissions; it is never monolithic. Every moment of negotiation over the understanding of sexuality in modern Japan reveals power functioning in myriad small ways—in the various conflicts between scientific and popular knowledge, the political uses of science, and the interactions between Japan's and other national cultures' knowledge in the field of sexology.

Power relations formed the various threads—some tightly knotted, some loosely woven—that came to constitute a complex texture of debates on numerous issues: the necessity of sex education in the broadest sense, to improve the physical and mental health of the populace on the one hand and to "liberate sex" on the other hand; the prevention of venereal diseases; the problem of masturbation (which was often collapsed into the new category of homosexuality) and its alleged consequences (including mental illnesses, venereal diseases, and tuberculosis); the legalization of birth control and other objectives of Japan's nascent women's movement; the fight against prostitution (which was most often a fight against prostitutes, rarely against pimps, and hardly ever against clients); the emergence of "positive" and "negative" eugenics; and eventually, the implementation of "racial hygiene" policies at the expense of sex research and education.

These debates were carried out in a heterogeneous, changing forum. I analyze shifts in the cultural meanings of sex and sexuality between various debates about sex and identify the main actors—scientific experts, administrators and politicians, media, and the wider public as represented by various social reform groups—involved in the construction and normalization of Japanese sexuality. Government agencies, scholars, and social reformers differed in their aims as well as their methods, but they were connected by a common desire to understand, document, and guide the sexual practices and attitudes of the Japanese populace. Even specialists' efforts to encourage members of the public to reveal details about their sex lives in order to gain data, legitimacy, and status for their goal of launching a "radical sex education" program *(kyūshinteki seikyōiku)* were grounded in arguments about "scientific expertise." Their expert status was contested, however, and was constantly being renegotiated.

Closely connected to the colonialist strategies I examine are the practices of medicalization and pedagogization that depicted the individual body as a miniature of the social, the national, and the imperial body. Throughout the late nineteenth century, the primary emphasis of these efforts was on the male body, thus designing the national body as decisively, if implicitly, male. The normalization of sex drew into its web all-male conscripts and soldiers who came to be considered constituent of the national condition, the consolidation of the nation, modernity, and progress—in short, who came to embody the Japanese nation to be achieved.

From the 1910s onward, these efforts seem to have been complemented or even superseded by a significantly increased medical and pedagogical interest in the female body. Curiously, when politico-economic activities decisively shifted toward imperialist actions in East and Southeast Asia, the expansive qualities of the (fertile) female physique appeared in the foreground of the discourse of sex, revealing a preoccupation with the womb, the uterus, fertility, and race. This singling out of the uterus as the most important organ of the female body and of the race may have had to do with obstetricians' anxiety about their status within the medical profession (Gallagher and Laqueur 1987:x–xi), but it also fed into efforts to elevate the value of women's reproductive organs for empire building.

Accordingly, the colonization of sex occasionally foreshadowed, or coincided and overlapped with, the Japanese imperialist penetration of East and Southeast Asia. In contrast to these external activities, efforts at national unity and imperial prosperity in the realm of sex and sexuality primarily produced processes and practices of "internal colonization," or battles against enemies within Japan. These battles were driven by a historically specific, multifold rhetoric that consisted of cries for defense and security and for liberation and truth, thus emphasizing in every historical moment how the sexual body has been (and is) part of a much broader current in political and cultural life.

The first pair of powerful rhetorical figures, defense and security, referred not only to military operations or planning but also to a general state of mind. Defense, once classified by Henri Lefebvre (1995 [1962]: 190) as the key element of the modern notion of well-being, represented a political and intellectual commitment to the protection of Japan against Western colonial powers, disease, and moral degeneration. By the 1890s, military surgeons and administrators had begun to plead for the defense of soldiers' health against prostitutes' venereal diseases. Around 1900, pedagogues set out to secure children from their own (subconscious) desires and the (sexual) dangers of a modern society. During the 1920s and 1930s, some sexologists took it upon themselves to defend what they perceived as sexual normalcy against perversion. And during the occupation era, officials called for the protection of impoverished girls from (sexual) seduction by the occupation forces—even while aggressively recruiting women to serve the nation as prostitutes (Kanzaki 1954a, 1954b, 1955). The rhetoric of defense and security was applied to and connected with perceptions of the national body, public health, and sexuality. It also tied in with the language of liberation and that of its counterpart, oppression.

While Foucault (1990 [1978]) and subsequent historians of sex and sexuality have questioned the assumption that repression was an evil reality and that a historical transition could be traced leading to emancipation, my study highlights the frequent recurrence—each time in a slightly different guise and at the hands of different actors—of the repression and liberation of sex throughout Japan's modern history. At the beginning of the twentieth century, medical doctors, pedagogues, and sex educators invoked the (necessity of) the liberation of sex in order to shed oppressive traditional beliefs and to unburden sex of mystification. Immediately after the end of World War II, officials in the ministries of education and health and welfare again declared sex and sexuality in need of liberation, this time from the militarist and fascist regulations of the wartime regime. For its proponents during the 1920s and 1930s, the liberation of sex implied the liberation of women from involuntary motherhood and from social inequity in general. In the minds of reformers of that era, a liberated sexuality would catapult the working class out of poverty. Very few of them imagined sexual liberation as a component or consequence of revolution; most insisted that its central tool was sexual knowledge based on scientific facts, or simply the truth about sex. While most historiographical accounts of sexuality in Japan focus on analyzing notions of gender and the erotic (Silverberg 1998), gender ambivalence and ambiguity (Roden 1990; Robertson 1989, 1992, 1998, 1999), homosexuality (Pflugfelder 1999; Robertson 1999), and other aspects of the eroticization of gender and sexuality (Muta 1992; Ueno 1990), I explore the obsession with the "truth about sex" and the use of the phrase as a discursive tool.

As much as negotiations over a modern understanding of sexuality in Japan intersected with concepts of nation and empire building and overlapped with debates about the nature of Japanese culture and the project of modernity, they also functioned to increase the premium placed on scientific-mindedness. On the one hand, scientific knowledge gained ground compared to other forms of knowledge claims. With respect to sexual practices, Yamamoto Senji, for example, forcefully proclaimed "seeking the truth" *(shinjitsu no tsuikyū)* as his goal (see Odagiri 1979a). On the other hand, knowledge about sex in modern Japan was perceived as dangerous to produce, possess, and spread. This book traces the specific activities and practices that complicated and diversified the discourse of sex by addressing questions of who was talking about sex, what they felt was at stake, and which state and private-sector institutions collected, documented, and disseminated material about sex and sexology.

One central idea was shared not only by the sexologists but by all participants in the modern and scientific-minded discourse of sex—an idea that would continue to inform ongoing arguments for and against sex education. Proponents and opponents of sex education were convinced that accurate knowledge would lead to "correct" behavior, and that the correctness of the latter could be measured by its social consequences. Advocates of divergent aims—such as individualization of birth control choices, improvement in the living standards of and liberation of underprivileged groups, and state enforcement of "racial hygiene" programs—could all successfully invoke science and the value of scientific-mindedness. Thus they contributed in very different ways to drawing more and more issues formerly not thought of as sexual under the umbrella of the science of sex.

The formation of the Japanese nation-state in the 1870s brought about new concepts of the populace as a social organism to be protected, nurtured, and improved by a public health system borrowed primarily from Prussia and other European countries. By the 1880s, the state had developed powerful instruments with which to investigate, manage, and control the health (more precisely, the sexual health) of the populace in order to build a modern health regime—the subject of chapter 1. Statistics and other forms of mapping the Japanese population seemed to play a modest supporting role for administrative mechanisms and military purposes. However, in Japan as in other countries, they also created new categories of people.

The new technologies of categorization and representation in social scientific terms created a national body that had not existed before. As Ian Hacking has suggested, its components were not "real" entities that awaited scientific discovery. However, once certain distinctions had been made, new realities effectively came into being. Far from creating a prioritized interest in a binary, dichotomous distinction between heterosexual and homosexual, the processes of "making up people" (Hacking 1999 [1986]:161–163) produced a great variety of sexual types— the syphilitic soldier, the masturbating child, the homosexual youth, the infertile (or frigid) woman, the neurasthenic white-collar worker, and the sexually and militarily impotent warrior.

Between the late 1870s and the early 1940s, debates on what had come to be known in Japan as the "sexual question" were as multifaceted as their participants were diverse. During that seventy-year period, a new system was established that enabled officials to undertake a detailed observation of the Japanese people in the name of public health.

The year 1872 marked one beginning of this new health regime, which was based on a new medical system and a strong emphasis on public hygiene and preventive medicine. Ann Bowman Jannetta (1987, 1997) has shown the enormous importance of this medical system in the prevention of epidemics in early modern Japan. I am interested in how the medical system contributed to the concern of the state and its agencies about matters of sexual practice.

The year 1872 also marked the introduction of compulsory elementary education for both sexes and compulsory military service for twenty-year-old men in Japan. Initially, soldiers and prostitutes were the main targets of investigation by the police and military authorities. They also were examined and observed by physicians and surveyed and documented by government public health agencies. Although only a small portion of the twenty-year-old male population was drafted for military service during peacetime, virtually all men of that age underwent a thorough medical examination and were categorized according to a four-tier system of physical fitness. Prostitutes were considered a necessary evil, mere instruments for keeping soldiers' and other men's sexual needs in check. They were regarded as primary carriers of venereal disease far into the twentieth century and were put under increasingly restrictive regulations in the name of the health and welfare of the population in general and soldiers and mothers and children in particular, all of whom were presumed "innocent."

In addition to conscripts and prostitutes, children were identified from the turn of the twentieth century onward as crucial to the health and future of the Japanese body politic. Their anatomical features were measured, their mental and physical conditions diagnosed, and their development closely monitored. Kathleen Uno (1991, 1999) has charted how social reformers at the beginning of the twentieth century widely promoted concepts of institutional child welfare. My approach allows me to examine how the newly developed academic fields of pediatrics and pedagogy identified children as sexual beings whose sexual desire (seiyoku) was recognized and repeatedly confirmed through hitherto unprecedented and regular examinations by a network of school physicians.

It was the new theories of child development that prompted discussions about the necessity of instructing children and youth on their sexuality and the obligation to help parents, teachers, and other social actors guide children's sexual development and maturation. In adults, an excessive sex life was perceived as a precursor to mental illness, tuberculosis, and venereal disease. In children, nervous exhaustion *(shinkei karō)* and masturbation were attributed to misdirected sexual desire. Hence, the sex education of children moved to center stage in the discourse on the improvement of the national body, a discourse that continued through the twentieth century.

In chapter 2, I analyze in depth the first debate on sex education printed in September and October 1908 in Japan's third-largest nationally distributed newspaper, the *Yomiuri Shinbun*. In this published debate, pedagogues and medical doctors presented their views on whether and how children should be educated about sexual desire. The confessions of children, ideas on masturbation and venereal disease, debates about normalcy and deviance, the responsibility of teachers and parents, the authority of experts, and the international character of sexual knowledge generated a discursive configuration that characterized the colonization of sex in children. Infantile sexuality was put under surveillance, became a "center of knowledge" (Stoler 1999 [1995]:142), was labeled both endangered and dangerous, and was exploited as a locus of defense: to defend the child came to mean to defend the nation. Infantile sexuality was of crucial importance because the child's body impersonated the empire's future.

Notions that connected the infantile body with the Japanese national/imperial body informed discussions and texts about sex throughout the first half of the twentieth century. By the second decade of the twentieth century, sexual issues previously discussed only within the boundaries of specialized journals of medicine, pediatrics, and psychiatry were capable of reaching the entire reading public of Japan, due to the introduction of universal education and the expansion of the print media market. The publication in 1908 of a series on the "sexual question" in the *Yomiuri Shinbun* was intended to provoke a sense of urgency among parents, teachers, scientists, and bureaucrats. It also effectively anchored the sexual issue in the public consciousness, as sex education became a perennial theme in general-interest papers and magazines, popular medical journals, and women's magazines.

The series of articles on sex education both broadened and deepened during the 1920s and 1930s. Self-appointed experts from the academic fields of zoology, biology, and medicine, as well as from education and the arts, attempted to create a new science of sex *(seikagaku* or *seigaku)*. These sexologists *(seigakusha* or *seikagakusha)* are the protagonists of chapter 3. They were a mixed bunch of men and a few women at the margins of academia who set out to push for the creation and popularization of sexual knowledge, the education of "the masses" about "correct" and "normal" sexual behavior, and the establishment of sexology as a field of knowledge.

Since James Bartholomew's (1989) path-breaking investigation into the formation of science, a number of scholars have studied the development of scholarly disciplines and scientific ideas in modern Japan, tracing histories of the social sciences (Kawai T. 1989, 1991, 1994), ethnography (Silverberg 1992), history (S. Tanaka 1993; Conrad 1999), and eugenics and racial hygiene (Doak 1997; Otsubo and Bartholomew 1998; Morris-Suzuki 1998; Otsubo 1999; Robertson 2001). Compared to many of the leading characters in these stories, sexologists were marginal to the academic world. But at the beginning of the twentieth century, sexologists shared—along with representatives of the younger generation of ethnographers, historians, and social scientists—the will to establish a new field of knowledge and change society in general. Sexologists were less interested in the formulation of a theory of sex or the design of a sexual paradigm than in a comprehensive sexual reform centered on what some of them tried to establish as purely scientific sexual knowledge. In order to mobilize allies from diverse groups in pursuit of this goal, they created a new discursive space in which to generate public controversy about sexual questions. The success of their efforts hinged on connecting various scientific groups and their allies with the wider educated public and with more specific audiences. Moreover, they had to win over powerful elites and institutions and to lobby continually to ensure their own legitimacy as experts and control over the production of sexual knowledge.

This heterogeneous group did not produce the "truth about sex" in a singular, esoteric way but rather pursued goals that were articulated differently by each player at different historical moments. Statisticians of the Japanese Bureau of Hygiene who documented venereal disease among prostitutes in the 1890s clearly had different goals in mind than did the editors of sexological journals who in the 1920s published graphic images to illustrate a set of detailed instructions on the insertion and function of intrauterine devices, or the censors from special units of the Special Higher Police (Tokubetsu Kōtō Keisatsu) who confiscated sexological journals but let advertisements for potency-enhancing products slip through their otherwise tight-knit network of social control.

The statistics produced by Japanese government agencies after the 1870s are different in nature from the results of surveys conducted in the 1920s by sexologists: the former were large, homogenous samples fo-

cusing on disease, while the latter were small, heterogeneous samples focusing on a broad range of questions on sexual behavior and designed
to explore the whole range of sexual practice and—in some cases—
to eventually draw a line between "normal" and "abnormal" sexual behavior. Similarly, knowledge about sex was transformed considerably
through the disputes on sexual questions that were engaged in by a variety of actors throughout the late nineteenth and the first half of the
twentieth century. What began as a controversy over sex education resulted in highly diversified debates on masturbation, venereal disease,
birth control, and prostitution.

Central to the discussion in chapter 3 are sexologists' attempts to
professionalize sexology through such measures as conducting an empirical survey of sexual practices (roughly two decades before Alfred C.
Kinsey's famous first report), founding sexological journals, and building alliances with other social reformers. Editors and contributing
authors repeatedly emphasized the importance of a "truly scientific"
knowledge of sex based on findings from the Japanese population rather
than results of sex research conducted in Germany, Austria, England,
France, or the United States. At the same time, they insisted that direct
interaction and exchange with the general populace would ensure that
sexual knowledge was adapted and disseminated to those who needed
it most.

The publication goals of each journal were spelled out in prefatory
editorials. For example, the editor's note in the journal *Sexuality (Sei)*
promised to guide young people's sexual development so as to ensure
that adultery, wild marriages, and abortions would disappear from society. Certain that critics would question the seriousness of the journal,
the publishers of *Sexuality* addressed mothers specifically, declaring that
they should at least have a look at the journal before dismissing it, especially as it had been approved as a professional journal by the authorities. "*Sexuality*," the editor concluded, "represents the view that it
is necessary to know about humans and to research them" (*Sei* November 1927: editorial).

Sexologists positioned themselves according to the needs and characteristics of their immediate audience, which was far from diffuse, undif-
ferentiated, or passive. The audiences they reached were the educated
public, various professionals, secondary school and university students,
and business groups. These audiences were of course historically
specific. In the 1880s, a typical seventeen-year-old girl from Tokyo most
likely had no formal secondary education. By 1925, however, she had a

good chance of attending one of 618 girls' high schools and of reading one of the books or journals on sexual questions that flourished at
that time.

Anticipating their audience's social makeup, sexologists posed as
experts on sexual questions when criticizing sociopolitical policies for
the prevention of venereal disease and as confidantes when asked by
members of the literate public for advice on sexual problems. They presented themselves as defenders of scientific freedom when criticizing
censorship of their publications and as progressive reformers when they
railed against the unscientific, superstitious nature of traditional practices and those promoted by the new religions (i.e., Omotokyō, Ten-
rikyō, and Hitonomichi Kyōdan). Japanese tradition was denounced as
uncivilized, and the authority of Western culture in general and of Western science in particular was emphasized to establish and ensure expert
status for these first self-trained Japanese sexologists.

Sexologists pursued the appropriation and popularization of their
special science with just as much enthusiasm as they engaged in actual
empirical research. Chapter 4 sheds light on the problems involved in the
popularization of sexological ideas within the politically, scientifically,
and socially controversial conditions of the production, collection, and
dissemination of sexual knowledge during the early twentieth century.
The boundaries between "pure" scientific knowledge and "unscientific"
popular knowledge were purposefully blurred; the popularization of
sexual knowledge thus was not a straightforward, top-down process that
disseminated preestablished scientific ideas to a less educated, anonymous public. Rather, in the case of sexology, it consisted of a set of strategies designed and deployed to further the development of a "science of
sex" outside the universities.

These strategies included public lectures followed by question-and-
answer sessions with local audiences, radio interviews with sexologists,
publication of articles in a wide array of media targeting different levels
of literacy and education, and extensive use of advice columns for sexual problems. The popularization of their ideas was crucial for sex reformers and researchers, who perceived the population as a whole to
be their laboratory. Their science was not to be developed within the
boundaries of academic institutions. It would flourish only if it grew
out of interactions with a wider public and only if it were based on alliances with other social reformers who would make the search for the
"truth about sex," along with the legalization of birth control and the
liberation of prostitutes and of the working class more generally, one of

their aims. Certainly these alliances brought about the mechanisms of social management Sheldon Garon (1997) has discussed with respect to religious groups, the women's movement, and the anti-prostitution movement.

Simultaneously, Japanese government officials continued to gather statistical data on physical and mental health as well as on venereal diseases; scientists adopted the vocabulary and content of Western science and tested them in Japanese contexts; and social movements made the reform of sexual habits and behavior their main agenda. Each of these three actors—government officials, scientists, and social reformers—assumed several roles. Government officials supported and relied on the work of some scientific and medical experts even as they hindered or rejected the research of others. Scientists doubled as social activists, founders of political parties, and party functionaries. Doctors treated neurasthenia and venereal diseases and also wrote novels and journalistic accounts about sex. Politicians founded movements to abolish prostitution. Women's rights activists translated works by Western sex researchers and circulated petitions to repeal abortion laws, among other legislation.

Invoking the rhetoric of scientific authority, sexologists insisted that sexology was a science and defended it against criticism from the more established academic disciplines. Treading a fine line between collusion with and distance from government institutions, Japanese sexologists countered repressive state measures with arguments based on public health and population policy. They found allies among members of women's rights groups who were working to introduce new ideas about and techniques of birth control. Their attempts to propagate sex education were supported by representatives of the anti-prostitution movement. Meanwhile, the reading public was won over both by informative articles about sex and by erotic-pornographic stories published in sexological journals as well as in general-interest magazines and newspapers.

The late 1930s and early 1940s were marked by an increasing militarism that left little space for individual decisions in terms of sexuality and other realms of life, and which was accompanied by a pronatalist ideology best illustrated by the slogan "procreate and multiply." A new discourse of eugenics and racial hygiene—borrowed mainly from national-socialist Germany—brought about laws that enabled physicians to legally perform abortions and sterilizations of people with venereal disease, alcoholism, epilepsy, and other diseases that were defined as "hereditary." The sex reformers' program of creation and dissemination of accurate knowledge about sex—which was directed toward the decrease of poverty, the promotion of lasting worldwide peace, the improvement of maternal health, the elimination of illegal abortions, and the improvement of the Japanese race—was hampered by the state's program of population growth, the object of analysis in chapter 5.

Albeit never completely out of sight, interest in the history of eugenics has been refueled by recent debates about euthanasia, scandals about forced sterilization of the mentally ill in some Western countries until very recently, and concerns about the reintroduction of the national-socialist concept of the "unfit." Matsubara Yōko's intriguing study and Sumiko Otsubo's ongoing work on the subject in Japan highlight crucial actors at the center of the crossroads of academe and the state between the late nineteenth century and the 1950s (Matsubara 1997, 1998, 2000; Otsubo and Bartholomew 1998; Otsubo 1999).

In this book, I explore what the rise of eugenics and racial hygienic thought did to the sexological project when, from the 1920s onward, sexologists were lumped together with pacifists, socialists, communists, and anarchists and regarded as a nuisance or even a danger to the imperialist state. While some of the more outspoken sexologists were silenced through house arrest, imprisonment, or, in at least one case, murder, others were won over by an ideology that was directed at the multiplication of healthy citizens through all possible means. Yamamoto Senji was fatally stabbed in 1929 when he spoke out against Japan's aggressive policy toward China. Abe Isoo, on the other hand, the founder of Japan's first socialist party and a leading crusader for what he called the "liberation of prostitutes," was celebrated for his promotion, in the late 1930s, of early marriages as an expedient means of increasing the population. Katō Shizue, eulogized today as the "grande dame of birth control" in Japan, did not speak publicly on birth control from 1937 to the end of World War II and, during the 1950s and 1960s, opposed the legalization of the contraceptive pill.

Debates about sex overlapped at times with eugenics, the science of "improving" the human race by controlling heredity. For example, in a reflection of an argument that was eugenic at its core, all participants believed that the spread of knowledge about sex would improve individual and social life and secure the future of the Japanese populace. However, sexology was a potentially explosive subject for two reasons, one concerning the nature of sexual knowledge itself, the other concerning the various publics that were supposedly in need of sex education. Like other intellectuals who advocated empirical research on Japan's social problems, sex researchers worked toward social reform and thus were often suspected—in some cases, rightly so—of sympathizing with socialist and revolutionary causes. In their eyes, the dissemination of sexual knowledge would help liberate the working class from its misery and women from their roles as "childbearing machines." Anticipating this view, some government officials translated the sex reformers' vision of a better society into a scenario of social unrest and disorder. They feared not only that women would turn the gendered order of society (as reflected in Japan's Civil Code of 1889) upside down if given the means to control family size, but also that the middle and upper classes, which were considered intellectually and morally superior, would contribute less to population growth than would the lower classes.

Beginning in the mid-1920's, the government implemented increasingly restrictive censorship regulations in order to shield the public from reformers' dangerous thoughts. In 1925, universal male suffrage was introduced but was simultaneously tempered by the Peace Preservation Law, which was based on a very broad definition of what constituted a violation of peace and social order. The law was aimed at the more extreme left-wing movements, but the vagueness of its wording and the possibility of loose interpretation meant that thousands of people, including many liberals and some sexologists, were arrested in its name.[1]

Thus, the sexologists' task was not an easy one. Negotiations about what kinds of sexual knowledge should be created and with whom this knowledge should be shared were undertaken on three main fronts. Representatives of established academic disciplines denounced the sexologists' knowledge as "obscene." Social reformist groups such as parts of the women's movement shared some of the goals of sex education but disagreed with others. And the influence of the state was felt most painfully in the form of censorship of sexological publications and the imprisonment and house arrest of sexologists. Yamamoto Senji's career is a good case in point, as it exemplifies the sexologists' antagonistic relationship to the various agencies of the state. Originally trained as a zoologist at the Imperial University of Tokyo, Yamamoto began to lecture publicly on human sexual development and practice. In 1922, he went on a lecture tour from Osaka to Kōbe, Nagoya, and other small cities throughout Japan. In Tottori, police observers interrupted his talk several times before they pulled him off the stage. The police report noted that Yamamoto had used technical terms but nevertheless had encouraged masturbation, approved of abortion, and talked about "other obscenities" (see chapter 3). As a consequence of the scandal he was fired from his positions at both Dōshisha and Kyoto universities.

Publications that dealt with sexual desire, theories of pregnancy, neo-Malthusian assertions, women's liberation, and critiques of the marital institution were viewed as a threat to social order and the educated middle and upper classes' willingness to reproduce and thus were subject to censorship.[2] Until censorship policies brought (explicitly) sexological publications to a halt in the late 1930s, the readers of that literature also played a role in decisions that involved the execution of censorship regulations. Journals directed at an academic readership faced less restraint than did those with a broader audience. During the late 1920s and early 1930s, sexological journals, termed *seiyoku zasshi* (literally, journals of sexual desire) by the authorities, were the journals most often censored or confiscated.

Despite the significant ruptures of decolonization and democratization after 1945, previous configurations of sexuality persisted and several alliances of important colonialist players remained intact. Many of the actors who had dealt with sexual issues before World War II, and in some cases during the war, resurfaced in the tense political arena of the immediate postwar years, when Japan was still under the control of the Supreme Commander for the Allied Powers (SCAP). The restrictive censorship policy of the early 1940s was not abolished at the end of World War II; rather, it continued in the form of neglect of sexology and sexologists in the immediate postwar period. The "*purely* scientific sex education" *(junkagakuteki seikyōiku)* as propagated by sexologists in the 1920s was rigorously replaced with "*purity* education" *(junketsu kyōiku)*, which was advocated by officials in the Ministry of Education, representatives of the Ministry of Health and Welfare, and members of newly founded sexological organizations.

The end of the empire brought other important shifts as well. Perhaps the most significant was that the prewar and wartime obsession with the uterus and female fertility was replaced by a new emphasis on the mutual sexual satisfaction of both partners. This shift once again focused on the female body—more specifically, on the clitoris and the vagina—and on female orgasm. Wilhelm Reich (1974 [1936]) had optimistically framed this shift as the "liberation of the female sex," while Henri Lefebvre concluded that "women's road to freedom was via frigidity, or worse: faked passion" (1995 [1962]:192). Foucault, in contrast, dismissed Reich's claims and simply noted that this shift was "nothing more, but nothing less . . . than a tactical shift and reversal in the great deployment of sexuality" (Foucault 1990 [1978]:131). The Japanese sexologists of the 1950s stuck to the older generations' rhetoric of liberation, as I will demonstrate in chapter 5 and the epilogue.

Some of the details of my study may seem bizarre or even comical. As I argue in the epilogue, however, some of the debates over sexuality in Japan—specifically those over the approval of the anti-impotence drug Viagra and the subsequent legalization of the low-dose pill in 1999, sex education and its relevance for the prevention of HIV and AIDS, sex research, and child prostitution—are again framed by the paradigmatic structure developed in pre–World War II Japan. Sexuality is discussed as a set of problems related to the necessity of defending and protecting girls and women from men, the populace from certain diseases, and the normal from the pathological. The liberation of sex is promoted to provide teenagers with more explicit sex education that includes information on HIV and other sexually transmitted diseases. Some participants in these debates even demand the truth about the variety of sexual behaviors actually practiced, not just what the majority admits to engaging in. The year 1992 was declared the First Year of Sex Education in Japan, by which time a media-generated AIDS panic had eased slightly. Subsequently, the Japan Association for Sex Education moved from supporting schoolteachers with advice and material on "purity education" to providing more concrete instruction on HIV and AIDS prevention to middle and high school students. Recently, child prostitution, euphemistically termed "compensated dating" *(enjōkōsai)*, has emerged as an issue demanding urgent address. While it was initially portrayed as deviant behavior by a few female juvenile delinquents, the Japanese media quickly suggested that thousands of "ordinary" female (and male) teenagers were willing to provide sexual services in exchange for expensive presents. Once again the discourse of sex, fueled by the media, educators, and the state, not only revolves around the questionable morality of present-day youth, but ventures to suggest that their disturbing behavior may reflect larger social problems occasioned by a modernity gone sour.

CHAPTER I

Erecting a Modern Health Regime

The military physician began to treat him with Salvarsan.
Syphilis was a severe illness in civil society, but particularly
so in the military. We nurses would whisper to one another,
"This one has the clap," or "That one has syphilis. Be careful. Don't get too close." . . . It was ironic that at the front
some soldiers suffered and eventually died from syphilis, here
where soldiers were severely injured and killed on the battle-
field every day. . . . The reason was that the military administration had installed field brothels where comfort women
were available. So it was hard to think poorly of them. The
comfort women were treated at the military hospital just like
the soldiers. I could not blame soldiers for visiting the brothels in their free time.

Anzai Sadako, *Yasen kangofu*

Anzai Sadako's journal, a memoir of her experiences as a field nurse on
the Chinese front, contains many entries about disease and death among
the soldiers she treated. The frequently emotional descriptions of her
everyday experiences and impressions reflect broader concerns that had
helped to create concepts of the "national body" from the formation of
the Japanese nation-state in the 1870s onward. Calling upon an increasingly complex configuration of bureaucrats, military officials, police,
physicians, pedagogues, and other men and women in public office,
these concepts focused on a populace to be regulated, protected, nurtured, and improved in order to establish what I will call a modern
"health regime."

This modern health regime was based on several sets of material and
imaginary physical entities. It tied individual bodies to the social body

that during the late nineteenth century was mostly referred to as the "national body" and had been transformed, by the early 1940s, into the
Greater East Asia Co-Prosperity Sphere. In this chapter I argue that the
first engineers of this health regime were most concerned with the "hygiene" of three groups—soldiers, prostitutes, and children—in various
attempts to protect and to improve the physical and mental condition
primarily of male subjects. Only during the late 1920s and early 1930s
did their attention shift to include other women and the population at
large. These engineers of "public hygiene" especially targeted sexual desires, sexual development, and sexual practices, as well as what they
identified as the consequences thereof.

The condition of the "Japanese nation's body and soul" *(Nippon
kokumin no nikutaimen to seishinmen)* seemed critical in relation to both
the defense of Japan against Western colonial powers and the handling
of East Asia (see Lone 1994; Ogi, Kumakura, and Ueno 1990; Matsubara 1993; Saitō H. 1993). The notion of the national body appeared in
several guises. Whereas some theorists leaned toward social reform *(shakai kairyōron),* others intended to find more direct means for the "improvement of the race" *(jinshu kairyōron)* in order to bring forth a civilized, modern, and above all, healthy population. These two approaches
to the establishment of a modern health regime, however, were not mu-
tually exclusive. In most treatises and public utterances, visions of social
reform overlapped with ideas of "racial improvement" and education.

The role of education in more or less systematic attempts at nation
building was debated widely among Enlightenment thinkers. In his famous work *Encouragement of Learning (Gakumon no susume,* 1872),
Fukuzawa Yukichi, Japan's most prominent educator and philosopher
of the Enlightenment, made a strong case for education as an effective
means of achieving national progress. Roughly twenty years later Fukuzawa's position had become somewhat less optimistic and more reminiscent of the Lamarckian belief in the inheritability of acquired characteristics. In a speech to a mixed group of teachers and students he said,
"If we endeavor to develop our good points and transmit these to our
descendants, who in turn cultivate them even more and pass them on to
their descendants, then there is no doubt that the descendents of even the
most ignorant will become heroes in the long run." However, he added
that one "cannot alter what a man has been endowed with by nature"
(quoted in Oxford 1973:174). In another of his works, *The Improvement of the Race (Jinrui no kairyō,* 1896), Fukuzawa proclaimed that

good fathers and good mothers were crucial for the production of good children.[1]

When enthusiastically promoting the improvement of the national body, some theorists singled out children, as Fukuzawa frequently did, while others approached the same goal by focusing on women, or, more specifically, mothers. Mori Arinori recast Fukuzawa's notion of good mothers in exclusively physical terms when he urged mothers to preserve their bodily strength. If they were weak, he argued, they would be unable to properly raise and protect their children, who were completely dependent on them (reprinted in Braisted 1976:252–253). Although Mori was perhaps the first and one of the most powerful educators of the early Meiji period to emphasize the importance of healthy female bodies in particular, other scholars and bureaucrats soon followed suit. Taking up Mori's notion of physically healthy and strong women, Nagai Hisomu voiced his concerns about the improvement of the race in slightly different and increasingly radical terms. An influential professor of physiology at the Imperial University of Tokyo, Nagai first presented his ideas on what he termed the "beautiful body" in 1907, in an article printed in a scientific journal, and then more extensively in 1916 in a 400-page treatise entitled *On Humankind (Jinseiron)*.[2] A review of the theories and methods of racial hygiene filled about a third of the book. According to Nagai and many other scholars of the time, the "struggle of existence among the races" *(minzoku to minzoku to no seizon kyōsō)* was two-sided. One side concerned the size of the population, the other its nature (Nagai 1916:265). Although customs, education, marriage practices, and reproduction rates were all important, the improvement of the "quality of mothers' bodies" was most crucial for the development of the Japanese race (Nagai 1916:288). About twenty years later, Nagai became a key player in drafting racial hygiene laws as a leader of the Japanese Association of Racial Hygiene, to which I shall turn in chapter 5. Here I wish to point out the variety of ideas about achieving the national body that existed during the late nineteenth century.

Still other Japanese intellectuals emphasized the racial component of physical differences that distinguished Japanese and non-Japanese peoples and agreed that humankind was divided into yellow, white, and black races. Accepting the view common among Western colonial powers, they considered "blacks" inferior to "yellows" and "yellows" inferior to "whites" (see Braisted 1976:439–446). Besides skin color, the brain seemed to offer further clues to racial difference. Respected philosophers such as Inoue Tetsujirō maintained that Western advantages in skull and brain size would translate into a competitive edge over the Japanese (see Gluck 1985:136). Physiologists who engaged in the creation of a "biochemical race index" claimed that the brain weight of Asians—then considered an indicator of intelligence—was lower than the brain weight of Caucasians but emphasized that Japanese men's and women's brains were weightier than those of Chinese, Koreans, and Formosans (Nagai 1928a:508–509). Claims of racial difference that positioned the Japanese below Caucasians prompted debates about how improvement would be possible. One theorist suggested that racial improvement was attainable through mass weddings between "whites" and "yellows" *(hakkō* or *shiroki zakkonron)* or blood transfusions to enlarge the body (Takahashi Yoshio, quoted in Saitō H. 1993:132; see also Ōta 1976:143).[3] Takahashi Yoshio's treatise *The Improvement of the Japanese Race* (*Nihon jinshu kairyōron,* 1884) was perhaps the most radical on the subject of racial improvement. Takahashi, a protégé of Fukuzawa Yukichi, argued that blood and learning determine and influence one another.[4] He also emphasized the importance of both character building and physical exercise and pointed out the advantages of mixed marriages between Japanese men and white women. While debates about the improvement of the race were common throughout the Meiji period, mixed marriages were not. Hence, Takahashi's suggestion provoked intense criticism by contemporaries who doubted that mixing races would result in an improvement of the Japanese race, arguing that even if it did, it would take a very long time (see Ōta 1976:49–50; Saitō H. 1993:132).

Takahashi's suggestion was not taken up by the authorities, but the concern about the condition of the national body voiced by him and other commentators governed the bureaucracy's immoderate interest in controlling people's lives in general and their sexual behavior in particular and in accumulating and disseminating scientific data on both.[5] This interest eventually brought about the development of several powerful instruments for channeling data into a state pool. Government institutions increasingly employed scientific knowledge to guide policies aimed at producing well-regulated human bodies that would constitute a better and more modern nation. Prompting the rise of statistical thinking and of practices of quantification, Japanese bureaucrats, philosophers, and scholars—and later, practitioners of medicine, psychiatry, pedagogy, psychology, and sexology—developed a more complex understanding of achieving the national body. The founding of the first government Association for Statistics (Tōkei Kyōkai) in 1880 vividly reflected this development, as did the creation of various bureaucratic units that began to carry out surveys and bring forth increasingly detailed quantifications and classifications of Japanese society (Kawai T. 1989; Takeuchi H. 1989).

Nationwide surveys, conducted from the early Meiji period on and motivated by efforts to build a powerful army and strengthen the economy, centered on what was perceived as beneficial and necessary for the nation-state's development. This systematic documentation covered agricultural production, population, topography, industrial production and work, welfare and hygiene, education, and the poor (Kawai T. 1989:13). Toward the end of the nineteenth century, the Meiji government began to recognize the necessity of gathering data stemming from statistical surveys and other social research on both the population and resources in order to achieve nationalist and imperialist goals and, to a lesser extent, to solve social problems. Social research institutes whose main agenda was the investigation of social problems were created more than thirty years after the Association for Statistics was founded, the Ōhara Research Institute for Social Problems (Ōhara Shakai Mondai Kenkyūsho) being the most important among them. Their researchers targeted particular social problems, surveying city life, Japan's colonies in East and Southeast Asia, social classes and social mobility, women's status, professions and work patterns, education, leisure and entertainment, consumption, housing, poverty, and crime (Kawai T. 1989:16).

The quantification and classification of the population's physical condition was considered one of the most important tasks in establishing a modern nation whose main characteristics were declared to be a prosperous economy and a potent military. As Stewart Lone has remarked, the Japanese government, at least during the late nineteenth century, was clearly more inclined toward a strong army than a rich nation (Lone 1994). Hence, the new methods of statistical research were first and most extensively applied to matters that were considered relevant for the establishment of potent armed forces, which in turn emerged as the prototypical site and agent of the building of a modern Japanese health regime. The army medical inspector general *(rikugun gun'i sōkan)* investigated and closely monitored the condition of conscripts and soldiers in more general terms. In civil society, the Central Sanitary Bureau began to gather data nationwide on health-related matters in general and, more specifically, venereal diseases among prostitutes. A school hygiene system provided schools all over Japan with the personnel and expertise to examine and document the condition of Japan's youngest generation.

Until far into the twentieth century, data accumulated by these three institutions—the Central Sanitary Bureau (later renamed the Bureau of Hygiene), the office of the army medical inspector general, and the school hygiene system—formed the foundation of administrative, medical, and pedagogical concepts of the physical constitution of the Japanese population and its future prospects. The average conscript served as the prototype for the establishment of a "biochemical race index" of the Japanese population and as a basis for prognoses regarding its potential for improvement. Prostitutes, regarded as both despicable and indispensable, emerged as the main carriers of venereal diseases (Matsuura 1912, 1926a–b, 1927, 1928, 1929; Nagai 1928b). Children appeared as vulnerable and manipulable symbols of the future in terms of hygiene and health, physical strength and national power. For many, their "body building" resembled the larger task of empire building.

As formulated perhaps most influentially by Gotō Shinpei (1857–1927) in 1889, the vision of a modern health regime adopted by the Meiji state reflected a national body that resembled a human organism and claimed an empire that was to be nourished, equipped, and nursed like one. In his treatise *Principles of National Hygiene* (*Kokka eisei genri*, 1889), Gotō emphasized the connection between a state's military power and the health of its populace. Gotō's vision of a healthy and militarily powerful nation was clearly influenced by Rudolf Virchow's concept of "social medicine" *(Sozialmedizin),* Otto von Bismarck's model of "social policy" *(Sozialpolitik),* and Herbert Spencer's theory of the nation as a "social organism." Gotō argued that human beings were not simply individual bodies but parts of a collective, which he termed "a state as human body." He explained that just as animals use claws and fangs to defend themselves, the national body should be equipped with weapons. It also should have a public health system, just as other living beings use their own means to take care of their well-being. Furthermore, it should have the economic means to secure its maintenance, just as other living beings have the ability to feed themselves (Gotō 1978 [1889]).

When Gotō's book was published, he had been affiliated with the Central Sanitary Bureau for fifteen years—an institution he declared to be the heart of the administration of hygiene in the Meiji government (Tsurumi 1937:298, 351). The Central Sanitary Bureau (Eiseikyoku) was established in 1873 as part of the Ministry of Education. Its founder and first director was Nagayo Sensai (1838–1902), another powerful engineer of the social and administrative aspects of Japan's modern health regime. He had studied medicine and had familiarized himself with theories and models of public health administration in Europe. Nagayo coined the term *eisei*—a translation of the German term *Gesundheitspflege* or *Hygiene*—after a visit to Prussia in 1872 (Marui 1980: 99). Accepted as a member of the Monbushō delegation to the Iwakura mission in 1871, Nagayo left Japan in November of that year. After a visit to Washington in January 1872, he reported that "the professors of medical schools and hospitals treated [us] like children and [we] were very angry" (quoted in Jannetta 1997:159). He and several others left the delegation, and Nagayo spent a month in England and then moved on to Paris and Berlin. It was in Berlin that he first became conscious of the sanitation or public health movement in Europe. Nagayo and other leading hygienists realized that "public health" referred not only to the protection of citizens' health, but to the entire administrative system that was being organized to ensure that protection. This system reached far beyond the traditional practice of medicine, with its focus on the relationship between individual doctor and patient. Instead, it was a state campaign aimed at society in the mass. It reached into the realm of public works, which were the responsibility of the state. It relied not only on medicine but also on physics, meteorology, and statistics, and it operated through the state administration to eliminate threats to life and to improve the nation's well-being.

For health officials in Europe, and, from the 1870s on, in Japan, improvement and maintenance of public health meant draining swamps and providing proper sewage disposal and clean water systems. It also meant educating the public about hygiene and keeping records to document the incidence of infectious diseases and the number of vaccinations. It involved the surveillance not only of physicians but also of local governments, which necessitated the collaboration of police departments. This vision of building a healthy and strong Japan through the offices of the state appealed enormously to Nagayo. Upon his return to Japan he wrote a medical code that covered education, medical practice, and sanitation regulations. The Meiji government accepted the code. The activities that Nagayo suggested administering centrally, however, were soon separated. Medical education remained within the Ministry of Education. Public health policies became the responsibility of the Home Department and were administered by the Central Sanitary Bureau (Jannetta 1997:158–160).

In 1874, the Central Sanitary Bureau was renamed the Bureau of Hygiene (Naimushō Eiseikyoku) and incorporated into the Home Department, where it became the most powerful of seven departments. One-third of the Home Department's budget was allocated to the bureau (Tsurumi 1937:303).[6] However, according to Nagayo, the amount was hardly sufficient to cover the costs of four divisions and a host of tasks. The bureau distributed the regulations for doctors' exams in the prefectures, was responsible for granting permission to open pharmacies, issued the regulations for health examinations of prostitutes for venereal diseases, and was responsible for various other hygiene matters (Tsurumi 1937:312).

The Office of Statistics (Tōkeika) was an important part of the Bureau of Hygiene. There, for the first time in Japanese history, the bureau's public health administrators began to collect data on the constitution of the Japanese national body. The careful inspection, measurement, and documentation of public health *(kōshū eisei)* was rooted in the hope of finding explanations for the high infant mortality rate, the high number of tuberculosis patients, and the spread of infectious diseases (Tsurumi 1937:303; Iwanaga 1994:79–118). The Bureau of Hygiene published its data in lengthy reports every two years and later also in English translations (Naimushō eiseikyoku 1893–1894).

Between the 1880s and the 1920s, the bureau documented a steady increase in mortality rates for infants less than one year of age. Public health officials ascribed this alarming development to chronic infectious diseases and what some of them perceived as the general deterioration of social life, which was, in Japan and elsewhere, associated with urbanization and industrialization. During the second half of the 1880s, the average mortality rate of infants less than one year of age per 1,000 normal births was 117. By the early 1890s, the number had increased to 147 per 1,000 normal births, and it reached 159 during the early 1920s (SBHD 1929:98–100). In comparison with eighteen European countries and New Zealand, Japan ranked fourth lowest in the latter half of the 1880s. Ten years later, the rise in its rate put Japan in tenth place; by 1910 it ranked fifteenth. By 1920, only Austria had a higher infant mortality rate, and by 1924 Japan had the highest infant mortality rate among these countries (SBHD 1929:101–102).

A high tuberculosis death rate was similarly worrisome to public health authorities. During the period under consideration, various forms of tuberculosis remained by far one of the most common causes of death, along with diarrhea and enteritis (SBHD 1929:104; Lebzelter 1926:

823). When the spread of acute infectious diseases slowed by the turn of the century, public health administrators shifted their focus toward chronic diseases such as leprosy, venereal diseases, and mental illness. Although less demanding of urgent attention—the mortality rate of syphilis patients, for example, was generally about 10 percent of the tuberculosis mortality rate and never increased to more than 20 percent (SBHD 1929:44–45)—chronic diseases were considered potentially disruptive to social stability due to their impact on the family, which increasingly became a central concern of Japan's bureaucracy.

The propagation of hygiene soon reached far beyond the boundaries and authority of the bureau. This was due to the cholera epidemic of 1878 and 1879, spread by soldiers returning from the battlefields of the Satsuma rebellion in 1877; to the founding of several hygiene institutions in the Tokyo, Osaka, and Kyoto prefectures; and, later, to the increasing number of publications on hygiene (Tsurumi 1937:311, 319). The definition of "hygiene" likewise expanded. For bureaucrats, military officials, physicians, and pedagogues alike, hygiene became a concept that not only linked but intrinsically intertwined rules of cleanliness with those of morality, the health of the body with that of the mind, the individual with society, and Japan with other modern nations (Imai T. 1906:243–245; Koide M. 1932:18).

For sanitation personnel in the military, hygiene included no less than knowledge of the importance of clean water, air, ground, and housing. Appropriate care of sick and injured soldiers was another important element. The discovery of the source and the prevention of "military diseases" *(gunbyō)*—a euphemism for venereal diseases in the military—made up an additional core element; a healthy diet and the correct maintenance of clothing, as well as a number of other factors that affected military life, were considered equally crucial (Mori 1886, 1888, 1889, 1886–1891, 1911).

For educators, hygiene came to cover all aspects of a child's development. They described hygiene as proper "care and maintenance of the body" *(shintai no yōgō)* that went beyond the bare "survival instinct" *(seizonyoku;* probably a translation of the German term *Überlebenstrieb).* Proper care and maintenance was declared the basis of a "moral person"; in fact, the care and maintenance of the whole self was to be recognized as both "a virtue and a duty" (Imai T. 1906:824).

Explanations of hygiene were integrated first into the manuals of military doctors and the textbooks of military academies and later into books for factory doctors and textbooks of ordinary secondary schools.

Under the banner of hygiene, cadets, soldiers, workers, and students learned to keep their bodies and clothes clean, store food properly, monitor their health, and make sure that enough fresh air and sunlight got into their barracks, schools, factories, and homes (Koide M. 1932; Yamai and Kinoshita 1982:376–378). Even booklets aimed mainly at instilling patriotism and loyalty to the emperor contained chapters on health and hygiene for adults and youth that were to be taken to heart (Mori 1907; Gotō 1926:90–96).[7]

Numerous sites of the enactment of the new concept of hygiene emerged during the Meiji era. In the remainder of this chapter, I will discuss three groups—soldiers, prostitutes, and children—that were particularly important because they strongly connected concerns about health, sexual practice, and national security. Systematic examinations in the Imperial Army and Navy enabled physicians to identify recruits as a social group with a high rate of venereal disease infection, a matter that eventually brought about the establishment of restricted-use brothels—mentioned in the epigraph to this chapter—that were controlled and administered by the military. Similarly, the Bureau of Hygiene began a survey of venereal diseases among prostitutes in order to try to justify their segregation from the rest of society. Finally, the introduction of a school hygiene system allowed school physicians to "discover" that children suffered from all kinds of ailments, many of which, they insisted, were caused by masturbation.

HYGIENE IN THE EMPEROR'S MILITARY

One of the most public manifestations of modern society has been the ability to mobilize armies on a national scale. However, as I will argue in the following pages, the modern national military was also one of the core organizations for the development of hygienic thought and practice. The Imperial Army and Navy was the first institution to attempt the administration and control of its members' sexual practices. The administration of soldiers' access to commercial sex was guided predominantly by concerns about their physical and mental health. Except for the women classified as "licensed prostitutes," whom I shall discuss in the next section, no other group was as thoroughly monitored. Large-scale survey data on the physiques of soldiers were used far into the twentieth century to assess the "physical constitution of the Japanese." Venereal diseases were first researched systematically in military hospitals. Antibiotics for the treatment of these diseases (Salvarsan) as well as devices for their prevention (condoms) were first introduced in the military (*Chūō Shinbun* 1913; *Hōchi Shinbun* 1916a; *Tōhoku Shinbun* 1916; Nagai 1928a), and it was the authors of hygiene manuals for the army and the navy who claimed that a combination of condoms and drugs—e.g., creams that had to be applied to the genitals before and after sexual intercourse (Odajima 1943[1938]:381)—were the most effective methods of disease prevention.

The Conscription Decree (Chōheirei shōsho), promulgated on 28 November 1872 as an imperial edict, laid the cornerstone for Japan's ability to mobilize its forces on a national scale. According to the decree, soldiers were to be drafted from all over the country to form the Imperial Army (Teikoku Rikugun), whereas the Imperial Navy (Teikoku Kaigun) depended on volunteers. Their primary task was declared to be the "protection of the nation."[8] The conscription system was long disputed among bureaucrats and ideologues, both before and after its introduction at the insistence of Yamagata Aritomo (1838–1922), then executive head of the armed forces and future commander of the First Army in the war against China.[9] Universal conscription was a revolutionary rather than an evolutionary act, insofar as it dispossessed the samurai of their arms monopoly and with it their status as a closed elite. Given that the samurai never comprised more than about 7 percent of the population and that their cultural norms relied on the outdated weapons of sword and bow, they were inappropriate in both numbers and methods for the kind of military organization required in modern war (Lone 1994:17–19). There was another logic behind the conscription system: In times of war, conscription provided a larger number of soldiers who could be swiftly drafted. During times of peace, men with military training who had returned to civilian life did not burden the military budget because they were not paid.

Some commentators insisted that a military of volunteers was preferable to one of draftees, and the many reforms of the conscription system, due in large part to the high number of young men avoiding the draft, hint at military officials' discontent with the organization. However, critics who doubted the value of the conscription system typically voiced their criticism in order to strengthen the military, rather than to reorganize it. In 1882 Fukuzawa Yukichi thundered in his critique *On the Military (Heiron)* that ten years after the introduction of conscription, no more than 740,000 men were serving in the military at any given time. Fukuzawa insisted that the Meiji government needed to invest more money in the development of the military (see Katō Y. 1996:20).

Fukuzawa and other critics of the conscription system accurately pointed out the relatively low number of soldiers compared to the number of young men classified as fit for service at the beginning of the Meiji period. In the first half of the Meiji era, only about one in thirty twenty-year-old men was drafted. Thus the number of soldiers first increased by less than 10,000 and later by about 20,000 per year. An increase in the disputed military budget, however, soon provided for a considerable increase in recruits. During the years from 1876 to 1880, the combined budget of the Imperial Army and Navy reached nearly 10.4 million yen, or 18 percent of the national budget (Katō Y. 1996:21). The number of conscripts examined between 1873 and 1900 went from 2,300 to 53,000, and in the course of the following seventy years, the Imperial Army and Navy grew to 5.9 million personnel, including officers and troops (Drea 1998:75).

Recruiting districts served as the administrative areas for managing the conscription process. The army medical inspector general was installed as the central authority for the physical examination of conscripts *(chōhei kensa)*, a move that marked the rather direct connection made by military personnel between the physical fitness of individual men and the national goal of building a strong imperial military. Each year, all twenty-year-old Japanese men had to report for this physical examination (see figure 1). The military administration learned each conscript's age, height, chest circumference, lung capacity, and weight from the examinations (which were held twice a year), and classified each of them in one of five classes according to fitness for service (Rikugunshō 1894: 190–194). Classes A, B, and C were considered different degrees of fitness for service. In class D were the "physically or mentally deficient," or those regarded as unsuitable for becoming soldiers, including criminals and dwarfs (Shimizu 1989). Young men in this class typically suffered from what the examiners termed "thin and weak bones" or an "insufficient development of the entire body." The examiners also noted that industrial workers (particularly coal miners, glass workers, and shoe factory and knitting mill workers) were in significantly worse physical shape than white-collar workers (Rikugunshō 1917:511; *Tōkyō Asahi Shinbun* 1917; *Yomiuri Shinbun* 1917). Class E men were ill at the time of the annual physical examination and had to report for reexamination and reclassification later that year or the following year (Drea 1998:78–79).

The first systematic physical examination after the introduction of conscription was carried out in Nagano prefecture. In December of

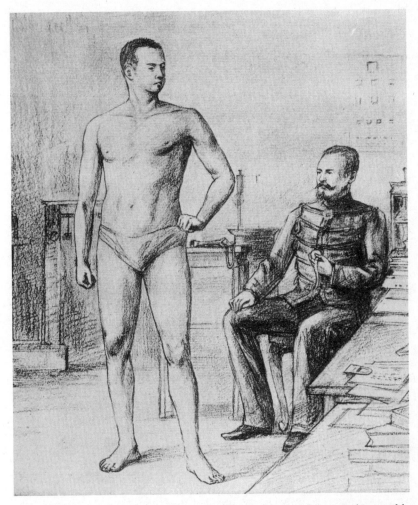

Figure 1. Kurushima Takehiko's *Everyday Use Encyclopedia 40: Indispensable Army Handbook for the People (Nichiyō hyakka zensho dai yonjūhen: Kokumin hikkei rikugun ippan)* contained this idealized sketch of a conscript and his examiner in a health examination office (Kurushima 1899: inside front cover).

1874, data from the first examination were made available to military administrators, and in 1876 the first nationwide data were published, documenting 2.9 million conscripts, almost 18 percent of whom were classified as class A or B (Katō Y. 1996:65).[10] After 1902, Japanese conscripts in Taiwan, and later, those in Karafuto, Manchukuo, and Korea were examined and drafted as well (see figure 2) (Katō Y. 1996:155).

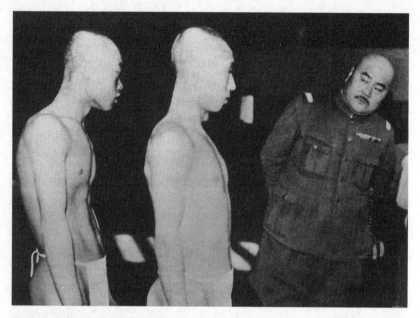

Figure 2. Men in the colonies had to travel to "mainland Japan" *(Nihon no naichi)* in order to be examined. Only when more and more people objected to this procedure because of the high cost of travel were conscripts examined and recruited in the colonies. After 1902, conscripts in Taiwan formed the Taiwan Reserve Force, those in Karafuto the Karafuto Reserve Force, and so forth (Katō Y. 1996:155). According to a military law of 1941, twenty-year-old Manshū men also had to undergo a health examination before they were drafted to fight in Japan's imperialist war in East Asia. Photograph from *Asahi Gurafu Sōkan: Warera ga Hyakunen* (Asahi graph summary issue: One hundred years of our history), 25 September 1968:120. Used with the kind permission of the *Asahi Shinbun*.

During peacetime, only class A men—those taller than 1.55 meters and in top physical condition—were eligible for conscription. Of these, an average of 20 to 30 percent were actually drafted to do 120 days of basic training and not more than 35 days of additional service per year thereafter (Drea 1998:78).

Recruitment officers and health examiners helped create the reputation of the male population in entire prefectures by documenting both their willingness to join the military and their physical capability to do so. They registered the conscripts' "character" *(seishitsu)* as simple and naïve, took note of stubbornness and bigotry, and were quick to describe as "lazy" and "effeminate" those who seemed to resent the military. In

徴兵検査

コノヱハ　徴
兵検査ヲシ
テキルトコ
ロデス。男子
ハ　マン二十
サイニナルト
ミンナ　徴兵
検査ヲ　ウケ
マス。

Figure 3. The physical examination of conscripts and numerous other military scenarios were explained to the young readers of illustrated books and magazines for children. This one is from the publisher Kōdansha, *Kōdansha no ehon: Nippon no rikugun* (Kōdansha storybook: Japan's army), 1940:52.

justifying their unfavorable evaluations of the conscript pool, recruitment officers also noted when the number of draft dodgers or men who "hated the military" was particularly high (Rikugunshō 1876:83–88).[11] While these evaluations of the conscripts' character served as a means to probe their willingness to serve, "physical quality" was really what examination officers were looking for.

Upon entering the physical examination office, conscripts learned the rules of the physical examination for conscripts. They were instructed on proper bodily hygiene, cleanliness of their clothes, and proper maintenance of equipment received on the day of their recruitment, and were warned not to attempt to escape recruitment. In addition to instructional pamphlets and posters providing warnings in recruitment offices, nationwide campaigns appealed to the public to report persons who illegally attempted to escape military service or who neglected to register, and reminded everyone that draft dodgers shamed the region (Katō Y. 1996:159).

Many potential soldiers awaited the physical examination with mixed feelings, and long after its introduction, draft evasion remained commonplace. After all, conscription had several worrisome implications for the recruit and his family, some of which were similar to the implications of universal compulsory education—most obviously, the loss of labor at home. When compulsory education was introduced in 1872, many Japanese families perceived schools to be detrimental to their interests because schooling robbed them of the use of older children's labor during prime daylight hours for a period of four to six years. Families were reluctant to enroll children in schools. Resistance took an active form in some areas during the early Meiji years as protestors razed and set fire to schools (Kosaka 1958:84; see also Uno 1999:40). Similarly, for the families of the young men, recruitment implied a loss of labor in times of peace as well as the risk of complete loss of their sons in times of war.[12] Moreover, neither martial spirit nor patriotism came naturally. To many men and their families, to die for the emperor and the nation seemed a strange idea, and resistance, at times violent, occurred all over provincial Japan (Katō Y. 1996:46–47).

This lack of patriotism in the wider population and the lack of commitment to the military service among recruits prompted military officials to take further steps. They tightened the regulations of the conscription system in 1883 and 1889 so that the categories of exemption became increasingly limited. Yamagata also drafted the "Imperial Precepts to Soldiers" ("Gunjin chokuyu"), which was introduced in 1882 in

order to "instill virtues of loyalty to the emperor and love of the country." The Imperial Rescript was a long (2,700-character) document distinguished by the use of such obscure Chinese characters that it was difficult even for a college graduate to read. The entire text was read to the
troops on special occasions, such as National Foundation Day (11 February) or Army Day (10 March). Recruits also had to memorize and
recite on command a shorter version of the rescript, "Five Principles of
the Soldier" (Kurushima 1899: inside front cover; see also Drea 1998:
81–82).

Despite the threats by the military that were posted in recruitment
offices, and despite village announcement boards and attempts at indoc-
trination, young men employed several strategies to escape the military's
call, some of which centered on the physical health examination. According to Ohama Tetsuya, guidebooks on how to escape military service were popular up to the eve of the Sino-Japanese war. The official
history of Tokyo explains that young students moving to the capital registered in certain wards where doctors would certify them as physically
unfit. In the far north of central Japan, there were even some who migrated to the undeveloped island of Hokkaido to escape (see Lone 1994:
17–18). Although it was a criminal offense if it was detected, some men
starved themselves in order to be underweight at the time of the examination. Others pretended that they could not see or hear well or even
injured themselves to escape the draft. Still others drank unhealthy
amounts of soy sauce to produce symptoms of heart trouble, and some
young men bought other people's birth certificates (*Yomiuri Shinbun*
1917). Recruitment officers of course were not ignorant of these illegal
practices. Quite the contrary, in their evaluations of the conscripts in
their districts they noted explicitly when young "unpatriotic men" *(hiko-
kumin)* attempted to "avoid the draft by using various illnesses as an ex-
cuse" (Rikugunshō 1876:87).

Those who were drafted were not always disappointed with military
life. Many realized that after the initial hardships of basic training, work
in the army had its advantages over farm work. Soldiers received relatively good food, and those in their second year enjoyed a considerable
amount of free time. Furthermore, the army accepted only the men who
were the most physically healthy. Being drafted as a class A soldier
was considered a mark of status and an acknowledgement of top physical condition. Once drafted, military doctors kept close track of the
soldiers' physical development (Iizuka 1968:95; see also Drea 1998:
79, 89).

MONITORING SOLDIERS' HEALTH

The health examinations of conscripts and other health matters in the military were administered by the Army Hygiene Council (Rikugun Eisei Kaigi), which was directly responsible to the Army Ministry (Kurushima 1899:17–18). During the late nineteenth century, it found that even class A conscripts were far from satisfactory to the military authorities. Among others, Chief Military Physician Dr. Mori Rintarō (1862–1922) set out to engineer the improvement of military hygiene in both word and deed.

In several ways, Mori's career was similar to those of the leading architects of Japan's modern health regime such as Nagayo Sensai and Gotō Shinpei. All three had studied medicine (Mori in the Medical Department of the University of Tokyo) and were sent to Europe to further their training (Mori was sent to Germany by the Army Ministry to study military hygiene). Like Gotō, Mori served in the army as a military physician and held a number of prestigious posts during his thirty-five years of military service. For four years, he was instructed by Germany's top hygienists, university professors Franz Hoffmann and Max von Pettenkofer, and university professors and military physicians W. A. Roth and Robert Koch, the founder of modern bacteriology. Mori served as a military physician in the wars against China (1894–1895) and Russia (1904–1905) and remained in the service of the emperor's army until 1916 (Maruyama 1984:vii–viii).[13]

Mori's *Army Hygiene Manual* (*Rikugun eisei kyōtei*, 1889) was published by the Army Medical Academy (Rikugun Gun'i Gakkō) exclusively for military physicians and other military instructors, but his *New Book of Hygiene* (*Eisei shinhen*, 1897) addressed hygienists more generally. Both served as textbooks for military education. Mori wrote the *Army Hygiene Manual* only one year after he had become an instructor at the Army Medical Academy. The concept of hygiene, Mori explained, included all practices that affected a person's health and aimed at health preservation and improvement and the prevention of disease. He urged military instructors and administrators to instruct soldiers on these ideas because the military was an important state organization (Mori 1889; see also Maruyama 1984:42, 85).

New concepts of military hygiene targeted not only the health examination procedures for recruits, cadets at military academies, and soldiers on active duty but also the hygiene conditions in military barracks.[14] In order to avoid the recruitment of sick men, examination officers were reminded frequently to check conscripts' physical condition carefully, particularly for lung diseases, which had been epidemic since the early Meiji years, and for skin diseases caused by cotton uniforms. By 1900, physical examination charts began to circulate in military academies, cadets received special lectures on hygiene, and their physical development was examined annually (Kaigunshō 1907:150). Newspapers began to report that due to the successful establishment of hygienic thought and practices, the physical constitution of conscripts improved steadily (*Hōchi Shinbun* 1916a; *Tōkyō Asahi Shinbun* 1917). The Imperial Army and Navy's annual reports also proudly noted that cadets were particularly heavy, well-built and well-fed compared to other men in the same age cohort—conscripts were on average 1.65 meters tall and weighed 58.6 kilograms (Rikugunshō 1917:577; Yamai and Kinoshita 1982:376–378). By the beginning of the twentieth century, the hygiene section of the armed forces' annual reports had expanded to several hundred pages that meticulously listed the physical condition of conscripts and soldiers serving in all parts of the Japanese empire and included data on about fifty different diseases and types of injuries (see, e.g., Rikugunshō 1917:364–499).

SYPHILITIC SOLDIERS

In addition to the health examinations of conscripts and the annual examinations of cadets and other soldiers, medical personnel in military hospitals and academies also carried out smaller-scale health examinations. These studies confirmed that one in ten recruits, or several thousand men, suffered from at least one of several kinds of venereal diseases *(karyūbyō)* (Fujikawa Y. 1908a:29; see also Rikugunshō 1894, 1897, 1917:505; Kaigunshō 1906:185, 1907:211, 1909:140).[15] The most common ones were gonorrhea, chancroid, and syphilis. Until effective medication was developed, the diseases were treated with various baths, painful injections, and treatments with special grasses and tinctures (Kariya 1993:22–23). However, venereal diseases often remained untreated and had severely damaging consequences. Gonorrhea and chancroid were not life threatening, but syphilis was. Up until the end of World War II, when effective medication became more widely available, syphilis attacked every organ in the body. It caused repeated skin eruptions and ulcers, brought about hair loss and deterioration of the nose, and in the final stages attacked the brain, turning the sufferer into a cripple (Sone 1999:178). As the former field nurse Anzai Sadako reported, patients eventually suffered loss of control over motor nerves, spinal cord phthisis, or progressive paralysis, as well as nervous and mental illnesses. Several entries in her memoir illustrated the lot of syphilis patients at the front. One of her stories read as follows:

> There was this erotomaniac patient with cerebral syphilis in the field hospital. He was quite a handsome man who had been in the war for six years. He frequented the field brothels all the time and had contracted acute cerebral syphilis. He was already seriously ill when he came to the hospital. Once he called out in a loud voice, "Come here, nurse. Come here!" I thought that something had happened. When I went over to him he said, "Your underpants look as if they may fall down any minute. Look, they are falling. Come quick. Show it to me. If you don't show it to me your buttocks will turn black. Please, show it to me!" He began to cry. Then he stopped all of a sudden. He wanted to tease us. Then he made a serious face and began to sing an obscene song. When he stopped he began to undress and do a striptease. (Anzai 1953:161)

In 1924, an average of 6 in 1,000 deaths in the population were ascribed to syphilis, with a wide range between regions—e.g., from eleven in Akita and Nagasaki to one in Shiga and Fukui. This mortality rate was comparable to those of other diseases such as dysentery (KRB 1927:128–129), and effective treatment was available only decades after 1909, when Paul Ehrlich and his laboratory assistant Hata Sahachirō developed Salvarsan 606.[16] Salvarsan was a poisonous yellowish powder consisting of an organic compound containing a small amount of arsenic and used in a dilute solution as a treatment for syphilis. At least in military hospitals, Salvarsan injections became routine treatment by the 1940s.[17] The mass production of the more effective penicillin, discovered by the bacteriologist Alexander Fleming in 1928, became possible only at the end of World War II.

The military health administration was interested in several characteristics of venereal diseases in the army and navy. Among these were the time of infection (before or after recruitment), the source of infection (classified either as several "kinds" of women or as "other"), the mortality rate of infected soldiers, and the cost of treatment.[18] Long-term documentation of venereal disease cases in military hospitals reveals that the rate of carriers of venereal diseases in the military increased per 1,000 soldiers examined from 21.9 in 1912 to 31.1 in 1926 (KRB 1927:1). The army responded to the increase in venereal disease patients by ordering weekly medical examinations of thousands of men and severely punishing those who were found diseased or seen entering a brothel. During the first Sino-Japanese war, the medical staff issued warnings that the Chinese were a promiscuous race and the country was rife with syphilis (Kaigunshō imukyoku 1900; see also Lone 1994: 149–150). The Siberian expedition from 1918 to 1920 provided another lesson for the Japanese army about the risk of venereal disease. During those two years, 1,387 men were killed in battle and 2,066 were wounded, but venereal disease casualties reached 2,012 (Allen 1984: 594). Soldiers' diaries from the Russo-Japanese war ten years later, however, indicate that the army eventually authorized certain brothels and even built others particularly for Japanese soldiers, in an attempt to control the sexual activities of soldiers and subjugate both soldiers and prostitutes under the authority of military physicians. Thus, prostitution within and outside of the military was geared toward the functionality of male sexuality through the use of female bodies in order to secure the power system within the military and over the empire. This practice was no secret in civilian society and was hardly a bone of contention there. Only occasionally did social reformers, most notably the Purity Society (Kakuseikai) and some women's groups that organized for the abolition of the licensed brothel system, criticize the establishment of brothels for soldiers. The military administration remained unimpressed when the monthly magazine *Purity (Kakusei)* published an article in which the wife of a Diet member stated her opposition to that particular policy. "As a mother," she declared, she would help her son escape the draft rather than expose him to state-sanctioned military brothels (Hinata 1911:43). When the article was published in 1911, the military establishment had already begun to systematically establish brothels in the vicinity of barracks (Chung 1997:222–223).

Among the regulations of the use of these military brothels were the following: Entry to a comfort house was authorized only for personnel attached to the army. Personnel entering the house had to be in possession of a comfort house pass. Personnel had to pay the required fee in cash and obtain receipts, in exchange for which they were given an entrance ticket and one condom. The cost of an entrance ticket was about 2 yen.[19] Ticket purchasers had to enter the room indicated by the number shown thereon. The consumption of alcohol inside the room was forbidden and the use of a prophylactic solution was mandatory. It was forbidden to have intercourse without a condom (Itō 1969:92–93).

Military administrations in Japan and elsewhere often justified this policy as an antidote to civilian rape, a serious problem in war zones everywhere, but particularly toward the end of 1937 during the occupation of Nanjing. At least as important a factor for the establishment of restricted-use brothels, however, may have been the widespread and unquestioned assumption that prostitution as a state-sanctioned institution was necessary. Men, and soldiers especially, had certain needs that had to be catered to. In this respect the military did not differ from the civilian male establishment. As much as military administrators strove to avoid criticism of the troops' behavior outside of bases, at the front or elsewhere in Japan's colonial empire, they were interested in protecting the designated "protectors of the Japanese nation" from unlicensed and thus potentially diseased prostitutes.

By the end of the 1930s, military-administered brothels were well established and, in addition to Japanese women, Chinese, Korean, and other women under Japanese colonial rule were forced into military sexual slavery.[20] There, ironically enough, both soldiers and prostitutes were examined for venereal diseases and other illnesses by the same doctors who collected data on both groups, albeit with a different degree of rigor. Health checks among the enslaved women were carried out mainly to prevent the infection of soldiers with venereal diseases. According to the survivors of the enslavement by the military, in some so-called comfort stations the women were injected with so many drugs that they had miscarriages, while in others no preventive measures were taken and venereal diseases were not treated at all. In contrast to the uneven attention given to venereal diseases, little or no notice was taken of cigarette burns, bruises, bayonet stabs, and even broken bones inflicted on the women by the soldiers (Jūgun ianfu 110-ban henshū iinkai 1992: 73, 106; Schellstede 2000:7, 22, 54–55, 78, 117).[21] Clearly, soldiers mattered much more than the prostitutes, as former field nurse Anzai pointed out in her journal:

> The soldier . . . was given a Salvarsan injection and all of a sudden could speak again. As he thanked the physician, the physician told him to never forget how he contracted the terrible disease in the first place and said, "You have a wife and children, right?" The soldier replied, "Yes. I have a wife and two children." "But still you like women and buy them frequently, right?" "Yes, I am not a man who dislikes women." We nurses were very embarrassed listening to this conversation and could say nothing. (Anzai 1953:159)

As Anzai's memoir and other records show, appeals to soldiers about the importance of preserving and improving their health were of limited success. Between 1912 and 1925, army physicians treated an average of

more than 5,000 soldiers annually who suffered from at least one venereal disease (KRB 1927:68). Varying considerably throughout this period, the number of patients ranged from a low of 4,370 in 1918 to a
high of 6,075 in 1922. The average number of venereal disease patients
in the Imperial Navy was considerably higher than in the army, but in
both branches, physicians claimed, the risk of infection depended greatly
on the area of deployment (KRB 1927:68–69).

Another worry for the health administration, in addition to the sheer
numbers of patients, was the time of infection. Almost 90 percent of
these soldiers were infected after they had undergone the physical examination of conscripts and had been found fit for service, probably because they visited a brothel on the eve of induction, before entering the
hardship of barracks life (KRB 1927:70–71). As for the source of infection, military physicians had to rely on information given to them
by the soldiers. The women they accused of infecting them with venereal
diseases were categorized into several groups, namely licensed prostitutes *(shōgi)*, waitresses and barmaids *(shakufu)*, geisha *(geigi)*, factory
workers *(kōjō)*, and wives *(tsuma)*.

While female prostitutes were widely stigmatized as sources of diseases that threatened men's health, shattered their families' happiness,
and potentially affected the physical and mental well-being of their offspring, military doctors and administrators drew direct connections between soldiers' venereal diseases and women in professions far beyond
the boundaries of (licensed) prostitution. Other young women, like waitresses or factory workers, whose sexuality was considered uncontrolled
and uncontrollable by their parents and employers, were commonly
characterized as promiscuous by military and civilian officials alike. In
1888, when explaining the causes of venereal diseases among military
conscripts, a journalist in Nagano even suggested that "entertainers and
prostitutes, female servants, and *komori*, female factory workers, and
widows are all responsible for these diseases" (see Tamanoi 1998:70).
And when the *Tōkyō Asahi Shinbun* noted the rate of conscripts infected
with venereal diseases (four in a hundred), it urged the authorities not
to forbid soldiers access to prostitutes but to tighten control of unlicensed prostitutes *(Tōkyō Asahi Shinbun* 1917).

According to a study by the military inspector general, about 70 percent of all recruits examined in 1920 and diagnosed with a venereal disease had reported a licensed prostitute or a waitress to be the source of
their venereal disease (KRB 1927:73). Another study based on the ex-

amination of 5.28 million twenty-year-old men found that the number
of diseased soldiers was lowest among those who came from rural areas
without licensed quarters (one out of a hundred), followed by rural areas with licensed quarters (two out of a hundred). According to this
study, three out of a hundred young men who originated from urban areas were carriers of venereal diseases, whether they came from cities
with or without licensed quarters (KRB 1927:79), confirming results of
other studies according to which venereal diseases were, at least for the
population of young men, primarily an urban disease.

Venereal diseases were troublesome for the military not only from the
perspective of national security but for economic reasons as well. The
period of treatment for a soldier diagnosed with a venereal disease remained consistent at about thirty days. The military kept paying their allowance during the time they were patients. The daily cost of one person's treatment constituted an additional cost of 30 to 50 percent of
a soldier's daily allowance. For example, in 1912, 337 patients received
an allowance of 61,294 yen, and another 24,581 yen was spent for their
treatment. In 1921, when the average number of patients throughout
the year—509—was considerably higher, the allowance increased to
92,604 yen and the cost for treatment to 37,138 yen (KRB 1927:62–
63, 66–67).

As military hygiene education regarding venereal diseases and punishment of infected soldiers by demotion or beating turned out to be
only partly effective, the authorities introduced more practical measures
(Jūgun ianfu 110-ban henshū iinkai 1992:104; Senda 1978:170). Condoms were made available for soldiers. During the late Meiji period,
condoms were imported mostly from the Netherlands and were distributed during and after the Russo-Japanese War (1904–1905), until the
first condom made in Japan, the Heart Beauty (Hāto Bijin), was introduced in 1909. Japanese condoms first came into widespread use at the
beginning of Japan's aggression against China in 1931, when soldiers
leaving their base were instructed to carry "hygiene matchboxes" (eisei
matchi), small boxes containing two condoms. From 1938 until the end
of World War II, rubber factories were put under the jurisdiction of
the military according to the National Mobilization Law (Kokka Sōdōinhō). Subsequently, condoms became legally classified as "munitions
of war" (gunjuhin). Especially considering the contemporary debates
about the availability and legality of contraceptives in civilian society,
to which I shall turn in chapter 4, it is important to note that by the end

of the 1930s, condoms were distributed in large quantities to soldiers. They were not classified as contraceptives, but solely as a means of preventing venereal diseases.

Condoms were accounted for and distributed by the Army Ministry's Bureau of Supplies and named according to imperialist practices, e.g., Attack Number One (Kōgeki Ichiban) and Attack Champion (Totsugeki Ichiban) for the Imperial Army and Iron Cap (Tetsu Kaputo) for the Imperial Navy (Ōta 1976:266; Jūgun ianfu 110-ban henshū iinkai 1992: 74; Watanabe Kazuko 1994; Chung 1997:229). They were specifically ordered by regiment commanders and distributed for use at the comfort stations. Ways to enforce the use of a condom, however, were of course limited, and practices varied from camp to camp. In 1942, 32 million condoms were distributed to the Japanese military, which meant a ration of twenty condoms per man each year. In some places, condoms also could be bought locally, and the managers of the comfort stations often provided condoms as well. In other camps, though, condoms were unavailable for long stretches of time, or soldiers washed and used them several times (Hayashi H. 1993:17; Jūgun ianfu 110-ban henshū iinkai 1992:74; Schellstede 2000:22, 54–55).

As a result, most of the more than 100,000 girls and women enslaved by the imperial forces and held in the comfort stations were infected with all kinds of diseases. Lured by false promises of employment, coerced, or simply abducted by military and police authorities, these women were forced to work as nurses, cooks, waitresses, and seamstresses during the day and were regularly raped and beaten, sometimes to the point of serious injury, by dozens of soldiers, only to be killed or abandoned at the end of the war. Moreover, they were not the only ones to suffer in this way: Women who engaged in prostitution unrelated to the military certainly did not do so out of "free will." Many were sold by their fathers and brothers or fled poverty or an abusive family only to eventually be stranded in a brothel within or beyond Japanese borders.

The system of forced prostitution was not unique to Japanese imperialism.[22] The comfort station system was not an exclusively Japanese invention; neither was it a military matter only.[23] The system was an extreme form of the colonization of sex and was closely intertwined with debates about and practices of the control of prostitution in civilian society at the time.[24] It is to these debates that I will turn in the next section.

FRAMING PROSTITUTES

We never forgot to disinfect ourselves when the man
was done. Near the bed in the corner of the room was
a basin filled with a red disinfectant solution. Each
time we finished we would carefully wash both the
man's and the woman's private parts and wipe them
with tissue paper. Because this solution chilled us
inside, we prostitutes hardly ever got pregnant. They
said it was to see if we had contracted a disease, but
every seven days, without fail, we had to go to the
hospital for an examination. Syphilis—if you had that,
you know, your body would rot. Your whole body
would be covered with pustules and you would die a
terrible death, or else you would go mad. We never
missed an examination, because we didn't want that to
happen to us.

Yamakawa Saki

As former *karayuki-san* Yamakawa Saki reports, by the time of Japan's
second war against China, prostitutes were well aware of the severity of
venereal diseases.[25] The system of health policies that singled out prostitutes as a source of disease was well established, because until the late
1920s the hygiene authorities in the Home Department were convinced
that only the control of prostitutes could curb the spread of venereal diseases in both the army and the wider population. It took the health administration several decades and an enormous amount of data about
the causes, the paths of infection, and the cures of venereal diseases
to acknowledge that the diseases could not be contained by regulating
prostitutes.

Attempts at systematically examining prostitutes were made in early
modern Japan (Fujime 1997; Burns 1998). Nationwide regulations for
the health examination of prostitutes—genital inspections and the examination of uterine secretions—were first introduced in 1876. However, only at the beginning of the 1930s was the long-held understanding that venereal diseases (now: *seibyō*) were a "civilization disease"
(bunmeibyō), rather than a "disease of the red-light districts" (formerly:
karyūbyō), transformed into quasi-legal measures (Abe 1924b; Amemiya 1928; Tagawa 1928; Doi 1934).

In order to inspect for gonococcus, doctors extracted uterine secretions with a loop, transferred them to a glass, and heated them over a burner. A liquid dye was added, then the specimen was rinsed with water and examined under a microscope. Syphilis inspections became more reliable when doctors began to use the Wassermann reaction in the 1910s.[26] Inspection for gonococcus usually took place once a week, those for syphilis once a month or once every two months. In both cases, a regular schedule was observed. According to a former inspector for the U.S. colonial Department of Sanitation in the Philippines who inspected Japanese prostitutes for syphilis from 1919 to 1921, those women who did not pass the inspection had to stop work until the following week. They were then hospitalized in the Oriental Hospital run by the colonial government. Gonococcus inspections cost three yen per visit, and syphilis inspections were ten yen per visit. The prostitutes paid the fees. Inspections were compulsory; prostitutes who did not show up were fined thirty yen for each missed inspection (Yamazaki 1999 [1972]:70).

The nationwide regulations in Japan for prostitutes' health examinations were frequently tightened as part of the Regulations for the Control of Prostitutes, the Regulations for the Enforcement of the Law for the Prevention of Infectious Diseases, or the Law for the Prevention of Venereal Diseases (Fujikawa Y. 1911:112; SBHD 1929:3). Article 425 of the Penal Code, promulgated in July 1880, called for three to ten days of imprisonment or a fine of between one yen and 1.95 yen as punishment for secret prostitution or lending premises to persons for the purpose of assisting secret prostitution (De Becker 1905:301). A stricter set of Regulations for the Control of Prostitutes issued by the Home Department on 2 October 1900 prescribed a preliminary medical examination by a physician as part of a formal application, submitted to the police station, to become a registered prostitute (De Becker 1905:336).

These regulations also called for frequent mandatory health examinations for all registered prostitutes and the hospitalization of those affected with a venereal disease. On 10 October 1900, a notification regarding the medical inspection of prostitutes (superseding the notification of March 1894) prescribed that all prostitutes were to undergo both regular and special inspections. Regular inspection was to take place once a week. Special inspection was obligatory under several other conditions: when a woman became a prostitute, when she had been resting outside the brothel and wanted to resume working as a prostitute after a lapse of seven days or more, when a hospitalized prostitute had recovered and was about to resume work, when a woman discovered that she was infected, and when a special inspection was considered necessary or expedient by a physician. Infected women had to seek proper treatment or face a fine of up to 1.95 yen (De Becker 1905:346). These new regulations also prescribed the brothel keeper's responsibility concerning the health of prostitutes. Brothel keepers were not supposed to infringe upon regulations relative to physical examinations and were supposed to advise ill prostitutes to seek medical advice and treatment (De Becker 1905:293).

The Law for the Prevention of Venereal Diseases (Karyūbyō Yobō Hō) of 4 April 1927 categorized venereal diseases as syphilis, gonorrhea, and chancroid (SBHD 1929:5). The Bureau of Hygiene documented a whole set of statistics on prostitutes and their environment. Among other information, it carefully recorded the number of prostitution quarters (yūkaku) in each prefecture; the affected cases classified by disease; and the affected cases per 100 examinations. By the end of the 1920s, 482 health examination offices and 223 hospitals for prostitutes (shōgi byōin) served 535 prostitution quarters (SBHD 1929:213–217).

In 1930 alone, 2.9 million health examinations were performed on a daily average of 47,436 prostitutes. Among these 2.9 million examinations there were 69,277 positive diagnoses for one of nine categories of disease: syphilis, gonorrhea, chancroid, ulceration, contagious skin diseases, tuberculosis, leprosy, trachoma, or "other diseases." More than two-thirds of the prostitutes with positive diagnoses suffered from at least one venereal disease, most commonly gonorrhea (34,798) and chancroid (16,369), while considerably fewer (4,297) suffered from syphilis (SBHD 1929:61, 213). On a national average, two in a hundred prostitutes were diagnosed with at least one venereal disease at regular health examinations, while between one and three in a hundred were hospitalized (KRB 1927:114–115).

The steadily increasing number of examinations, from 1.77 million in 1896 to 2.9 million in 1930, demonstrates the great importance for the national body that the hygiene administration placed on the health examinations of prostitutes. In 1896, 4.06 percent of those examined were diagnosed as infected, while the official infection rate in 1930 was only 2.17 percent of those examined (Naimushō eiseikyoku 1893–1894, 1895, 1897, 1900, 1910, 1930).[27]

This development, however, may have been related to the establishment of hospitals for prostitutes, which resulted in less frequent examination of the same infected prostitutes. Some prostitutes may have undergone the examinations several times a year while others avoided the examination offices entirely; because it was examinations, not persons,

家　庭　雜　誌

通　俗　醫　學

第四卷　　第拾壹號

公娼存廢と
性病問題號

東京　　日本通俗醫學社發行　　大阪

Figure 4. By the late 1920s, information on the consequences of and advice for the treatment of venereal diseases dominated medical and household journals. *Popular Medicine (Tsūzoku Igaku)*, for example, regularly printed instructive articles and chose "Prostitution and the Problem of Venereal Diseases" as its theme for the November 1926 issue. (For extensive coverage of venereal diseases, see, e.g., *Tsūzoku Igaku* January 1930:161, September 1930:129, August 1933:124, February 1935:170, August 1942:80.) Used with the kind permission of the Kyōto Ika Daigaku Library.

that were counted, it is unclear how great the number of infected prostitutes was. Apart from that, the examinations first became mandatory on 18 July 1926 with the enactment of the Venereal Diseases Prevention Bill (Karyūbyō Yobō Hōan), but they were systematically applied only to registered prostitutes (Murakami 1926). Illegal prostitutes were estimated at several tens of thousands (Kagawa 1926:8). According to a 1925 official count, there were 48,291 barmaids and waitresses who worked in the coffee houses and dance halls built during the late 1920s and 1930s, and they were also rumored by the sensationalist media to have wild sex lives. However, they were just as neglected in the official health statistics as the 79,348 (1925) geisha, three-quarters of whom, according to estimates, likewise engaged in prostitution (Garon 1993b:712).

Special hospitals for the treatment of prostitutes with venereal diseases were first founded in Tokyo (1874), Osaka (1879), and Kyoto (1886), and a few years later in other prefectures and seaport towns (Kariya 1993:144). Because the prostitutes' savings rarely covered the hospital costs, the brothels for which they worked were supposed to prepay the costs (Kariya 1993:147). While this arrangement officially was tolerated out of a desire to control and regulate prostitution, or rather, the prostitutes, the courts that dealt with the cases of prostitutes forced them to pay back their debts to brothel keepers, a practice that suggests the legislation protected the trade more than the prostitutes (De Becker 1905:366–367). In 1927, 1,854 patients from the previous year and 58,308 new patients were treated in hospitals for prostitutes located all over Japan. Most of them were treated in hospitals in Osaka prefecture (835), Tokyo prefecture (637), and Kyoto prefecture (371), followed by the Nagasaki, Fukuoka, Mie, and Aichi prefectures (SBHD 1929:266–268).

Joseph E. De Becker, an international lawyer who spent most of his life in Japan and wrote several books on the Japanese legal system, emphasized that these low figures must be regarded with great suspicion. They not only contradicted the experience of medical practitioners in other countries but also were misleading in light of the statistics published by the Yoshiwara Hospital in Tokyo, where the number of infected prostitutes was considerably higher.[28] Indeed these suspicions were confirmed by examinations that were carried out beyond the auspices of the Bureau of Hygiene. In Kanagawa prefecture, more than 5,000 infections in 36,000 examinations were recorded in 1880 (Kariya 1993:154–155). In an examination in 1914, the recorded syphilis and gonorrhea infection rates among the examined prostitutes was as high as 20 percent (Takemura T. 1980:148). In addition to its other consequences, gonorrhea was the cause of incurable internal diseases and, in many cases, infertility, particularly for women. Syphilis also took a significant toll on prostitutes' bodies, and it and its complications were the most common causes of death among prostitutes (Sone 1999:178).

Most civilian physicians in modern Japan agreed with their military surgeon colleagues that licensed prostitution was a necessary evil that served as a safety valve against rape, seduction, adultery, "unnatural vices," and illicit prostitution. They also pointed out that the rate of syphilis cases had diminished considerably after the system of inspection and control was inaugurated. Medical doctors throughout the Japanese empire affirmed that since the introduction of inspection and enforced hospitalization, the more severe types of syphilis had become less common (Mori 1891:207). European medical practitioners also noted that syphilis among the Japanese was exceptionally mild and severe cases were rare. Whereas prior to the Meiji era it was quite common to see people whose noses had been eaten away by syphilis, one author noted, this sight had become uncommon by the beginning of the twentieth century (De Becker 1905:312–313).

However, not everybody embraced the health examinations for prostitutes. Some hygienists, medical doctors, and proponents of the prohibition of public prostitution criticized the examination policies on two fronts. They argued that the legislation for the health examination of prostitutes reinforced the view in the wider population that only prostitutes were carriers of venereal diseases (Ieda 1936). Another concern was that it lulled potential brothel customers into the false belief that they were safe from venereal diseases because the prostitutes were examined, while in reality—these critics speculated—only half of the registered prostitutes underwent frequent examinations (Matsuura 1912, 1927; Murakami 1926; Yutani 1932).

The conditions in the hospitals for prostitutes further discredited the government's health policies. After a prostitute had been in the hospital for three or four days, if she happened to be a popular woman, some brothel keepers bribed the hospital to have her discharged as soon as possible. Doctors and nurses in hospitals for prostitutes were poorly trained and may have given a clean bill of health to women infected with venereal diseases. De Becker also suggested that the low salaries paid in hospitals for prostitutes were unlikely to tempt the most capable medical practitioners to remain in service for any length of time (De Becker

1905:357). Moreover, physicians sometimes discovered cases that would have been impossible to conceal from an examiner. In those cases, brothel keepers requested counterfeit certificates stating that a change of air was necessary for a woman's health. Armed with these certificates, keepers pretended that the patient had gone into the country, when in reality she was carefully hidden in the brothel and secretly treated by a physician (De Becker 1905:366).

While both soldiers and prostitutes were examined for venereal diseases by state authorities out of a concern for the national body, the procedures applied to both groups as well as their effects could not have been more different. Venereal diseases appeared prominently in military records and reports, but they represented only one type of a few dozen diseases soldiers were checked for. By the end of the Meiji era, the examiners of soldiers' bodies had produced the most comprehensive stock of data ever made available to population planners in Japan, symbolically representing the normal and normative Japanese physique and widely used in comparative physiological treatises. Along with many other techniques of health improvement and preservation, physical examinations of conscripts—and through them, of the Japanese populace at large—clearly served to standardize and optimize their health and fitness.

Health examinations of prostitutes, in contrast, focused on venereal diseases. Hence, while attempts were made to detect venereal diseases by means of periodic inspections, internal diseases often were ignored, and brothel keepers forced women suffering from syphilis and other diseases to continue their work (De Becker 1905:354–357). Despite the frequently repeated claim that prostitutes were necessary to contain the overflow of men's sexual needs, they were declared a source of disease and a health hazard to men and their innocent wives and children, and thought of as the latrine of the modern state. Thus their health was not considered worthy of protection or improvement for its own sake. The women themselves were considered negligible and could be (and were at times) disposed of.

Only between the implementation of the General Mobilization Law (Kokka Sōdōinhō) in 1938 and the Law for the Strengthening of the National Body (Kokumin Tairyokuhō) in 1941 did legislation for the prevention of venereal diseases undergo a significant shift away from the focus on prostitutes and toward coverage of the entire population. Then, the largely preventive policies of the late nineteenth century were gradually substituted for by proscriptive legislation that culminated in the implementation of the National Eugenic Law, which I shall discuss in chapter 5. Before eugenic concepts came to the fore, however, Japanese physicians, pedagogues, and bureaucrats turned their attention to children, who they came to perceive as another pillar of the modern health regime.

EXAMINING CHILDREN'S BODIES

Children, Masuda Hōson noted in his *Social History of Children (Jidō shakai-shi)* in 1924, have not been cherished or loved by all cultures at all times. On the contrary, whether in China, Western countries, or Japan, instances of abandonment and infanticide had been common. Writing his book at a time of intense discussions about and significant improvements in children's health and education, Masuda described the Edo period (1612–1867) as an era in which duty and filial piety on the part of children overshadowed concern about their well-being (Masuda 1924:229–230). In his book, Masuda was concerned primarily with the ideals of a warrior class parent-child relationship. However, ordinary children's relationship to their parents and their role in the household began to undergo significant changes as well when—in addition to barracks and brothels—schools and other institutions of education and training became further sites for the enactment of the new concept of hygiene.

By founding public schools and mandating first four, then six years of education for children of both sexes, the Meiji government aimed at controlling the socialization process in order to further state goals. To begin with, the introduction of compulsory education in 1872 (at the same time conscription was introduced) had a negative impact on the household division of labor and on family livelihood. This stirred resistance to state policy, mainly among ordinary households that were dependent on their children's domestic or wage-earning labor for their survival. The government adopted various strategies, such as reducing the duration of compulsory education, lowering tuition, and founding special institutions to educate poor children and soothe aggrieved families, to counteract this resistance. It likewise continued to promote school enrollment and to send out truant officers to compel school attendance. By the early twentieth century, enrollment rates suggested that ordinary families throughout the nation had come to accept compulsory schooling. However, registration rates may have suggested a brighter picture than was the reality. Autobiographies and oral histories reveal that children of all ages were routinely kept home from school when their families required extra labor (Uno 1999:39).

Throughout the late nineteenth century, pedagogues urged teachers and parents to vigorously impress upon children the virtues of cleanliness (Watanabe Y. 1886; *Dai Nihon Kyōiku Zasshi* 1888). However, while the battle against infectious diseases had taken off in the 1880s—when the police became one of the chief protectors of public hygiene and were given the responsibility of isolating patients, intercepting traffic, and in other restrictive ways trying to prevent the spread of infectious diseases—effective hygiene regulations for children were only put in place at the end of the 1890s. The results of a fact-finding mission of officials from the Ministry of Education in schools all over Japan revealed that children were shockingly weak and suffered from all kinds of diseases. Claiming children as agents of hygiene and at the same time styling them as vulnerable victims of social menace, pedagogues and medical doctors insisted that children needed to be measured, protected, and instructed for their own good and for the welfare of the nation. Subsequently, pedagogues and physicians began to promote a program of physical exercise and cleanliness to balance the emphasis on scholastic training that dominated school education at the time. In 1898, a set of policies for the prevention of infectious diseases and disinfection in schools came to replace the simpler rules of cleanliness that had been part of the School Regulations (Seitō kokoroe) of 1877 (Naka 1977: 202; Okamoto 1982:124; Nomura 1990; Muta 1992).

According to this new set of policies, the most worrisome diseases that affected children in schools included measles, whooping cough, influenza, mumps, German measles, and chicken pox. Tuberculosis and skin and eye diseases were also common but not specific to children. At schools, preventive measures and hygiene measures were introduced and developed at the initiative of Mishima Tsūryō, an official in the Division of School Hygiene in the Ministry of Education. From the early Meiji years onward, the general school regulations had prescribed that children with certain diseases be denied admission, but only under the guidance of Mishima were important steps taken to improve hygiene conditions in schools and prevent the infection of children there.

A new committee of school hygiene was founded in the Ministry of Education in 1897. The committee consisted of nine people from the fields of medicine and hygiene. Mishima became its first president. The committee's achievements were numerous. Regulations for elementary school equipment were introduced in 1892; regulations for school architecture followed in 1894; the School Cleanliness Law and the Physical Examination Guidelines of School Students (which substituted for a physical strength exam from 1889) were passed in 1898; and a hygiene system for public schools established in 1899 was expanded in 1900 to include all other types of schools and kindergartens. These achievements laid the foundation not only for healthier children but also for more children surviving into adulthood (Naka 1977:205). In 1901, Mishima became responsible for the Division of School Hygiene in the Ministry of Education, which had been established in 1898 by imperial decree as the central authority in a new system of school physicians. It gave a new type of physician, the specialist in children's health, complete access to the bodies of children and adolescents. Medical specialists in children's health had existed before pediatrics was established as an academic field in Japan, but Tokugawa-era and early Meiji specialists typically had been trained in Chinese medicine. The first courses in pediatrics were taught at the University of Tokyo in 1888 but research on children's health in Japan began only around 1900 (Naka 1977:203).

Although the school hygiene system was built much slower than Mishima had hoped, with 30 percent of schools covered in 1902 and 80 percent of schools covered in 1918, the system received international praise as early as 1904. At an international convention on hygiene in Brussels, the director of the Belgian school hygiene division noted of the Japanese system that the world was now to learn from Japan rather than the other way around (Naka 1977:206). By 1902, more than 9,000 school physicians had been hired. Of these, 8,700 worked at primary schools, which about 55 percent of the children under the age of eleven attended, while the others were affiliated with teacher seminars, middle schools, and girls' schools (Leuschner 1906:790–93). These physicians did not merely inspect the schools, but also sought opportunities to invite pupils and parents to discuss sanitary matters related to their homes. It was this system that prompted an English admirer of Japan's "national efficiency" to declare that "nothing is neglected in the calculations to improve the national physique and provide Japan with able-bodied citizens in every branch of national life" (Stead 1905:133).

During the Sino-Japanese war of 1894–1895, the quality of boys' bodies became especially crucial for the strength of the nation, and "military-style exercise" *(heishiki taisō)*, advocated since the early days of the Imperial Army and Navy, was practiced in secondary schools (Tsuji 1884; Ōmura 1886; Kojima 1942). Many Japanese intellectuals of the time were already familiar with the social Darwinist idea of the survival of the fittest. At wartime in particular, the ideal of not only a strong army but an army of strong men was propagated. The short stature and physical weakness of Japanese troops in 1894 was a major concern for the forces, and many found that this concern could best be addressed in the schools. Outgoing Education Minister Inoue Kowashi (known to his opponents as the "nervous minister") took the initial step of ordering more physical exercise for elementary schoolchildren, as well as military exercises accompanied by the singing of war songs for more advanced elementary boys. Pupils also were encouraged to lead a healthy lifestyle, and those who lived in towns and habitually took a carriage to school were advised to walk (Lone 1994:96–97). In this way, children rapidly became a critical resource for the production of knowledge and the development of pedagogical theories. Children allowed access to a means of controlling and guiding society. Symbolically, they united a number of agents who helped achieve a modern health regime. Representatives of psychology, pedagogy, and medicine assigned a key position to children, their education, and their health care.

School hygiene programs were implemented mainly to control the spread of infectious diseases that particularly affected children but also to fight the spread of tuberculosis and tracheitis, which had occurred in epidemic proportions after the Sino-Japanese War. Children were told not to use the handkerchiefs or towels of other children and, in moral education and sports classes, were educated about the principles of cleanliness and instructed to take care of their bodies. By official decree, all children were examined twice a year. As with the health examinations of conscripts and soldiers, data on primary school pupils were carefully documented. Their height, weight, chest circumference, general constitution, sight, and hearing were systematically measured. The results of these measurements and all illnesses diagnosed were noted in a student's graduation certificate, which had to be produced at the entrance examinations for secondary schools (Narita 1995:68). At the beginning of the twentieth century, illnesses, morphology, and athletic abilities were central in these examinations, which became ever more detailed. Pupils were examined for a long list of conditions including scrofula, malnutrition, anemia, beriberi, pulmonary tuberculosis, headaches, chronic diseases, nervous dejection, and exhaustion. Newspapers frequently reported the results of these examinations, pointing out the improvement of the physical constitution of girls and boys. Attributing health and national strength to children's increasing height and weight, newspapers noted with satisfaction that upper-class children especially,

Figure 5. Children's textbooks, storybooks, and magazines emphasized the importance of proper hygiene for children. The back cover of this Kōdansha storybook from 1940, for example, featured an advertisement for a toothpaste, but also urged children to "play well," "eat well," and "sleep well." This particular copy was available at a dentist's office.

and girls in particular, were becoming taller (*Chūō Shinbun* 1913; *Jiji Shinpō* 1914; Shimoda 1914; *Yomiuri Shinbun* 1915a, c; *Tōkyō Asahi Shinbun* 1916; *Hōchi Shinbun* 1916b).

School physicians and pedagogues referred to these examinations when they reported that children and adolescents in urban areas suffered from headaches, exhaustion, melancholia, a pale complexion, or other forms of unsatisfactory physical or psychological development. When at the beginning of the twentieth century pedagogues and medical doctors began to accept the "discovery" of the sexual instinct in children, they not only blamed overwork, bad air, and the lack of exercise but also "psychological exhaustion" *(shinkei no karō),* neurasthenia, and masturbation for these ailments (Shimoda 1904a:415–420; *Miyako Shinbun* 1917).

By the beginning of the twentieth century soldiers, prostitutes, and children were—to different degrees and in different ways—represented in and incorporated into a complex set of power relations. These power relations were created by the quest for knowledge and surveillance, as well as ultimately for control and the desire to refashion the physique and psyche of imperial subjects and—by extension—of the empire. Considering that soldiers featured prominently in these attempts, it is not surprising that the language of the health regime's engineers was inherently militarist and expansionist. Administrative control was exercised and extended in order to "protect" and "defend" the soldiers from prostitutes, the children from themselves, and the empire from its pathological subjects. Sex became the locus of these struggles, which were increasingly modeled not only by military and civilian health administrators but also by experts from a number of fields, including medicine, pedagogy, and psychiatry, who were situated at Japan's leading institutions of higher education. It was these experts who eventually triggered a massive debate about sexual desire in children, the subject of the next chapter.

CHAPTER 2

Debating Sex Education

In Germany sexual issues are treated not only from the perspective of morality, as in Japan, but also in a scientific way.
As a result there is hardly anyone in Germany over twenty
who still masturbates. An overwhelming number of books
about masturbation and works about other problems related
to sexual desire are published there.

Habuto Eiji, *Doitsu shōnen no imawashii seiyoku*

Habuto Eiji was a gynecologist and a tremendously prolific writer of
popular books on sexual issues during the 1920s and 1930s. In 1913,
he had just returned to Japan after two years of studying medicine in
Germany when the newspaper *Tōkyō Nichinichi Shinbun* printed a
short article on his experiences and impressions of German sex education and research entitled "The Detestable Sexual Desire of German
Youth" ("Doitsu shōnen no imawashii seiyoku," 12 November 1913).[1]
The newsworthiness of Habuto's statement reflected a heightened interest in "scientific" sex education, which had been discussed controver-
sially by pedagogues, medical doctors, writers, and bureaucrats of the
public health administration for more than a decade.

SOME ESSAYS ON INFANTILE SEXUALITY

Within and outside of the school hygiene system that had emerged during the last decades of the nineteenth century, pedagogues and medical
doctors were the first scholars to occupy themselves in their professional
journals with questions of children's sexual desire. In November 1898,
in the same year that the Division of School Hygiene was established, educational psychologists Takashima Heisaburō (Takashima Beihō), Matsumoto Kōjirō, and Tsukahara Keiji founded the journal *Pediatric Research (Jidō Kenkyū)*. *Pediatric Research* was one of the first pediatric

journals to provide a forum, mainly for medical doctors and pedagogues, for discussing children's development in a comprehensive manner (Takashima 1898–1899). Half a year later, contributors to the journal began to discuss sexual desire in children, a subject that soon became the focus of a much broader debate that would continue for many years to follow.

In the May 1899 issue, *Pediatric Research* printed an article on the causes of "Psychological Illnesses among Children" ("Jidō ni okeru seishinbyō") in which masturbation *(shuin)* was noted as one factor leading to the occurrence of these illnesses (Matsubara 1993:232). Soon other pediatricians articulated similar views in the *Journal of Pediatrics (Jika Zasshi)* in contributions such as "Dangers during the Growth Phase" in the May 1900 issue or "The Malady of Venereal Diseases" in the February 1901 issue. In 1900, medical doctor and distinguished historian of medicine Fujikawa Yū (1865–1940) submitted an article to *Pediatric Research* entitled "The Sexual Instinct in Children" ("Jidō ni okeru seiyoku").[2] In it, Fujikawa provided information about the medical aspects of sexual desire *(shikijō* or *seiyoku)* in children and suggested that children masturbated because they were not properly educated about sexual matters by their parents or by their teachers (Fujikawa Y. 1900).

In this article and later, in other scholarly journals and general-readership newspapers and mass-circulation magazines, Fujikawa argued that the Japanese population had to be given "scientific" information on children's sex drive. He considered it his mission to provide that information (see, e.g., Fujikawa Y. 1907a–b, 1908a, 1912, 1915, 1919a–d, 1923, 1924, 1928). When he launched his own journal entitled *Humankind: Der Mensch (Jinsei—Der Mensch)* in 1905 (see figure 6), Fujikawa wrote an editorial describing his goals, which can be summarized as follows. First, *Humankind: Der Mensch* would set out to provide solutions for the social and psychological problems of mankind. Second, it would lay the cornerstone for collaborative research about these problems between East and West. And third, it would contribute to research on the history of humankind. Fujikawa envisaged a readership of a great variety of professionals, among whom, he hoped, would be lawyers, bureaucrats, pedagogues, theologians, physicians, anthropologists, and other scientists who shared his concerns "about the great problems of humankind" (Fujikawa Y. 1905: 1).

Mishima Tsūryō, founder and first director of the Division of School Hygiene in the Ministry of Education, was one of these intellectuals. On 20 March 1906, the *Journal of Pediatrics* printed a lecture that Mishima

Figure 6. The first issue of the journal *Humankind: Der Mensch* (*Jinsei—Der Mensch,* 1905) vividly illustrated the complexity of the concept of appropriation from Western science: above the Japanese name is the German subtitle *Der Mensch*. Below that, the earth can be seen in front of the rising sun, flanked by the sun god Apollo (right) and the German war god Baldur (left). Used with the kind permission of the Meiji Shinbun Zasshi Bunkō, University of Tokyo.

had given at the first International World Conference on School Hygiene in Nuremberg in 1905, which was, coincidentally, the year August Forel's influential book *The Sexual Question (Die sexuelle Frage)* was published in Munich. Perhaps the most powerful pediatrician of his time, Mishima clearly agreed with Fujikawa on the necessity of sex education. In his article "Sexual Questions of School Children" ("Gakkō seitō no shikijō mondai"), Mishima proclaimed that indeed the German notion of "sexual pedagogy" *(Sexualpädagogik)* was the most effective prophylactic measure for preventing both masturbation and venereal diseases. Mishima's article provoked a great deal of discussion among school directors and teachers. He urged them to enlighten children on the "dangers of venereal diseases and their evil consequences" in relation to sexual desire and encouraged teachers to consider sex education at least for middle schools, girls' schools, and high schools (Mishima 1906).

A few regional projects were set up in which teachers made initial attempts to introduce sex education at schools (Furukawa M. 1994:117). Some invited medical doctors like Fujikawa to their schools to talk about hygiene and the functions of the sex organs *(seishokki)* as well as the potential risks of their use. However, it wasn't until 1908 that the quest for sex education spilled over the boundaries of scholarly journals and local sex education projects to become a public issue that was debated on a national scale.

THE "SEXUAL PROBLEM"

By the end of the first decade of the twentieth century, debates about sexual issues had begun to reach the entire reading public of Japan. From 1 September to 13 October 1908, the *Yomiuri Shinbun,* a nationally distributed newspaper, serialized the views of prominent pedagogues and medical doctors on what they termed the "sexual problem" (alternatively referred to as *seiyoku mondai* or *seimondai).* Founded in 1874, the *Yomiuri Shinbun* is one of the oldest modern daily papers in Japan. With a circulation of 60,000, it was also the third-largest newspaper after the *Asahi Shinbun* and the *Mainichi Shinbun.* However, it was the first to print the phonetic syllable writing systems *hiragana* and *katakana* next to less common Chinese characters in order to facilitate legibility for a less educated readership. This printing technique corresponded with the maxim of the press, which was that important information should be printed in a form understandable to all (Minami H. 1965:334; Muzik 1996:83–84).

The *Yomiuri Shinbun* debate on the "sexual problem" both represented and contributed to an increasing interest in children's sexual desire and its proper guidance by continuously broadening the new arena of discourse on sex. It heightened the sense of urgency regarding sex education among scholars, bureaucrats of the health administration, teachers, and parents. It was particularly significant because it presented the sexual problem to a huge, heterogeneous readership that was not necessarily scientifically literate. The debate in the *Yomiuri Shinbun* also introduced an entire repertoire of new ideas. Among these were opinions on masturbation and venereal disease, "normalcy" and "deviance," the responsibilities of teachers and parents, the authority of experts, and the internationalism of sexual knowledge. It helped generate a discursive configuration that came to inform talk and texts about sex throughout the first half of the twentieth century.

Almost all of the contributions were rooted in the conviction that the creation of and instruction on "correct" knowledge about sex was necessary in order to improve the Japanese national body. According to the participants in the debate, the idea of protecting or improving the national health or national hygiene legitimated a tight network of examination, control, and surveillance through schools, parents, and children themselves. "Correct" knowledge about sex was to be obtained through "scientific" methods. These methods included the solicitation of confessions from children, observation and interrogation by parents and teachers, diagnoses of school physicians, and empirical data on the sexual behavior of Japan's young. "Scientific" knowledge about sex had to be completely severed from religious customs and social traditions.

The frequently recurring metaphors of (necessary) disclosure versus (previous) suppression highlighted the larger purpose of sex education, namely protection, prevention, and regulation, and have accompanied the discourse of sex ever since. As I shall show in the following chapters, however, the labels "liberation" and "suppression" were reconfigured frequently and promoted or condemned by players with radically varying agendas. I shall turn to the postwar rhetoric of "sexual freedom" in chapter 5. Here I am interested in the emergence of the preoccupation with infantile sexuality and the sex education of children and youth. On the one hand, children were to be protected from both their own (unconscious) desires and the corrupting dangers of modern society—since a "fallen society" threatened to destroy the education of children, even those from the best homes. On the other hand, the national body had to be protected from those children who could not be prevented from in-

dulging their desires and who thus became mentally and physically diseased. Hence, instruction on sex that would eventually emerge from
"scientific" knowledge was to be prophylactic and preventive in nature.
It should aim at preventing dubious sexual practices (e.g., masturbation
or intercourse with prostitutes) and their supposed consequences (e.g.,
neurasthenia, venereal diseases, and unwanted pregnancies).

Initially, the debate was framed as an exchange of opinions on sex education *(seiyoku kyōiku* or *seikyōiku mondai)*, but it came to be pursued
in a far more complex manner. The contributors raised a great number
of questions. What exactly did "sex education" mean, what should be
said, and why should sex education be carried out? Who was authorized
to speak and who was to remain silent? What was the right age for children to be enlightened on sexual matters? The sheer range of these questions indicated that the new interest in the implications of children's sexual desire had consequences beyond the boundaries of certain scholarly
disciplines. The debate demarcated the "intellectual field" (Bourdieu
1980), which the sexual problem came to colonize for itself and which
engendered a dense web of tensions over individual and state responsibilities, self-control and happiness, disease and the concern for the national body. It was also interwoven with negotiations about the authority of experts who strove to distinguish themselves from lay people by
insisting on the necessity of "scientific" knowledge.

DEFINING THE CHILD

For the contributors to the series in the *Yomiuri Shinbun,* sex education
was based on two techniques of inquiry: encouraging children to speak,
and making children investigate themselves and their own behavior.
Yoshida Kumaji (1874–1964) argued that the term "children" had to
be carefully and clearly defined, since education about sexual desire
might harm children of certain age groups (Yoshida K. 1908a:5). Ironically, however, he suggested including everybody from infants *(akago)*
to adults *(otona)* in the definition of "children" *(shitei)* because sex education was important for everyone.[3]

The question of the age range of childhood was not taken for granted;
pedagogues had attempted to define the child in terms of age prior to the
debate in the *Yomiuri Shinbun.* Imai Tsuneo, for example, published a
monumental work, *Family and Education (Katei oyobi kyōiku),* two
years before the debate appeared in the *Yomiuri Shinbun.* This work explained that the "infant phase" *(nyōjiki)* referred to infants up to the age

of eight months, "childhood" *(jidōki)* covered children up to the age of seven, and "late childhood" *(jidō kōki)* referred to children between the ages of seven and fourteen or fifteen and was followed by adolescence and adulthood (Imai T. 1906:176–177). The authors of the series in the *Yomiuri Shinbun* were not as explicit regarding the age of children they discussed, and they vacillated among the four phases that Imai had outlined. Thus the categories "children" and "adolescents" appeared in equal proportions in the debate, and sex education was situated in the home as well as in elementary, middle, and high schools. However, regardless of the age at which participants suggested children receive sex education, most agreed that ignorance and error had to be combated and sex had to be liberated from mystification.

PREVENTING HARM

A few authors steadfastly opposed sex education of any kind and retreated to the notion of the nature of the Japanese as essentially different from that of people from the West, where sex education was perceived as necessary and legitimate (Yoshida K. 1908b:5). This difference in nature stemmed from a number of things, including the Japanese diet, which lacked meat and alcohol, and—as noted in the first chapter—an awareness of a relative physical weakness that had been commented on in military hygiene reports and in the physical examination reports of school physicians. Yoshida, for example, reasoned that people in the West ate a lot of meat and frequently drank beer and wine for lunch and dinner. Both of these customs, he claimed, typically increased sexual desire. Little wonder, then, that the negative effects of increased sexual desire were much more common among Western youth, and thus sex education there was justified, while in Japan its necessity was far from proven (Yoshida K. 1908c:5; see also Katayama 1911). Yoshida warned that Japanese translations of German books that maintained that more than half of German elementary school pupils masturbated did not sufficiently legitimate the introduction of sex education in Japanese schools (Yoshida K. 1908b:5). He also demanded that nothing should be done at all in terms of sex education before detailed empirical studies were carried out at Japanese schools to prove its necessity.

I shall analyze the first sex surveys, conducted at the beginning of the 1920s, in chapter 3. Here I wish to emphasize that unlike Yoshida, most of the participants in the debate were convinced that sex education was as necessary in Japan as in any other modern nation. The actual content of sex education, however, was controversial. While some insisted that it was vital to convey accurate knowledge about sex, others cautioned that the amount of knowledge was crucial. As evident from the *Yomiuri Shinbun* debate, sex education covered a wide variety of topics, ranging from exercise and training in willpower and self-control to explicit explanations about sexual awakening, the development of the sexual organs, and related aspects of the transition to adolescence and adulthood. Families and elementary schools were responsible for laying the groundwork for sound ethics and morals, declared Mukō Gunji, professor at the prestigious Keiō University, but it was also the duty of the state to raise a "morally strong people." Sex education for children was thus one of the most crucial tools for nurturing "national moral health." The warrior ethics of premodern Japan *(bushi no dōtoku)* should now be enforced by a "social system of punishment" *(shakaiteki seisai)* consisting of the family, schools, and other institutions (Mukō 1908b:5).

Most pedagogues who contributed to the debate in the *Yomiuri Shinbun* agreed that sex education was necessary primarily to avoid the "horrible consequences of masturbation" (Mukō 1908a:5). Yubara Motoichi, head of the Tokyo School of Music (Tōkyō Ongaku Gakkō), suggested discussing sexual desire in a way that would "not embarrass" young boys and girls. Masturbation, he argued, should be mentioned rarely, only if absolutely necessary, and only after consulting a doctor (Yubara 1908:5). For the founder and director of Japan's first Medical School for Women (Tōkyō Joi Gakkō), Washiyama Yayoi (later Yoshioka Yayoi), masturbation was "the most terrible ailment related to the sexual instinct." Regarding sex education, she asserted that the only purpose of the sex drive was reproduction and any abuse would have fatal consequences. Washiyama, the only female participant in the debate, reasoned that ignorance led students between the ages of fifteen and seventeen to masturbate. Since masturbation did not lead to satisfaction, they masturbated frequently and had to bear unimaginable consequences (Washiyama 1908a:5). Mukō, along with most of the pedagogues who participated in the debate, wholeheartedly shared Washiyama's conviction that sex education served mainly to avoid the "devastating consequences of masturbation" (Mukō 1908a–c).

However, pedagogues and medical doctors agreed that attempts at avoiding masturbation in order to escape its harmful effects were a tricky matter. Since sexual desire would awaken eventually no matter what was done about it, the essential decision to be made was not *if* sex education should take place but *how* youth, who possibly masturbated, could be

told that they must not masturbate, without provoking those who did
not to try it. Mukō and other participants in the debate did not question
the sexual drive in children but rather strove for an appropriate means
of controlling youth and protecting them from "everything bad," be
it masturbation, "impure women," or venereal diseases. According to
Mukō, sexual desire should serve the purpose of reproduction alone,
and any other use should be considered a "sex crime" (Mukō 1908e:5).

Other authors vigorously advocated a more comprehensive sex education that would teach children everything about the dangers of sexual
desire. They thought that children should no longer be told that they
"descended from trees" (Inagaki 1908:5). Instead, sexual knowledge
should be "popularized" *(tsūzoku-ka suru)* in order to avert the danger
to the nation's health and welfare represented by masturbation and venereal diseases. Ignorance of sexual matters was seen by proponents of sex
education as directly linked to "neurasthenia" *(shinkei suijaku)* or—
more precisely—"sexual neurasthenia" *(seiteki shinkei suijaku),* which
was repeatedly diagnosed by physicians of middle schools, and ascribed
to "sexual immorality" *(seiteki fudōtoku)* both within and outside of
the *Yomiuri Shinbun* debate (Mukō 1908a:5).

Shimoda Jirō, a colleague of Yoshida's at the teachers' college, subsequently presented a competing view of the causes of neurasthenia. He
suggested that students who suffered from too much learning and too
many exams would develop neurasthenia and other neurological diseases. After graduation they would not be able to live "normal" lives,
and some might even die. Many preparations were necessary for life
in a modern society like Japan and thus, Shimoda argued, the number of
subjects in schools had increased. "Human strength" *(ningen no chi-
kara),* however, he emphasized, has always been and still was limited.
He concluded that if the brain were overused from an early age, neither
the body nor the mind would fully develop (Shimoda 1904a:406–407).
Most contemporary pedagogues, including those who participated in
the *Yomiuri Shinbun* debate, disagreed with Shimoda on the issue of
neurasthenia. In contrast to his position, they generally agreed that there
was a direct connection between masturbation and neurasthenia. No
matter whether they propagated or opposed sex education in schools,
they were convinced that excessive autoerotic practices, rather than too
much school work, led to paleness, loss of appetite, forgetfulness, indif-
ference, melancholy, and poor scholastic results, predominantly among
male youth (Mukō 1908b:5; Minami R. 1908a, c; Washiyama 1908b:5).

Anxieties about neurasthenia, just like concerns about prostitution and venereal diseases, were shared by specialists in schools as well as in military academies and hospitals. Preoccupied with neurasthenia's causes and consequences, health administrators in the military and the national government's public health administration began to view neurasthenia as a precursor to more serious illnesses that could occur epidemically and eventually challenge military discipline and combat capabilities, or even the nation's social order and stability. Medical experts employed by militaries throughout the world insisted on the enormous role that psychic predisposition played in the onset of all war-related disorders (Rabinbach 1990:267). Accordingly, the Imperial Army and Navy's medical staff began to record nervous diseases *(shinkei-kei byō)* among soldiers and officers as early as in 1878, when some physicians began to make connections between a venereal disease infection, consequent suffering from nervous maladies, and eventual attempts at suicide (Rikugunshō 1879; Kaigunshō 1897:170). By the end of World War I, categories for nervous illnesses listed in the military's annual health reports had been expanded from one to eleven different kinds. These nervous illnesses were recorded in the army and the navy stationed throughout the Japanese empire and included "neurasthenia" and "hysteria" as separate categories (e.g., Rikugunshō 1917:140, 151, 364, 403, 432, 466, 492). Medical doctor Hirota Motokichi was especially concerned with neurasthenia when it occurred among military men: "It is especially important to ensure that military leaders do not suffer from neurasthenia. They have to keep their nerve until the very end of a war, for example, and suffering from neurasthenia would be dangerous in the case of military leaders who operate under a lot of pressure. . . . Without a strong physique and mind, nothing new and good can occur" (Hirota 1919:134, 138).

However, in civilian society too, associations between sexual practices, mental and physical ailments, and challenges to the social order of the nation had become commonplace. Ōkuma Shigenobu (1838–1922), an immensely influential figure in politics and education, addressed this concern in a powerful speech to the participants of a conference on mental illnesses in 1922. Ōkuma promoted a law that would regulate the lives of the mentally ill. His appeal clearly was dominated by the idea of social order and the potential challenge posed to that order by the "chronically ill":

Insanity occasionally becomes infectious. This infection can be terrible, spreading ceaselessly among the people. A society, or even a state, can eventually become morbid. I suppose that a nation like Russia might be affected by insanity. In the beginning, it was neurasthenia, then it became psychosis, and finally it turned into a pathological attack which would lead the nation to end in a complete failure—a revolution. Being insane produces a peculiar effect. Because, once affected by insanity, even the Japanese, who have been known for a unique loyalty to their Emperor, may exhibit a disloyalty. . . . Insane persons should be taken care of by the state. Why? If they are neglected, the infection will make the nation increasingly morbid, and the entire society will become confused and out of control. (Quoted in Nakatani 1995:15)

Ōkuma defined the attributes of insanity as infection, moral degradation, and threat to social and national integrity. He argued that decadent public morals—indulgence in alcohol, art, and literature—prevailed among Japan's youth, causing neurasthenia. In Ōkuma's eyes, the contagiousness of immorality was associated with the infectiousness of mental disorders, both of which were equally devastating because they threatened people's morality and caused social turmoil.

Medical doctors, bureaucrats who dealt with public health policies, and pedagogues alike perceived neurasthenia as a pathological phenomenon caused by an excessive and misled sex life, of which masturbation and prostitution were but the most obvious manifestations, manifestations that could result in venereal diseases as well as tuberculosis. These connections were fueled by the belief that tuberculosis was not a disease in its own right but was a form of syphilis (Johnston 1995:48, 190, 197, 289).[4] Moreover, it was also commonly believed that the development of insanity followed a pathological evolution that was disastrous for the individual and society—similar to that of venereal and other infectious diseases. Extensive autoerotic practices, which were commonly stimulated by alcohol and "bad literature," would lead to neurasthenia. Neurasthenia, as a preliminary stage of psychosis, would bring about pathological consequences and eventually culminate in moral degradation and social chaos. Hence, masturbation was but one expression of insanity.

Participants in the *Yomiuri Shinbun* debate were equally concerned about the spread of venereal diseases and the threat they posed to national health. Here too, health interests intermingled with moral claims. For Fujikawa, for example, people who were convinced that sex education increased sexual desire were ignorant about education. He argued that a "morally oriented education" that treated the "sexual problem" ambivalently actually prevented a solution to a problem that had to be "attacked swiftly" (Fujikawa Y. 1908a:5). Yubara also was convinced that ignorance posed an even greater danger than any sex education possibly could, regardless of whether the latter was carried out at school or at home (Yubara 1908:5).

"Immoral behavior," or individual morality for that matter, was a rather complex construct as reflected in the *Yomiuri Shinbun* debate and the more comprehensive pedagogical works of the time. Imai Tsuneo explained that individual morality was in fact threefold. There were the "morals of the body," including all practices that involved one's physique, "external morals," which concerned all things outside of oneself, and "morals of the mind" (Imai 1906:822). While "external morals," or the risks and challenges of modern society, were considered outside the grasp of an individual, the training and hygiene of the mind separate from and in addition to that of the body was frequently emphasized. Shimoda Jirō, for example, considered "mental hygiene" *(seishin no eisei)* no less important than physical cleanliness. "Mental hygiene" was crucial in the education of both boys and girls because mental weakness would eventually harm and weaken the body. Referring to Herbert Spencer's work *Education* (1880), Wilhelm Löwenthal's *Outline of Hygiene in Education (Grundzüge einer Hygiene des Unterrichts,* 1887), and the works of several other German, French, and British pedagogues and philosophers, Shimoda emphasized the importance of the balance between body and mind. He argued that an overdose of knowledge, if accompanied by a lack of physical exercise, could provoke rather unwelcome results in a child (Shimoda 1904a:405). Minami Ryō, director of the First High School (Daiichi Kōtō Gakkō, which was later integrated in the pedagogical faculty of the University of Tokyo), expressed similar concerns when he suggested that mothers instruct their sons by employing the following words:

> We become fathers and mothers through body and soul. That means that both body and soul are important. If parents' bodies are bad or their souls rotten, the body of the child will be bad and its soul rotten too. The man's seed is very important. Since his seed turns into a shoot from which a new person arises, you must take care day and night to keep your body and soul healthy and pure so that on the day you become a father you will not regret anything. Keep pure that part of your body which is the source of children and grandchildren. . . . Happiness depends on whether one has adequate self-control. No matter how much obscenity you see or hear, keep your distance from it. You must carefully concentrate on preserving your purity. (Minami R. 1908b:5)

Concern about the physical and mental consequences of venereal diseases and the conviction that female prostitutes (male prostitutes never appeared in this debate) were their source led Shimoda to explain that sex education must serve to keep youth from the dangers of contact with "impure women" *(fuketsu na onna),* who he suspected not only populated the traditional red-light districts but also waitressed in the new beer halls (Shimoda 1908c:5). As appropriate reading matter he recommended a book that underlined the importance of sex education by describing the horrific consequences of an infection with a venereal disease.[5] Although some people would attempt to end their lives by throwing themselves into the Kegon Waterfalls (a popular site for suicides), at least society, he argued, would remain undamaged. Referring to the content of the book, Shimoda explained that in many cases infection with a venereal disease resulted in blindness, sterility, mental retardation, and physical deformities in the offspring of the infected person (Shimoda 1908c:5). Yoshida assented, emphasizing that infection with a venereal disease meant nothing less than undermining the very basis of the state by damaging the entire national body (Yoshida K. 1908a:5).

GENDERED TROUBLE

It was not always made clear in the sex education debate whether the focus was on boys, girls, or both. Although some considered coeducation *(danjo kongō kyōiku)* an important prerequisite for boys' and girls' getting used to the other sex and "meet[ing] them in harmony," cautious pedagogues like Mukō warned that physical proximity might have the disadvantage of enabling children to touch one another. However, he felt that if some subjects were taught separately, coeducation in others would not have negative effects on children (Mukō 1908d:5). Inagaki Suematsu, a colleague of Mukō's at Keiō University, steadfastly defended the existing model of coeducation in elementary schools, if only because coeducation in these schools was sanctioned by the Ministry of Education and also "favored in the Protestant countries of the Western world." He was more wary of the possible negative effects on the development of pubescent students at middle school age. However, Ingaki noted, because coeducation had become the well-established ideal in "civilized" societies, Japan had to become accustomed to it as well. Once coeducation at the middle school level became common in Japan, it would not cause great damage. Inagaki also appealed to readers of the *Yomiuri Shinbun,* arguing that instead of confronting the "sexual problem" with resistance and mistrust, they should give it sufficient attention and allow it to be "liberated from mystification" (Inagaki 1908:5).

Shimoda agreed that children needed to know about the "most important issue in human life," but rejected coeducation at the middle school and high school levels because pubescent boys and girls were at a very "sensitive age." He also questioned whether the Japanese in general and Japanese children and youth in particular were ready to take on the sexual issue (Shimoda 1908a:5, 1908b:5). Sexual desire might be natural, he argued, but modern human beings had to overcome nature to a certain degree. Sex education should not be forced on students, Shimoda cautioned, as some of them might be mentally unprepared for it. Also, sex education could provoke and irritate students who had not yet developed adequate self-control (Shimoda 1908b:5).

Most participants in the debate had no doubts about masturbation and "same-sex love" *(dōseiai)* being common among boys in schools, factory dormitories, juvenile reformatories, and prisons (see Ōsugi 1992 [1930]; Roden 1980; Pflugfelder 1999:283). However, directors and teachers of girls' schools, who represented the majority of participants in the *Yomiuri Shinbun* debate, "knew" that masturbation was also rampant among girls. Psychologists and gynecologists might justly criticize the fact that girls were left to grow up in "sexual ignorance," one of them reasoned, but if girls would only refrain from reading "obscene novels" and if they were not harassed by men, they would know nothing about sex and everything would follow its natural course (Shimoda 1908b:5). Pedagogues were preoccupied with the age of sexual maturity for girls, which was perceived as closely related to their reaching full body height. They suggested that one had to be particularly cautious with girls around the age "when their development is faster than that of boys." Studies based on the school hygiene examinations had found that the majority of Japanese girls reached sexual maturity, defined as their first menstruation and the growth of their breasts, by the age of thirteen, while boys reached sexual maturity by the age of fourteen. At this age, proper care and maintenance of the body *(shintai no yōgo)* was considered crucial, precisely because "sexual desire [occurred] before girls and boys were able to develop a strong will and make proper judgments" (Imai T. 1906:824). Minami phrased an ideal lecture on sex education by a mother to her daughter as follows:

You have come so far that you can produce the sprig from which a human arises in your body. This is also visible externally. Do not be surprised by it. It does not mean anything. You are completely healthy. You will bleed for two or three days and during these days you will feel your body intensely. That will happen once every four weeks and is only the proof that you have grown up. However, it is important that you do not overwork, and that you wash yourself carefully and take better care of yourself during these days. This is not simply an experience but the preparation for you to become a mother one day. Therefore you must take proper care of yourself. You might worry about when it will happen and it is indeed an important time but please be pleased with yourself that one day you will be a mother. (Minami R. 1908c:5)

The preoccupation with girls' future as mothers of (it was hoped) numerous healthy children was responsible to a large extent for a great number of articles written in pedagogical journals and other magazines after the turn of the century. These articles dealt exclusively with girls' education, hygiene, sex education, and physical training. Emphasizing the supposed "special characteristics" of the female mind and physique, these authors insisted that girls' and women's sexual desire was inseparably pervaded and guided by their desire to have children. They also declared women's sexual desire to be weaker than men's, or they discounted it altogether (Shimoda 1904a, 1904b; Nagai 1916; Narita 1995).[6] In any case, however, most pedagogues thought that as a precautionary measure, girls also should be educated on sexual matters (Washiyama 1908b:5). Pedagogues and medical doctors found it quite disturbing to detect signs of exhaustion in girls, which they assumed stemmed from autoerotic practices. When occurring in girls, neurasthenia seemed even more worrisome than in boys. Shimoda Jirō and other pedagogues believed that neurasthenia increasingly occurred in girls as an effect of schooling, to which they had only recently been subjected. According to Shimoda's logic, higher education affected girls much more severely because they had been denied an adequate education for such a long time. Now girls could study, but as a result their menstruation became irregular, their faces pale, and their bodies and souls weak. Since he feared that neurasthenic girls eventually would give birth to neurasthenic infants, Shimoda urged the authorities to reform school curricula so that more time could be invested in both the "hygiene of the body" and the "hygiene of the mind" (Shimoda 1904a:412–413; see also Adachi 1930).

Masturbation was often collapsed with homosexuality. Although lesbian encounters at girls' schools were thought to be quite common, some authors suggested that masturbation and/or homosexuality among girls was not as "animal-like" as that among boys (Kuwatani 1911; *Fujo Shinbun* 1911, 1912; Furuya 1922; *Hentai Seiyoku* 1924a–b; see also Robertson 1998, 1999). Among others, Yamamoto Senji (1889–1929), Japan's first sex researcher, whose achievements I shall discuss in chapter 3, pursued this view and claimed that "purely platonic" relationships among girls were erroneously being judged as sexual because the predominantly male staff at girls' schools were unfamiliar with the female psyche. Hence, male teachers regarded "homosexual love among girls" *(shōjokan no dōsei renai)* as a pedagogical problem. Yamamoto castigated them for equating "platonic love" *(puratonikku rabu)* among girls, who "simply hugged each other without any carnal trick and who remained yearning," with the "psychotic group forms of masturbation and sodomy common in boys' dormitories" (Yamamoto Senji 1924b: 39–42).[7] He criticized schoolmasters for scandalizing the "completely harmless" behavior of girls, and for battling it unnecessarily with draconian measures. As a result of unjustified punishment, girls would only develop a strong sense of shame, which itself could have disastrous effects on their lives. Yamamoto urged schoolmasters to implement sex education at their schools not only for students but also for male and female teachers, in order to enhance their poor knowledge of the female psyche and physique (Yamamoto Senji 1924b:39–42).

   In contrast to the weak, harmless, or even absent sexual desire attributed to girls, the authors of the series in the *Yomiuri Shinbun* and other commentators consistently presented sexual desire in boys as aggressive, destructive, and, above all, potentially uncontrollable, reiterating earlier assumptions about male sexual desire that I discussed in chapter 1. Hence Minami, for example, suggested that boys had to be warned and, if necessary, intimidated in order to sufficiently emphasize the importance of self-control. According to Minami, sexual desire should be described to boys as an "animalistic power" that held them imprisoned. It was to be likened to the power that made people steal someone else's food and drink when they were hungry and thirsty. Besides drawing comparisons with other basic needs, teachers should point out to their male students that the "reproductive drive" was more important than eating and drinking. Just as for horses and dogs, the "seed [wants to be] inserted into the female body," but, unlike animals, humans had to be wary of all kinds of temptations related to physical desires. Minami urged teachers to point out to their male students that "happiness [would] entirely disappear from their lives" should they "succumb to temptation" (Minami R. 1908d:5).

If a boy or man were led astray by temptation, Minami warned, sexual desire would take over, as its only purpose lay in the transmission of fluid. Hinting at the consequences of venereal diseases, Minami encouraged teachers to emphasize that the sex drive was concerned with neither the health of parents nor the health of an unborn child. Again and again, teachers should plant the thought in their students' heads that the "eruption of sexual desire" was "as strong as a storm." In a storm, a boat might tip over. Likewise, if young men did not control their sexual desire, they would "sink like a boat in a storm" (Minami R. 1908d:5).

Cautious pedagogues also warned that not all teachers were fit to give such a tough lesson to their students. Only mature teachers who possessed adequate teaching experience, had a solid sense of morals, were themselves entirely "free of sexual desires," and were able to speak "scientifically" about the sex drive were declared adequate (Mukō 1908e:5; Washiyama 1908b:5; Shimoda 1908b:5). Yubara referred to "Western works" on the research of masturbation and suggested that teachers should speak about sexual desire in a way that did not provoke a sense of shame in youth. He also suggested that girls and boys not only be educated separately but also by a person of their own sex—i.e., girls by mothers or female teachers and boys by fathers or male teachers (Yubara 1908).

CLASS DISTINCTIONS

When talking about youth in general or pupils at girls' schools in particular, participants in the *Yomiuri Shinbun* debate were implicitly referring to children from middle- and upper-class homes, many of whom attended institutions of secondary education. By the time of the *Yomiuri Shinbun* debate, more than 98 percent of elementary school–age children attended elementary school and more than 300,000 male and female students received some kind of secondary education (see Marshall 1992:81, 219). In the minds of members of the upper and emerging middle classes, the educated upper class was considered morally superior, and Mukō—among other intellectuals—appealed to its members not to shy away from what he considered to be their responsibility. He urged them to take their responsibility seriously and build a social system of punishment for "crimes against national health," so that sex education for children would eventually become unnecessary. Until then only the upper class, privileged by education, could prevent children from doing harm to their bodies and souls (Mukō 1908c:5).

Participants in the debate spoke confidently about male and female children and adolescents who attended their schools. The sexual nature of relationships among the working class and particularly among young female factory workers, however, seemed far less clear to them. Many middle- and upper-class educators, physicians, and social reformers suspected female factory workers to be promiscuous and "undutiful." Physicians who examined female factory workers believed that many of them masturbated regularly. In light of the lack of education among workers in general, they assumed that there were more women in factories than among the upper and middle classes who were prone to sexual indecencies. They frequently underlined their assumption by pointing out that "industrious working-class people's sexual desire was stimulated by living in small, crowded housing" (Yoshida S. 1925; Ieda 1939).

In 1925, Hosoi Wakizō, the author of *The Sad History of Factory Women (Jokō aishi)*, reported on women who had secretly taken short pieces of pipe home from the factories and inserted them into their vaginas. Others used potatoes for the same purpose and eventually had to see a doctor because the potatoes could no longer be removed. Tall girls pressed their bodies against the machines, thus sexually arousing themselves while working (Hosoi 1996 [1925]:317). Pointing out that only the better-equipped factory dormitories provided a futon for each girl, and that in most cases two girls shared a futon, Hosoi also suggested that the cramped conditions might have furthered their activities. In the morning, Hosoi reported, one could find at least 30 percent of the girls in "strange positions," another 30 percent had unintentionally embraced each other during sleep, and 40 percent had intentionally done so. Hosoi concluded, "The phenomenon of lesbianism is quite common and includes a wide range of practices ranging from mutual psychological love to extremely lustful activities, which are accompanied by a strong sense of jealousy" (Hosoi 1996 [1925]:316–17).

Hosoi Wakizō had been working in a factory since the age of thirteen and remained a worker and socialist activist at a cotton spinning factory until his death at the age of twenty-nine. In his book he wrote that female workers and a factory physician with whom he was acquainted had told him these stories. Hosoi emphasized the difficulties in studying the psychology of factory women. He noted that he had eventually succeeded because he had lived with them from dawn to dusk, observed their daily life, collected their songs, studied their psychology from a medical perspective, and tried to clarify the relationship between their psychology and their physiology (Hosoi 1996 [1925]:317).[8]

From the issues aired in the *Yomiuri Shinbun,* Hosoi's book, and a variety of other records, it is clear that most pedagogues and physicians were convinced that sex education in general and at schools in particular would have a positive effect on sexual morals and behavior (Yoshida K. 1916).

FLAWED PARENTS

While an important role was ascribed to schools, parental responsibility with respect to sex education was another highly contested theme in the debate. Some contributors to the debate questioned whether parents were suitable to judge the maturity of their children and therefore to determine the right time for sex education. Some participants in the debate considered parents the authorities best qualified to observe their children and elicit their responses. However, they argued, it was imperative for sex education to employ even more intrusive techniques of surveillance. Sex education had to make youths so self-conscious that they would "carefully observe and investigate" themselves (Washiyama 1908b:5). In order to prevent "immoral behavior," these writers suggested, parents should speak with and interrogate their children. If they found out that their offspring had in fact "been bad," the more cautious educators believed that it would only do harm for parents to disclose too much to their children (Mukō 1908a:5). Others suggested that parents lacked the necessary sensitivity to teach their children about sex because they knew too little themselves or because their own sexual morals were less than desirable.

Parents were urged to choose the appropriate words carefully so that their children would "shudder at the idea of contravening their parents' advice" (Mukō 1908a:5). Mukō, for example, found it inadequate to teach children that they were different from animals and instead urged parents and professional educators to highlight the specifics of human nature. He felt it more appropriate to explain that in the world of all beings, humans were in a "superior position" and that even "lowly animalistic sensual stimulation" was part of the "highly developed" human being (Mukō 1908b:5). If parents "were not ashamed to relish having sex while sharing a bedroom with their children," he concluded that they should sleep in separate rooms, because otherwise children might remember not only "the good" but also "the bad" (Mukō 1908a:5).[9]

Like Mukō, Washiyama considered it unlikely that parents were capable of educating their children on sexual matters, because they typically knew very little about "physical hygiene." Parents could determine symptoms if they—as they should—observed their offspring adequately. Headaches, a pale complexion, weak eyes, passivity, melancholy, stomach aches, and tuberculosis were all understood as definite signs of indulgence in masturbation. However, the very important task of sex education should be taken over by schools as a distinct subject (Washiyama 1908a:5, 1908b:5).

The lack of faith in parents' abilities expressed by some of the contributors to the *Yomiuri Shinbun* debate reflected the importance and sensitivity ascribed to sex education by professional educators, medical doctors, and other guardians of the health of the national body. It also pointed to an older conviction, according to which parents and especially young mothers should not be given extensive authority over childrearing if older, supposedly more trustworthy, family members were present. Early modern advice tracts had tended to undermine mothers' relationships with their children. They held that women's many faults impeded their ability to properly socialize children. Children would become better adults if reared by more "virtuous" men, such as fathers, grandfathers, or pedagogues, and men comprised the bulk of pedagogues far into the twentieth century (Uno 1999:37–39).

After 1890, a new pattern of child care had emerged in city households that were no longer productive units. Particularly influential were the family patterns of the new urban middle-class households whose breadwinners filled the expanding ranks of salaried employees. The upper reaches of the new salaried class included influential professionals, such as the educators who voiced their opinions on sex education in the *Yomiuri Shinbun* debate and other forums, bureaucrats, technicians, managers, and journalists. In their homes, women and children became dependent consumers as the family shed many of the productive tasks that women and sometimes children continued to perform in rural and urban enterprise households.

These broader changes did not have an immediate impact on the literate classes to which the authors and many of the readers of the *Yomiuri Shinbun* belonged. Thus, when some participants in the debate on sex education insisted that parents should act as primary caretakers and provide sex education for their children, they expressed a rather progressive view of parenting. Only around the advent of the twentieth cen-

tury did the family ideology, which formed the base of the Meiji constitution promulgated in 1889, spread into pedagogical treatises and into
literate middle- and upper-class households. In minimal accordance
with the new state-initiated emphasis on parents as the primary educators of children, promoters of sex education declared parents to be
crucial primary authorities for closely observing children and making
them talk.

This modern family ideology stylized love and marital fidelity between husband and wife as the "pinnacle of reason and emotion," and
Meiji intellectuals declared it the "greatest pleasure in human life"
(Kōda Ryūzō, quoted in Ueno 1990:507). Now, the family was to be
a place of mutual love, respect, and care and was viewed as the core
unit of social stability and progress. Pedagogues insisted that the family
was the base and primary training ground for a person's entire moral
education. Given this important role it was the parents' primary duty
to provide and maintain peace and happiness in the family (Imai T.
1906:4, 14–15).

In reality, these duties, prescribed by the Civil Code and reinforced by
contemporary print media, rested with mothers, who found themselves
pressed to conform to their ascribed gender roles as "good wives" and
"wise mothers." These roles entailed a strict commitment to their families and subordination to their fathers and husbands. Love, be it for
one's spouse or children, did not always come easy, and often wives
ended up striving to make up for a husband's flaws in order to save the
family. Trapped in a marriage with an adulterous, abusive, or in other
ways less than caring husband, a despairing wife often put on a happy
face and wound up raising her husband's illegitimate children in addition to her own, or managed without the help of a maid in order to
avoid having her husband harass her (Yamada 1989 [1983]:357). Even
when a husband allegedly had molested his daughter or made his wife's
sister pregnant, a woman was unlikely to find a way to break either the
union or the family bonds (Tsūzoku Igaku 1925:60–62; Yamada 1989
[1983]:355).

Male pedagogues rarely addressed these problems when they outlined the ideal roles of mothers and fathers in the education of children
at home. In his contributions to the Yomiuri Shinbun debate as well as
in his other works, Shimoda propagated the roles of mothers and fathers. He argued that the mother was the child's best educator because
she took care of the child from birth and thus was "one with the child"

(dōshin ittai). Since the child experienced how to feel and act with other people through the mother, being educated by the mother was, in Shimoda's view, very important for the child. Because the mother represented the inside, and the father the outside of the house, a mother's love was physiologically and psychologically very different from a father's love. If one compared the family to a ship, Shimoda wrote, the father would be the captain and the mother the machinist (Shimoda 1904a: 320–322).

Mukō announced that he was "against telling children as little as possible about the sexual instinct" and warned that the danger of children "doing something bad" would prevail if this topic was not discussed in families (Mukō 1908a:5, 1908b:5). Hence, he criticized those parents who avoided responding to children's questions on sexual matters. Pointing out the "dangers of modern society," he suggested that parents who did not talk about sexual matters with their children probably thought that their children were completely innocent, but they had forgotten about the impurity of society. If parents failed to provide sex education for their children, children would be unable to develop as proper moral beings or to acquire knowledge of their physiology and the pathologies caused by certain sexual practices (Mukō 1908b:5).

Despite the reevaluation of parents as primary educators, pedagogues often doubted their judgment and repeatedly came to the conclusion that parents were probably the best of all the poor choices available, which included sensationalist newspapers and magazines, obscene paperbacks, and bad friends. Minami deemed the parents' role relatively positive, since they were the most capable of knowing when the right time had come for their children to learn about sex. Because of the different ages at which children mature, Minami favored parents as sex educators. Minami was also the only contributor to the debate who made concrete suggestions for what exactly should be said to girls and boys who were to be sexually enlightened. Referring to the German physician and pedagogue Friedrich Wilhelm Förster's concept of willpower, which was to be developed in a child in order to properly control the sex drive, Minami suggested that self-control and willpower were more important than knowledge about sexual desire: "Physical things are not so important. One has to imagine the psyche as the basis for morals and personality. To be sure, one must take preventive measures to counter immorality, since today, as much as in the times of the old Greeks, unnatural forms of satisfaction of the sexual instinct cause major mischief" (Minami R. 1908b:5).

EXPERT KNOWLEDGE AND WESTERN FRIENDS

The debate in the *Yomiuri Shinbun* was dominated by pleas for a sex education that would pass on knowledge about sexual desire and its supposedly related risks to individuals and the nation. This knowledge, its proponents thought, should be passed on to children, youth, parents, and through parents to all groups in society that could not be reached by schools and other educational institutions. The participants in the debate appointed themselves as experts on what kind of sex education was true or false, right or wrong, morally just or objectionable. Even those who were inconsistent in their stance on the matter generally approved of sex education by parents or schools or both, if only to avoid having less competent agents carry it out and end up causing more harm than would have been caused by no education at all.

The debate followed an explicit demarcation of scholars and other professionals whose authority was rooted in academia from other agents of potentially misleading advice. The new naturalist literature, which Shimoda called "obscene novels," was denounced by a mostly older generation of literary critics as "pornography" or "unhealthy erotic writing." Other intellectuals agreed with Shimoda. A few months prior to the *Yomiuri Shinbun* debate, the mass-circulation magazine *The Sun (Taiyō)* had dedicated the majority of its New Year's edition to the question of whether young men and women should be allowed to read these novels. One of the contributors thundered that the new literature "full of adultery" caused great damage in youth, stimulated "low instincts," led to individualist, liberal ideas, and propagated a negative world view (*Taiyō* 1 January 1908, quoted in J. Rubin 1984:121–122). Literary scholar Oguri Fūyō countered that the naturalist school did not make sexuality a theme out of pure pleasure, but rather because knowledge about sex was too important for youth to be ignored (*Taiyō* 1 October 1908, quoted in J. Rubin 1984:122). Authors of the naturalist school attempted to turn against the "old morals and customs" and highlight the importance of "correct sexual knowledge" for Japan's youth. They looked with scorn and disdain at the old customs. The new authors saw themselves as combatants against the nonscientific view of humans and attempted to "boldly [make] sexuality and desire a part of human reality" (*Bungei Jihyō* 1 January 1908, quoted in J. Rubin 1984:123).

A few months after the *Yomiuri Shinbun* debate came to an end, authorities confiscated the July edition of the literary magazine *The Pleiades (Subaru)*. They argued that one contribution to the edition,

Mori Ōgai's "Vita Sexualis" *(Wita sekusuarisu)*, endangered public morals.[10] In the autobiographical text, first-person narrator Kanai Shizuka, a professor of philosophy, describes his sexual development over the course of the first nineteen years of his life. The chronicle of increasing sexual awareness begins with Kanai's first glance at erotic woodblock prints as a child and leads up to an encounter with a professional courtesan. Almost immediately after it was banned, critic Uchida Roan deemed the text a "valuable educational document," adding that in the West the secrets surrounding reproduction had long been a subject of scientific research. Only in Japan did the "traditional unscientific morals and hypocrisy" continue (*Asahi Shinbun* 6, 7, and 8 January 1910, quoted in J. Rubin 1984:92). However, the participants in the *Yomiuri Shinbun* debate doubted the capability of literature to replace sex education as they imagined it.

The vocabulary of the dichotomization of experts on the one hand and laity on the other served as "rhetorical demarcation work" (Hilgartner 1990:520) to monopolize the discourse on sex. It was employed to secure the status of expert knowledge against all other forms of knowledge and the experts themselves against all other speakers. In this way pedagogues and medical doctors strove to obtain authority over an entire series of decisions. They were to decide what kind of knowledge was recognized as "scientific," "true," and "valid." They also were to decide to whom and to what degree this knowledge should be disclosed. In addition, they insisted that they knew best where, when, and by whom sex education should be carried out.

These pedagogues and medical doctors were indeed experts in their fields. Many had written lengthy books on pedagogical or medical issues, had published in the most prestigious journals, and held powerful positions in Japan's most respected educational and academic institutions. Some of them had studied in Germany or elsewhere in Europe, were members of their respective international professional associations, and had presented their work at international conferences and in other professional forums. Fujikawa Yū was among those who represented Japan at the International Hygiene Exhibition in London in 1884 and in Dresden in 1911. He was in good company. The *Catalogue of Exhibits from the Imperial Japanese Government* (*Katalog der von der Kaiserlich Japanischen Regierung ausgestellten Gegenstände*, 1911) was written by leading representatives of Japan's modern health regime. Among the authors were Kitazato Shibasaburō, a microbiologist and director of the Research Institute for Infectious Diseases; Doi Keizō, founder of the

Japanese Society for the Prevention of Venereal Disease (Nihon Seibyō Yobō Kyōkai);[11] Hata Sahachirō, director of the Imperial Dermatological University Clinic Tokyo, who together with Paul Ehrlich had developed the first medication for the treatment of syphilis; and Fujikawa Yū (*Katalog* 1911:41).[12]

Out of professional convention as much as necessity (i.e., a lack of "allies" in Japan), scholars, educators, and scientists enhanced their expert status by appointing Western scholars as authorities to confirm and justify their claims. Whether speaking favorably of willpower training, emphasizing the necessity of implementing sex education in schools, or questioning parents' ability to enlighten children and youth on sexual matters, they called on Western scholars and pointed out over and over again the significance of the condition of the national body. Western scholars, theories, and institutions mainly meant those from Germany, as well as, to a lesser extent, Britain and France. The advanced German medicine and comparatively authoritarian German pedagogy appealed most to Japanese pedagogues and medical doctors until the early twentieth century, in a way continuing the process of widespread adoption and adaptation foreshadowed by government institutions during the first half of the Meiji era (Bartholomew 1989). Apart from a few exceptions, these Western scholars remained anonymous in the *Yomiuri Shinbun* debate. Their works were cited mostly in references to the order of things in the West and served primarily to underscore the Japanese authors' own opinions.

This strategy of referring to internationally circulating ideas, theories, and research results was not specific to Japan, the beginning of the twentieth century, or writings on sexual matters.[13] Such references were evoked in order to achieve recognition for new ideas or fields of research in other national settings as well (Okamoto 1983b; Hirakawa 1989; Nye 1991:387–388). Britain's sexologists pointed to their German and French colleagues (Porter and Hall 1995:278), Chinese sex reformers looked to both the West and Japan (Dikötter 1995; Shapiro 1999), Russians compared their sexual issues to those of Western Europe (Engelstein 1992:1–13), and Americans tried to fend off the sexological writings of Europeans (Gevitz 1992). For Japan, the use of "the West" as a rhetorical figure had several functions. References to the West opened a discursive space for the demands for sex education and sex research and the claims of their propagators to cover ever more terrain. The debate in the *Yomiuri Shinbun* was just one of many stages in the expansion of discursive space that facilitated the colonization of the "sexual problem" by pedagogy and medicine and thus by both education and scholarly inquiry. "The West" was used as a synonym for certain claims to truth and the importance of scientific knowledge in general.

The participants in the *Yomiuri Shinbun* debate had no sympathy for what they referred to as Japan's "tradition." Instead, they denounced whatever they felt had to be overcome as "old traditions," "false beliefs," or "heterodoxy." The appearance of experts marked the break with "false, unscientific interpretations," which were confronted with "correct, scientific, modern, civilized knowledge." The proponents of sex education and sex research sided with a great portion of the educated classes in this respect. The educated middle class supported the prohibition of public nudity and exuberant dancing at folk festivals (see Muta 1992; Nomura 1990). Its members also felt that certain religious rituals, such as phallic worship to promote fertility, endangered Japan's new status as a "civilized" country. Police commonly justified their actions against these practices by classifying them as "superstition and absolute nonsense" and pointing out that they negated the "rationality of modern science" (Garon 1994:353–354).

Participants in the debate further criticized the (supposed) secrecy surrounding the "sexual problem" in Japan and praised Western sex research. They criticized Japan's educational system, which had deprived girls of higher education for such a long time. They pointed out the (supposed) equality of the sexes in the West. In an attempt to justify their claims of women's nature as different and inferior to men's or as sensitive and untrustworthy, they castigated Confucian gender norms for rendering women sick (Nagai 1916:277, 284), only to praise ancient Greek and highly misogynist nineteenth-century German and Austrian philosophers, including Arthur Schopenhauer and Otto Weininger. They were able to read accurately both Western and Japanese sources, whether on the relationship between venereal diseases and prostitution or the results of physical examinations of conscripts or students and their implications for the health of the national body. Whether the texts and theories they referred to were statistical, sociological, or medical, and whether the studies they resulted from were literary, historiographical, or philosophical was of secondary importance. All of them seemed suited to heighten the demand for sex education and to emphasize the necessity of comprehensive empirical sex research in Japan.

Participants in the debate on sex education frequently and explicitly associated themselves with Western science and Western scholars, em-

phasizing their importance for Japan as a modern nation. This incorporation of "Western friends" in the *Yomiuri Shinbun* debate took various
forms. One was the notion of the earliest Western work. Yubara, for example, mentioned "the earliest [Western] work" on masturbation, entitled *Onanie* (Yubara 1908:5). He did not note the author's name or
a publication date but he was most likely referring to *L' Onanisme ou
Dissertation physique sur les Maladies produites par la Masturbation*,
authored by the Swiss physician Simon Auguste André David Tissot and
originally published in 1760 but widely read only in the nineteenth century (see Hirschfeld 1926:286; Braun 1995:27–100).[14]

Other frequently used figures of speech were references to the "famous Western scientist" and the "well-known Western scholar." Underscoring the rhetorical function of references to the West that has been
emphasized by several scholars of modern Japan (see, e.g., Barshay
1988; Robertson 1998), Japanese authors sometimes presented the
work of "a famous Western scholar" in ways contrary to its reputation
in the West. Minami, for example, presented the doctor and sexual pedagogue Friedrich Wilhelm Förster as "*the* Western authority" on sex education (Minami R. 1908b:5). In Germany, however, Förster was considered a radical opponent of sex education. There, Magnus Hirschfeld,
an influential sexologist and hygienist at the Institut für Sexualwissenschaft und Eugenik in Berlin, considered Förster's recommendations—
such as his suggestion to "appear quietly in the evening, take off the
boots silently, close the door in a disciplined manner, keep conversation
muffled with respect for those who want to rest" in order to prevent sexual arousal—to be simply naïve and lacking any sense of reality (Hirschfeld 1926:104).

Participants in the *Yomiuri Shinbun* debate also referred to works
more precisely, but these instances were exceptions rather than the rule.
Shimoda, for example, explained that it was the "famous American psychologist" George M. Beard who coined the term "neurasthenia" in his
book *American Nervousness: Its Causes and Consequences* (1881). In
fact, Beard was a New York physician who had coined the term "neurasthenia" in the 1860s.[15] Shimoda added that the phenomenon dated
back to the time of Hippocrates in ancient Greece, although its occurrence as a "developmental disease" *(hattatsubyō)* was observed only at
the end of the nineteenth century. "The German pedagogue" Wilhelm
Erb, wrote Shimoda, made this observation in *About the Increasing
Nervousness of Our Time (Über die wachsende Nervosität unsrer Zeit)*,

published in Heidelberg in 1893. Eventually, neurasthenia was studied extensively by "England's most prominent sexologist," Havelock Ellis, in *Man and Woman* (Shimoda 1904a:407).[16]

This strategy of "bringing in Western friends" enabled Japanese sexologists and other intellectuals to ally themselves with the project of modernity itself, emphasizing the feeling of being up to what José Ortega y Gasset would call the "level of the times" (Ortega y Gasset 1985 [1929]: 23–24). "Modern" and "modernity" were insisted upon as a mode, set against the traditional modes of the past. In these intellectuals' texts, the term "modern" expressed a consciousness of a new life superior to the old life, and at the same time an imperative call for Japan to rise to the "level of the times." Setting their modern concept of sex education against what some perceived as "old, unscientific, and superstitious beliefs" symbolically provided these authors and their claims with a future by banishing Japan's tradition "below the level of history" and into the pre-Enlightenment past. "Modern," noted Henri Lefebvre (1995 [1962]:168) more than thirty years later in an influential text on the meaning of modernity, was a word that had been used in triumphant self-justification as a means of relegating to the past everything that those who spoke did not consider part of themselves.

The *Yomiuri Shinbun* debate made sexual desire an issue of education and public debate, and it was not long before other print media followed suit. The same year, the monthly *Central Review (Chūō Kōron)* summarized Fujikawa's views on sex education (Fujikawa Y. 1908a). In September 1911 another monthly, *New Review (Shinkōron)*, printed more than seventy pages of articles on "theories of sexual desire" *(seiyokuron)*, triggering a wave of similar publications.[17] And in January 1912, only a few months before Habuto Eiji reported his observations about Germany, the *Central Review* further stirred public interest and concern by printing the comments of schoolmasters of middle and girls' schools, as well as teachers' colleges, about whether their male and female students were provided with "knowledge about sexual desire" *(seiyoku ni kan suru chishiki)*. As it turned out, almost two-thirds of these schools were still pondering the questions discussed in this chapter, while in one-third of the schools some kind of sex education had begun to take place (*Chūō Kōron* 1912). It would be almost ten years before Yoshida Kumaji's precondition for sex education would be fulfilled and teachers could ground their sex education in Japanese empirical sex research— the subject of the next chapter—rather than in Western theories and findings.

CHAPTER 3

Sexology for the Masses

My science is not born from reading and thinking alone; it
also arises from my lectures, journeys, and conversations,
from answering audiences' questions, from correspondence
with readers and students, and from the advice on life that
I attempt to give.

Yamamoto Senji, "Milieu and
Background Intellectual of My Own",1921

In February 1925, Yamamoto Senji, a thirty-six-year-old bachelor of science, explained how he conducted sex research, as he had done before.
This time, however, he chose to publish his explanation in the first issue
of a small journal entitled *Birth Control Review (Sanji Chōsetsu Hyōron),* published in Kamokyō ward in Kyoto. Yamamoto and his friends
sold this first issue of the *Birth Control Review* to a few professors and
physicians in Kyoto. A few months later, three thousand copies of the
fourth issue were printed and sent to subscribers all over Japan (*Sanji
Chōsetsu Hyōron* 1925d:40). Yamamoto directed readers who were interested in "purely scientific research" *(jun gakujutsuteki kenkyū)* to his
more scholarly publications and explained that this particular article
was meant to grab the attention of "non-experts" or "ordinary people"
(senmon gakusha naranu ippan no hitobito).

On the remaining pages, he acknowledged that in Japan and elsewhere, economic and social changes had brought more and more people
to large cities, where they lived in ever more crowded settings. These
modern transformations of social life, he continued, had resulted in
an increase in sexual problems, horrible crimes, family tragedies, the
growth of prostitution, and the spread of venereal diseases. Many people,
Yamamoto observed, were seeing doctors to receive treatment for these
venereal diseases, but others turned to dubious pamphlets and magazines promising "secret remedies." Entire theories about human sexual-

ity and, for that matter, humankind were being formed exclusively on the basis of the study of sick people. Thus, he wrote, people had come to associate "sexology" *(seigaku)* exclusively with writings on venereal diseases and "perverse sexual desire" *(hentai seiyoku)*.

Yamamoto conceded that these books were not entirely useless for people who were infected with a venereal disease; however, he stated, they might lead perfectly healthy people to develop negative attitudes about sex, associating it exclusively with disease and perversion (Yamamoto Senji 1925a:31–33). Reevaluating the sexology practiced by physicians, he demanded that it be enriched by biology, economics, jurisprudence, political science, history, folklore, and other "cultural sciences" *(bunka kagaku)*. Praising the invaluable impact sexology had had on the social system, the arts, and the sciences in Western countries since World War I, Yamamoto suggested that sexology in Japan should proceed in the same direction. In his view, sexology in Japan should aim at producing great scholars of sex similar to Britain's Havelock Ellis and Germany's Iwan Bloch, Hermann Rohleder, and Magnus Hirschfeld (Yamamoto Senji 1925a:33), and he clearly imagined himself as such a figure.

In Yamamoto's eyes, sexology in Europe had done away with many stereotypes there. If sexologists and other courageous people failed to disseminate new knowledge about sex in Japan, Yamamoto declared, "Life can not be lived in a correct way" *(jinsei wa tadashiku sugosu koto wa dekinu)*. The new knowledge about sex, which he had set out to create, based on Japanese empirical data, and wished more readers of the *Birth Control Review* to welcome, rested on a statistically defined normalcy. Driven by and based on the study of "normal life" *(heisei no seikatsu)*, its primary task was the study of healthy people's "normal sex lives" *(jōtai no seiseikatsu)* (Yamamoto Senji 1925a:33). Yamamoto was aware that terms like "healthy" and "normal" (he also used the word *seijō*) were far from self-explanatory and highly problematic. However, he rarely said more about this matter than that he was interested in a sexology that was not exclusively concerned with pathologies. It is clear that he saw himself and his fellow sexologists as being at a distance from physicians, if not in opposition to them, as they only dealt with sick people. By the mid-1920s, Yamamoto Senji had become one of the most important proponents of the study of sexual behavior in Japan.

Systematically acquired data, Yamamoto suggested, should be a requirement for bringing to "the masses" a "purely scientific sex education" *(jun kagakuteki seikyōiku)*. Yamamoto and his friend Yasuda

Tokutarō, who later would become a medical doctor and historian of sexuality, adopted the rhetoric of earlier proponents of sex education when they condemned confession and scandal stories in entertainment magazines and some women's journals for their frivolous treatment of sexual issues (Yamamoto Senji 1921e, 1924a–b). They also declared war on "ancient sexual knowledge," which they saw as resting on superstition and "false folklore"—a reference to the Buddhist commandment for asceticism and what they perceived to be the related "false ideas of sexual hygiene," as well as the "feudal repression" of sexuality that unnecessarily burdened youth (Yamamoto's own childhood and youth, he once confessed, had been overshadowed by a fear of sex) (Yamamoto Senji 1921).

Born in 1889, Yamamoto grew up in the sheltered environment of a bourgeois family that ran an inn in Kyoto. In a brief autobiographical account of his life, Yamamoto noted that as a child, he was interested mostly in flowers and plants. After the first year of middle school, his parents allowed him to move to Tokyo to learn gardening, which he did. Following the recommendation of one of his teachers, he attended an English course in the evenings. He read Japanese translations of Western scientific works and soon also read books in English. Among these were Charles Darwin's *On the Origin of Species* and Havelock Ellis's *Studies in the Psychology of Sex,* which he eventually classified as "a symbol for the new century" and translated into Japanese (Yamamoto Senji 1921f: 74–77).[1]

In 1907, Yamamoto went to Canada, where he initially planned to stay for five years and study to become a botanist. He went back to school and graduated from a public high school in Vancouver. In addition to perfecting his English, he acquired skills in German and French and learned some Latin and Greek. In contrast to many students of the early Meiji era who were sent abroad on government stipends (Bowers 1970), Yamamoto had to earn his own living. Initially making ends meet with house and garden work, he later took up work in a laboratory and became increasingly interested in biology. He continued his studies of evolutionary theory and developed an interest in socialism. Still in Canada, equipped with a "cleverness that made [him] disregard the opinions of others" and with "a strong intellect and an aggressive determination to dry the tears of the oppressed"—he decided to "discover under the microscope something meaningful for the welfare of humankind" (Yamamoto Senji 1921).

In 1921 he abandoned his original career plans, returned to Japan,

and began to study zoology, first at Dōshisha University and then, from
1914 on, at Kyoto University. After completing his studies in Kyoto he
continued his studies at the University of Tokyo, where he not only occupied himself with his zoological studies but also attended lectures on
physiology, gynecology, dermatology, and urology. In 1917 he earned a
bachelor of science degree and graduated under the guidance of Professor W. Watase, a former professor at Clark University and the University of Chicago. Ironically foreshadowing his future professional engagement, Yamamoto's thesis was entitled "The Spermatogenesis of the
Japanese Water Salamander" (Yamamoto Senji 1921:514).

In 1920 Yamamoto was accepted into the master's course in biology
at Kyoto University and began teaching biology at Dōshisha University.
Two years later he also accepted a lectureship for a three-semester
course entitled "Outline of the Sciences" at Kyoto University. The course
was open to second-year students and drew a heterogeneous group of
about 140 seventeen- to twenty-year-olds, all male, majoring in political science, economics, literature, and other fields in the arts and humanities. Initially he conceived the course as a human biology lecture
and taught a wide range of subjects, including human reproduction and
development, genetics, eugenics, cell theory, the theory of evolution, and
the human life cycle (see Odagiri 1979b:509, 576).

Adjusting the course more and more to what he believed interested
students most, Yamamoto gradually turned it into a sex education
course. His introductory remarks were phrased as a "warning for misunderstandings that may easily arise" (Yamamoto Senji 1921a:51). He
explained that the "science of sex" *(sei no kagaku)* did not encompass
all of biology and acknowledged that there were many other important
biological issues besides reproduction. As his lecture was a biology
lecture—implying that it was not a lecture in medicine, pathology, or
psychiatry—Yamamoto announced that he would not be dealing with
venereal diseases or research on perverse psychology but with perfectly
"normal" sexual phenomena from a biological perspective. Informing
the students that they would become familiar with many technical terms
and foreign (European) words, he said that using technical scientific ter-
minology was unavoidable for the subject matter and also necessary to
escape "obscene associations." He recommended the middle school
textbooks in physics and natural history to graduates from professional
schools and urged them to take a look also at the textbooks from girls'
schools (Yamamoto Senji 1921a:51–53). Because sex education commonly was ignored as a subject in schools, Yamamoto went beyond the

boundaries of an introductory course and eventually designed an "Outline of Sexual Knowledge" focusing on general questions of conception, reproduction, and human development (Yamamoto Senji 1921f). Eventually, the "Outline" became a multilayered effort, not only to enlighten students on sexual issues, but also to create knowledge about sex in ways unprecedented in Japanese history in an attempt to establish a new intellectual field at the fringes of academia.

PIONEERING SEX RESEARCH: FOR TRUTH AND FREEDOM

Positioning himself and other academics as both "creators of knowledge and at the same time original researchers and brokers of knowledge" (Yamamoto Senji 1921a), Yamamoto revised his courses at Kyoto University and Dōshisha University and developed a model for systematic sex education. He distributed questionnaires to several hundred students who had attended his courses.[2] The questionnaire was entitled "Light, some light!"—supposedly Goethe's last words on his deathbed—and the respondents were asked to fill it out carefully "for the sake of truth and freedom" (shinri no tame, jiyū no tame). "To create the future culture, we first have to awake and gather facts about ourselves," it proclaimed. Suggesting that Japan could create something other than its "unique contributions to world culture of bean-jam buns and rickshaws," the questionnaire urged students to cooperate in the building of a new culture. On a less dramatic note, it also reminded students that perversion (hentai) and normalcy (jōtai) were not defined well enough to be differentiated from one another, and the survey would be a means of clarifying the distinctions between the two (Yamamoto Senji 1921g:323).

The first nine questions of the survey concerned the familial situation of the respondents: the date and place of their birth; where they had lived the longest; the schools from which they had graduated; the professions of their parents, older brothers, and themselves; the number, age differences, and sex of their siblings; the age and sex of their children; and their religious beliefs and tendencies of thought. In order to ensure anonymity, respondents were told to leave any of these first nine questions blank if they did not want to answer them (Yamamoto Senji 1921g:323–324).

The remaining eight questions concerned students' reactions to Yamamoto's lecture. Among them were questions about the good and bad effects of the course and other, more specific ones about the course:

whether the respondents had felt sexually stimulated—i.e., had felt
mental excitement, erections, or had experienced involuntary ejaculation—at any point in the course, and if so, how it had occurred; whether
they felt that there were incorrect, prejudiced, or disagreeable elements
in Yamamoto's lectures; whether they had any further questions;
whether the source of their knowledge prior to the course had been
people, physicians, or books; whether they thought that Yamamoto
should publicize his course and lecture to a broader audience or only to
educated people; and finally, whether they had any other thoughts or requests concerning the course (Yamamoto Senji 1921g:324–325).

Pleased with the results of the survey, Yamamoto summarized the
answers and published them, together with a commentary, as a small
booklet, which he distributed to the students. Hoping that they would
become as convinced as he was that the overwhelmingly positive response of students could only be interpreted as further proof of the necessity of sex research and scholarly sex education and would then approve of his sex education method, Yamamoto also sent the booklet to
more than a hundred "educated people" for comments. Among them
were prominent democrats and socialists, including Kagawa Toyohiko,
Sakai Toshihiko, Yoshino Sakuzō, and Oka Asajirō. Different versions
of his summary appeared consecutively in two large newspapers, the
Ōsaka Asahi Shinbun and the *Tōkyō Asahi Shinbun,* and in the magazine *Outlook (Taikan),* whose editor was none other than Ōkuma Shigenobu, former prime minister, foreign minister, and chancellor of
Waseda University (Yamamoto Senji 1921b–d).[3]

The support of the print media and other concerned intellectuals further encouraged Yamamoto to launch a larger survey that would not just
contribute to the improvement of his course and serve as a tool to push
for sex education, but in fact would comprise a considerable body of
statistical data on Japanese men's and (to a lesser extent) women's sex
lives.[4] Yamamoto and his colleague and friend from the Medical Department at Kyoto University, Yasuda Tokutarō, began to carry out a
more comprehensive survey. Ten years younger than Yamamoto, Yasuda
was on his way to becoming a medical doctor and sexologist who would
translate some of the major works of Sigmund Freud into Japanese and
also write one of the first historiographical accounts of homosexuality
in Japanese history (Yasuda T. 1925, 1935).[5] Inspired by the omnipresent "remedies" for masturbating youth in medical and popular magazines, he had carried out a small study among medical students to gather

information on the actual extent of autoerotic practices among young men. Between 1922 and 1928, Yasuda and Yamamoto conducted a large-scale survey based on Yamamoto's first questionnaire that eventually covered the responses of five thousand men and a small number of women. Respondents came from diverse social backgrounds and included students from several universities and workers' schools, white- and blue-collar workers, farmers, teachers, physicians, and pharmacists (Yamamoto Senji 1924c:218).

Yamamoto presented an initial report on male students entitled "Statistical Survey of the Sex Lives of Japan's Male Students" ("Nihonjin dangakusei no seiseikatsu no tōkeiteki chōsa") to the Kyoto Medical Association and published it in the *Kyoto Medical Journal (Kyōto Igaku Zasshi)* (Yamamoto Senji 1923). An extended version based on the answers of more than one thousand respondents was published as a series of articles in the *Journal of Physiology (Seirigaku Kenkyū)*, another reputable journal edited in 1923 and 1924 by Ishikawa Hidetsurumaru (1878–1947) (Yamamoto Senji 1924c; see also Odagiri 1979b:514).

Both researchers were driven by doubts about the power of medical studies to describe and explain sexual behavior in "healthy bodies" *(kenkōtai)*. They hoped that the new science of sex, and their surveys for that matter, would contribute to the liberation of young people from "falsehood and menace." Those who "loved the truth" and those who trusted in the impending "happiness for humankind" were called upon to participate in Yamamoto and Yasuda's investigation and tear down the walls that had been erected by the authors of medical studies of venereal diseases and the potentially dubious sexual practices of what Yamamoto and Yasuda believed to be a small number of people (Yamamoto Senji 1924c:208–209). They again emphasized their conviction that it was not yet clear what exactly could be described as "normal" sexual behavior and development. One of the goals of the survey was to establish reliable indicators of "normal" and "healthy" sexuality, which Yamamoto and Yasuda imagined would emerge from statistical calculations done on the responses of a large number of people.

Initially, Yamamoto and Yasuda—and with them, probably the majority of the middle and upper classes—imagined a close correspondence between the level of education and what they referred to as "sexual morality" *(seidōtoku)*. Their assumption that the educated urban population possessed higher moral standards due to class heritage and education identified them as typical representatives of the urban edu-

cated elite, who commonly insisted that the educated classes had to fulfill a particular responsibility as moral role models for the rest of the
population.[6] In the survey, sexual morality was defined by cultural practices and divided by class. It reflected the social status of partners in instances of first sexual intercourse and the circumstances under which the
young men surveyed had first been confronted with sexual activity (of
others).

What kind of answers did the survey generate? In response to a whole
set of questions on their first sexual intercourse, more than half of the
young men surveyed indicated that they had had their first sexual intercourse before the age of eighteen.[7] Among the men who had entered the
workforce after middle school, almost half had had a prostitute as their
first sexual partner. Another 30 percent had their first sexual encounter
with an "unmarried woman," 14 percent with a "married woman," and
a meager 1 percent with their wives (Yamamoto Senji 1924c:223). Some
of these young men explained that they had been enticed by older colleagues at work to spend evenings in the red-light districts. One young
man reported that he realized that he had become an adult when he
turned twenty and became interested in the opposite sex. Upon this realization he began to stroll about the red-light district and engage in sex
with strangers every night (Yamamoto Senji 1924c:238; see also Okamoto 1983a).[8]

Yamamoto and Yasuda found that the rate of prostitutes as first sexual partners was still relatively high, 33 percent, among men who were
attending or had attended high schools and universities. Phrasing their
interpretation as social critique, they argued that the high rate of young
men who had chosen prostitutes as their first sexual partners was merely
a reflection of two social nuisances. In their view, blame was to be placed
on both the capitalist order of Japanese society and the "nationalist education" (kokka kyōiku) of Meiji and Taishō Japan, which had overem-
phasized the training of personality and the cultivation of character.
Under the enormous pressures of capitalism, the two sex researchers
concluded, young men could not help but consider sex as a site of mere
economic exchange and an escape route from the many expectations put
on them as patriotic citizens (Yamamoto Senji 1924c:207). They defended Japan's youth against social critics who observed that by the end
of the 1910s, collective efforts toward a national goal had ceased. Youths
were criticized for their lack of interest in the state and for a general lack
of a coherent existence. They were perceived as disinterested, colorless,
and either lacking ambition or exclusively focused on their own social

advancement *(risshin shusse)* and ignorant of social issues and goals (see Harootunian 1974:10).

Although Yamamoto and Yasuda saw young men's casual indulgence in sex with prostitutes as problematic, they blamed neither youth nor prostitutes but the capitalist order of society that made sex a commodity. Critical of the notions of "national unity" and "national goals," and aware of the great class differences in Japanese society, Yamamoto promoted the advancement of a new "culture" and "society" (he never spoke of the "nation" or the "empire") that was, in his eyes, based on the dissolution of capitalism and the liberation of the working class from its miseries. Although Yamamoto and Yasuda insisted that men, particularly those who lacked an appropriate upbringing, perceived women primarily as objects of desire (hindering the development of mutual respect), they also concluded in their report that sex education had to be provided for all social classes. The sexual practices across class boundaries that came to light in their survey, Yamamoto noted, were simply an expression of the pressing need for a "sexual enlightenment movement for the masses" *(taishū ippan ni taisuru seiteki keimō undō)* (Yamamoto Senji 1924c:286).

Yamamoto and Yasuda also were interested in the question of when the respondents learned about sexual intercourse, and again they drew class-related conclusions from the survey results. One factory worker wrote that he had first become aware of sexual intercourse when he was ten years old and happened to watch two "juvenile delinquents" *(furyō shōnen)*, who were two years older than he was, having sex with an older woman from their neighborhood. Another factory worker reported that he first realized that men and women have sexual intercourse when he went upstairs in his parents' restaurant one night and found the waitress engaged in sexual intercourse with a guest. Yet another reported that he was with a theater group when he was nineteen years old and one of his friends "taught him the taste of male-male love" *(nanshoku)*. From these examples and others primarily provided by workers, Yamamoto and Yasuda concluded that the circumstances for the initial awareness of sexual intercourse varied according to class and that particularly in uneducated young members of the working class, first sexual encounters were characterized by coincidence and unpreparedness. They suggested that there would be more examples similar to these three if they questioned only workers instead of the mixed group covered by their survey (Yamamoto Senji 1924c:251).

Another of their assumptions, which was shared by many of their contemporaries, was contradicted by the results of the study. As discussed in chapter 2, masturbation was generally established as a pathological matter that warranted cautious social control. Pedagogues and medical doctors commonly had argued that "normal" and "healthy" children succumbed to masturbation only because of negative social influences. A set of fifteen questions in the survey were designed to provide detailed coverage of the first instance of the respondent's awareness of the sex drive, various types of ejaculation, and masturbation.[9] According to the survey's results, most respondents had first become aware of their sex drive between the ages of six and twelve. Yamamoto and Yasuda classified both of these ages as times of crisis. According to the survey, the first was marked by the entry into a new social environment and separation from the parental home, the second as the onset of puberty. The first sexual experience was commonly associated with masturbation. Some young men explained that they had found out about the pleasures of masturbation by themselves, but many described a situation in which they had been either told about or taught masturbation practices by older friends. One of them was taught the tricks by an older pupil in elementary school at the age of eight. For others, the crucial experience had occurred while living in dormitories with several other youth or in barracks after they had been drafted (Yamamoto Senji 1924c: 254–255).

Although Yamamoto and Yasuda acknowledged significant age differences in regard to the first instance of masturbation, another result was much more important to them: They found that 96 percent of their respondents had masturbated and 86 percent had experienced nocturnal emissions. Based on these figures, they concluded that masturbation was not a pathological phenomenon that needed to be fought with medical treatments and repressive education. They declared it simply a normal feature of sexual behavior that occurred inevitably and had no negative effects on young men's healthy development (Yamamoto Senji 1924c:255; see also Oshikane 1977:169).[10] In order to underscore their point that masturbation was normal, they coined new terms for the development of human sexual behavior. In an effort to dissociate masturbation from moral judgments, Yamamoto introduced and used *jii* (*ji* = self, *i* = consolation) in place of terms with questionable connotations, such as *jitoku* (*ji* = self, *toku* = defilement), *shuin* (*shu* = hand, *in* = lasciviousness), and *akuheki* or *warukuse* (bad habit).[11] When an audience member who was worried about the harmful effects of masturbation approached Yamamoto, he typically responded in a sedate manner:

I am very happy that you have trusted me with your innermost secret. I already have been asked many questions like yours . . . and would like to answer in the following way: You say that you believe in the horrible consequences and permanent damage of masturbation. As I already have said on other occasions, this habit is completely normal for adolescents like you. It is unnecessary to talk about it, as there are simply no psychological or any other harmful effects. In former times, people believed that masturbation was something horrible. As I already have said, however, masturbation does not cause damage. When you enter into a healthy sex life it will disappear by itself. (Yamamoto Senji 1921f:104–105)

Questions like this one from the audience at his lectures further encouraged Yamamoto in his attempts to show the normalcy of certain sexual activities previously considered pathological.(or at least a cause of pathologies). His efforts to normalize masturbation were based on the statistical findings of his surveys, but they were also driven more generally by his insistence on a transnationally and transculturally universal character of sexuality. Hence, in his report, Yamamoto positioned himself by implication in opposition to biological essentialists who insisted on the uniqueness of the Japanese "race" or the peculiarity of Japanese culture and were skeptical of Western science and its application to Japan. Yamamoto and Yasuda viewed their study as proof of Sigmund Freud's theory of sexuality (Freud 1962 [1905]), which had motivated Yasuda's interest in conducting the survey in the first place. They also emphasized the similarity of their results to studies carried out by Havelock Ellis, Magnus Hirschfeld, and other European sexologists (notwithstanding the selectiveness of these researchers' samples), siding with them on the question of the internationalism of sexuality and sexology. In their eyes, the similarity of young Japanese men's sexual development to that of young Western men proved that there were no biological or "racial" differences that were not eclipsed by individual ones. Yamamoto especially (and Yasuda in later years) was equipped with a solid knowledge of European sexology, and by the beginning of the 1920s had already published translations and reviews of German and English publications in the field (see, e.g., Yamamoto Senji 1922a–b).

The fact that the name for their new science, *seigaku*, derived from the German name *Sexualwissenschaft* also is highly significant. The term *Sexualwissenschaft* had been coined by the medical doctor and "special physician for sexual illnesses" Iwan Bloch in an extensive study entitled *The Sexual Life of Our Time and Its Relation to Modern Culture (Das Sexualleben unserer Zeit in seinen Beziehungen zur modernen Kultur,* 1919 [1906]).[12] In his book, Bloch demanded an independent science of sex that did justice to the biological as well as the cultural aspects of sexuality. In his view, the science of sex had to consolidate "all other sciences, general biology, anthropology and ethnology, philosophy and psychology, medicine, literature, and the study of culture in all of its dimensions" (Bloch 1919 [1906]: prologue).

Yamamoto's interpretation of the results of his survey highlighted the sameness and equality of all races, an observation that was also central to some European sexologists' guiding principles. Hirschfeld, for example, proclaimed that there were "no two countries on earth with the exact same sexual arrangements," but that these dissimilarities were not rooted in a difference of "sexual aptitudes" or "natural instincts," which he believed to be entirely the same in peoples and races as entities. Rather, the differences in sexual customs were determined by the great variety of forms of sexual expression. Consequently, for Hirschfeld the role of a "scientific study of human sexuality" lay in pioneering and being a precursor to nothing less than "human sexual rights" (Hirschfeld 1935 [1933]:12). Similarly, Yamamoto and other sex reformers envisaged happiness and the liberation of the masses from wrong and oppressive beliefs. The equality of all races and the equality of the masses was as much an element of their sexology as their socialist politics.

SEXOLOGY FOR THE MASSES

By the time he and Yasuda completed the survey, Yamamoto had been engaged in debates about the role of science and scholars in society for many years. As far back as his time at the University of Tokyo, Yamamoto had been discontented with the dominant practices in science. He had found it difficult to adapt himself to the aristocratic atmosphere at the University of Tokyo and to make friends among the "young lords at the most luxurious institution supported by the impoverished taxpayers of this country" (Yamamoto Senji 1921b:51). He later wrote a manifesto for the comprehensive reform of the scientific world of biology. In an essay for the newspaper *Ōsaka Mainichi Shinbun*, "The Disillusionment of the Taxonomists," Yamamoto attacked the rigidity of biological research in terms of its domination by taxonomy and propagated what he termed a "genuine biology" characterized by more dynamic research methods.

Yamamoto strongly believed in a "science for humankind" *(jinsei no tame no kagaku)*, which for him was equivalent to opening up the academy and making scientific knowledge comprehensible and accessible to the wider public. He felt that especially in his field of biology, which was meant to "center on human society," too little was done to make scientific knowledge available to the wider public. The main reason the general public did not understand biology, Yamamoto argued, lay in its specialization. Biological research was done "on single trees without seeing the entire forest." The experimental methods that dominated biological research were incapable of explaining the entirety of individual and social life. In Yamamoto's view, the "science for humankind" had to strive to become more integrated. He viewed demography as a crucial set of techniques for measuring births, deaths, disease rates, population growth, marriages, politics, society, education, religion, hygienics, the health system, and medicine. This set of techniques was meant to complement the commonly used methods of inquiry, which he considered reductionist (Yamamoto Senji 1927e:492).[13] Sexology was of course not the only field that emerged out of discontent with scientific practices in established academic institutions.

Other Taishō intellectuals shared Yamamoto's concerns about scientific theory and practice, the uses of science, and the role of scholars in contemporary Japanese society. During the 1920s, representatives of the newly flourishing fields of the social sciences and humanities brought this understanding of science to the fore.[14] It was marked by a number of shifts that were characteristic of scientific practices. For example, the blending of social theory and activist involvement was characteristic of Taishō intellectuals' concept of the social sciences. For many, interest in the social sciences in general and sociology in particular rested less on the necessity of developing analytical models and more on an acute awareness of social problems (Soviak 1990; see also Hoston 1992:299). This previously common overlap between scholarship and political activism was first criticized as limiting the universities' autonomy and freedom in the second decade of the twentieth century, when university professors also became actively involved in party politics.[15] The professionalization of journalism, as well as a steady increase in the number of educational institutions (universities, teachers' colleges that also engaged in research, and private research institutes), had two important effects. First, they prompted a dissolution of the previous monopoly over the creation and validation of knowledge. Second, they brought about the end of the University of Tokyo's dominance as the single recruitment pool for the bureaucratic elite.

Society had changed rapidly during the years of World War I, and a wave of internationalism and liberalism swept the intellectual world.

Discontented intellectuals and students protested against inequalities in society and joined farmers and laborers in pressing the government for reforms (Mitchell 1973:319). Progressive leaders with liberal and socialist leanings like Yoshino Sakuzō, Takano Iwasaburō, Kawai Eijirō, Suzuki Bunji, Abe Isoo, and Yamamoto Senji aimed at mass mobilization and strove to gain support for reforms among the wider populace. They came from socioeconomic backgrounds that were decidedly different from those prevalent in the Meiji era and attempted to open the political system to citizens who did not belong to the small political elite. They promised more effective possibilities for social reform through the academic and semi-academic world of the university, schools, political and social movements, and the print media than were possible from posts within the government.

The liberal Ōyama Ikuo, for example, felt that the "democratization of knowledge" was a requirement for an orderly democratization of politics. He believed that only a scientific method of social analysis would provide a theoretical guide for social change (see Duus 1982:429,432). Cultural critic Tsuchida Kyōson pointed out the lack of theories in the social sciences that were based on the social realities of Japan and pressed for empirical social research. In a similar vein, he castigated academia for its ignorance of "events of the day" and its lack of "social interest." Often intermingling with socialists and other social activists, sociologists insisted that their field be based on empirical research within Japan rather than theories and concepts that emerged from Euro-American societies. The sociologists' call to examine and perhaps separate from Western theoretical concepts was invariably tied to the efforts to make social problems visible and pressure the government into solving them (see Soviak 1990:94–95).

It was no longer mainly alumni from the University of Tokyo who were behind the progressive powers of the Taishō era. Social reformers and scholars came in equal proportions from samurai, agricultural, and mercantile families. The establishment of a new political awareness was achieved primarily by a steadily growing class of intellectual workers who attempted to capture new intellectual, social, and political terrain. They presented themselves as the chief interpreters, creators, and popularizers of knowledge. Many saw socialism as a model for the solution to social problems. As Fukuda Hideko observed, the socialists who were beginning to raise their voices on behalf of social justice and political freedom were the true heirs of the early Meiji people's-rights movement (see Hane 1988:51). The manifesto of the first Society for Sociology

(Shakai Gakkai), founded in 1896, for example, stated that "we must study the principles of sociology and research actual social life in order to control and avoid social problems" (see Kawamura N. 1990:64). After the dissolution of the Society for Sociology, Christian socialists such as Katayama Sen, Murai Tomoshi, Abe Isoo, Kōtoku Shūsui, and Kinoshita Naoe, who for the most part had studied in the United States, founded the Society for Socialist Studies. Amateur sociologists who were not interested in socialism, such as Katō Hiroyuki, Takagi Masayoshi, and Motoyoshi Yujirō, founded the Society for Sociological Studies in the same year.[16]

Empirical studies on Japanese culture and society that concentrated on social problems came to be regarded with increasing distrust, whether they concerned workers' lives and urban slum populations, like the studies of Kagawa Toyohiko (1880–1960), or sexual practices among Japan's youth. Kagawa Toyohiko, a Christian social reformer involved in the labor movement and founder of the Japanese Salvation Army, published *Research on the Psychology of the Poor (Hinmin shinri no kenkyū)* in 1915 and *Crossing the Death Line (Shisen o koete)* in 1920. His investigations were based on interviews with the inhabitants of Kōbe's slums and were reason enough for Kagawa to be under close surveillance by the authorities of public order. In 1921 he was arrested for the first time for his interest in poverty as a social problem and his involvement with the labor movement (see Ōta T. 1980:103–104).[17]

Like the students of sociology, economics, and political science who struggled to ground their respective disciplines in Japanese society rather than in Western theory, Japan's first sex researchers strove to consolidate changes in scientific practice with broader social change and to establish a science of sex. An important effect of these attempts was the increase and diversification of creators and popularizers of knowledge about sex. While some sexologists clearly welcomed and profited from such an increase, others opposed these "nonscientific" writings and strove to establish themselves as "scientific" authorities on sexual knowledge. Their attempts to do so were manifested in various activities. Public lectures were one way of exchanging sexual knowledge with a diverse audience, including medical doctors, mine and factory workers, and teachers and students. Sexologists presented information on sexual development, discussed the results of their research, and gave advice on sexual problems in specialized journals, women's and household magazines, and household medical reference books.

Using diverse instruments and methods to gather data about sexual practices in contemporary Japan, sexologists emulated the young generation of scholars in other emerging fields. Survey data were supplemented by information from personal letters from people who had attended their public lectures or read their books and journals. Conversations and discussions after public lectures also found their way into the sexologists' publications. They considered all of these efforts legitimate for the creation of a body of knowledge based on continuous interaction between sexologists and their audience. The latter was not only the receiver but at the same time the object of this new knowledge, and thus was involved in its creation in a complex way. The sexologists saw themselves as forerunners of a new and better society, and they saw possibilities for decisive change.

Yamamoto and Yasuda's continuing survey on sexual behavior was a major step in that direction, but they did not stop there. Yamamoto in particular extended his authority through public lectures at other universities, schools, farm and labor unions, and community and city halls. Between September 1921 and February 1924, he lectured in thirty places in addition to giving his regular lectures at the Universities of Kyoto and Dōshisha. Among these other sites were the Kyoto Prefectural Medical University, the University of Tokyo, Waseda University, two free universities in the Niigata and Nagano prefectures, and the Osaka Labor Union School, which had been established by socialist labor union leaders (see Hane 1988:152). He spoke at meetings of teachers' organizations, to several teachers' unions in Tottori, Kōchi, and other cities, and to teachers of all types of other schools, including elementary schools, girls' schools, and universities. He spoke to young company recruits and farm youth groups and accepted invitations from publishing houses and labor unions to speak to subscribers and laborers (Yamamoto Senji 1921g:322, 1924c:218). In 1925 he reported that 13,000 people had come to hear his lectures in Osaka, Kyoto, and Nagoya, and many more had attended his lectures in Kōchi (Shikoku), Sakai, Yoneko, Matsue, Miyatsu, Sonoe, Imazu, Nagoya, Nara, Nagano, Okayama, Kagawa, and Tokyo (Yamamoto Senji 1925a:36).

A lecture normally lasted two hours and included time for discussion. However, Yamamoto often was invited to do a lecture series of ten hours or more. He meticulously recorded information about the event. He noted the organization or person who had invited him (usually a representative of the organization or group), and listed the site of the lecture (often a public assembly building). He documented the size of the audiences (between 30 and 170 at a time), and the number of people who had returned his survey (between 4 and 57 percent). He also documented the dominant professions of his audiences, their age, and occasionally other information (e.g., "Ten-hour course for factory workers," or the exact title of his talk). The gender of the audience was not listed separately but Yamamoto noted on five separate occasions that both men *and* women were among the audience (Yamamoto Senji 1921g:322, 1924c:218).

A poster announcement for one of his two-hour talks included the main topics of his talk:

TWO-HOUR LECTURE ON SEX EDUCATION:
OUTLINE OF SEXUAL KNOWLEDGE

Yamamoto Senji, Lecturer in the Department of Science at Kyoto University

Contents: (1) The essential accurate knowledge about reproduction, which is of such great importance to life; (2) Knowledge about the construction of the male and female sex organs; (3) The male sexual apparatus: sperm, testicles, vas deferens, sperm production, ejaculation, urethra, penis; (4) The female sex organs: ovaries, Fallopian tube, uterus, vagina, and hymen.

Break: Answering questions

(5) Sexual diseases and their prevention; (6) Emission *(isei)*, masturbation *(jii)*, sexual intercourse; (7) Menstruation, conception, pregnancy, birth.

The Lecturer's Goals: (1) Until now, young people, misguided by information whose validity is questionable, have been faced with grievous worries in their blind search. If we have accurate knowledge, we must ensure that it is used in order to lessen harm and suffering. We should not waste our energy, but rather pass on accurate knowledge immediately.

(2) There is a comparative lack of knowledge on how common *(jinjō)* men and women live their lives, since many scholars have busied themselves with the morals, habits, and customs of the past . . . and in doing so, have dealt with nothing but diseases. We must first of all get to know ourselves. Therefore, the lecturer, a scholar, will speak about this phenomenon for a general audience. (Yamamoto Senji 1921g:320–321)

One of these public lectures resulted in the sudden end of Yamamoto's academic career. In 1922, he went on a lecture tour from Osaka to Kōbe, Nagoya, and other small cities. On 17 April he spoke in Tottori. After several warnings by police observers, his talk eventually was interrupted and he was pulled off the stage. The police report noted that Yamamoto had used technical terms but had nonetheless encouraged masturbation, approved of abortion, and talked about "other obscenities" (see Odagiri 1979b:514–515). As a consequence of the scandal he was fired from his position at Kyoto University and shortly thereafter

from Dōshisha University. This sudden but definite exclusion from academic institutions certainly contributed to Yamamoto's intensified involvement in the education of laborers and his engagement in the Labor
Farmer Party (Rōdō Nōmintō). From January 1924 on, Yamamoto
worked as a teacher at a worker's school in Osaka and as the editor of
an educational section of the press for the Labor Farmer Party. When a
labor school was opened in Kyoto in April of the same year, he became
its director. In 1928, as one of two representatives of the Labor Farmer
Party's left wing, he was elected as a parliamentary representative in Kyoto (see Scalapino 1967:34).[18] By the time of his election, his sexological journal *Sex and Society (Sei to Shakai),* which had been one of more
than a dozen such journals, had ceased to exist.

SEXOLOGICAL JOURNALS AND THE SCIENCE OF SEX

There are people who want to read about sexuality but
are embarrassed because they doubt the educational
value of our journal. The youth of today read about the
experience of being seduced or about wedding-night
memories in women's magazines—texts that are poorly
written and have hardly any content. Mothers, you
must at least take a look at our journal *Sexuality*! Our
journal has been approved as a professional journal
by the responsible authorities. . . . *Sexuality* pursues
the viewpoint that it is necessary to carry out research
on humans and acquire knowledge about them.
[*Sexuality*] is a unique journal that carries out crucial
research. Recruit even more readers! We put our hopes
in you.

                                        Sei November 1927

Sexuality (Sei; see figure 7) was but one of a dozen or so sexological
journals founded between the late 1910s and the early 1930s, when the
number of sexological books and specialized journals, as well as sexological articles in women's magazines, popular science magazines, and
general periodicals, exploded. The remarkable increase in the number of
publications on sex was widely acknowledged all over the nation. Newspapers reported in various fashions about this phenomenon, in tones
sometimes alarmist, sometimes approving.[19] Even though academic institutions were not eager to acknowledge the emergence of a new field

Figure 7. The spring 1920 issue of Akiyama Yoshio's journal *Sexuality (Sei)* dealt almost exclusively with "female sexual desire" *(fujin seiyoku)*. The mission statement of the journal features poems by Friedrich von Schiller and Johann Wolfgang von Goethe dealing with desire and sacrifice. The cover shows an adaptation of a scene from Goethe's *Faust* depicting Mephisto.

of research and teaching, sexology did become situated at the fringes of academia. The science of sex was furthered by the writings and other activities of scholars, journalists, medical doctors, biologists, bureaucrats, and other intellectuals and social reformers who identified sex and sexuality as the pivotal point of debates about society and social reform, whether they feared for national security, demanded freedom or social control, or insisted on the "truth about sex."

By the 1920s, this group of scholars and professionals could rely on a continuously expanding school education system and increasing literacy among all classes. Both factors had led to a significantly larger readership than had existed in previous decades. For men, literacy had improved tremendously during the first decade of the twentieth century, when the portion of illiterate conscripts dropped from 23 percent in 1899 to 0.5 percent in 1929 (Kiyokawa 1991; Nagamine 2001:162). Literacy among women virtually exploded with the expansion of secondary schooling during the 1920s. In 1930, readers could choose from more than 11,000 magazines and journals, and the population of 65 million bought 10 million daily newspapers. The numbers of readers who subscribed to one or more newspapers or magazines significantly increased as well, and more and more people borrowed their neighbors' or friends' copies or went to local libraries to read newspapers, magazines, and books (Kimura 1992; Maeda 1993 [1973]; see also Silverberg 1993:123–124).

White-collar households were willing to spend between 3.3 and 8.7 yen per month on reading material, and many subscribed to more than one newspaper and/or magazine. An unmarried staff person of a magazine with a monthly income of 60 yen, for example, spent 3.3 yen on reading material, while the three-person household of a trading company employee with a monthly income of 150 yen budgeted 7.5 yen for newspapers, magazines, and other reading material. The rather luxurious household of a manager with a monthly income of 215 yen could afford to spend 8.7 yen on reading material, including a newspaper, two women's magazines, a foreign magazine, and other reading material for the manager, his wife, three children, and a maid (*Sarariiman* May 1929; quoted in Nagamine 2001:225). According to a female reader survey published in 1926, 77 "modern girls"—including female students, typists, train conductors, sales clerks, café waitresses, actresses, and nurses—enjoyed reading more than 30 different magazines (*Fujokai* October 1926; quoted in Nagamine 2001:110). According to a 1923 survey on leisure behavior, newspaper and magazine reading had become one of the two favorite leisure activities (the other was book reading) of the working class (see Nagamine 2001:164), allowing for the development of a "low scientific culture" (Sheets-Pyenson 1985).

In these publications, ranging from general interest newspapers and magazines to women's and household magazines, readers of all walks of life found articles by sexologists, advertisements for sexological publications, and reports on the authors' activities in the realm of sex research, sex education, and sex reform. These print media helped some individual sexologists attain a more prominent status and contributed significantly to the dissemination of their ideas. Publishing houses realized that sex helped boost their circulation numbers to new heights and used it—often packaged as scandal and confession stories—to increase their commercial success.

Akiyama Yoshio's editorials in *Sexuality*, quoted above, informed readers that young people's "false sexual development" needed to be guided in a better direction to ensure that "adultery, wild marriages, and abortions" would soon become practices of the past (*Sei* October 1927, editorial). He hoped that a balanced blend of "erotic tales, reports from experience, narratives and scholarly essays" would enlighten and entertain readers enough so that they would pay the relatively hefty price of 40 sen for one issue.[20] He also offered free public lectures on "sexual love" *(seiai kōen)* for a minimum of thirty people and encouraged readers to contact him about that possibility (*Sei* October 1927, editorial).

Founded by Akiyama in 1918, *Sexuality* was one of the sexological journals that had survived the Kantō earthquake in 1923 (*Sei* December 1926, editorial). A typical issue brought together a diverse group of proponents of sex research and sexual enlightenment. The spring 1920 issue was a special "issue on women's sexual desire" *(fujin seiyokugō)* and included articles on the importance of (female) chastity, a comparative history of prostitution systems, and notes on consanguine marriage by Sawada Junjirō, an immensely prolific writer on sexual issues. The literary critic Sawada Keiko (Sawada's wife) contributed an article on the various roles of women in the home and society. Abe Isoo (1865–1949), a graduate of Dōshisha University and professor of economics at Waseda University, expressed in his contributions to the journal his concern about the impact of work on women's reproductive ability. Abe cofounded the Social Democratic Party in May 1901 (with Kōtoku Shūsui, Katayama Sen, Kinoshita Naoe, and others) and the Social Mass Party (1932–1940) and was an omnipresent public figure throughout the first half of the twentieth century, coupling scholarly engagement with political activism (see Kawamura N. 1990). He also was a cofounder of the Purity Society (Kakuseikai), which guided the anti-prostitution movement as of July 1911 under the slogan "liberation of prostitutes" *(geishōgi kaihō)* and published the monthly journal *Purity*. At the beginning of the 1920s, Abe became a leading representative of the Tokyo arm of the birth control movement—the subject of chapter 4.

Classifying childbirth as one of the most "important factors in human development," Yokoyama Masao, a statistician from the Census Bureau (Kokusei Chōsa-kyoku), contributed an article to the special issue of *Sexuality* in which he presented Japanese women's birth rates and compared them to birth rates of women in twenty-three other countries.[21] Based on his experiences as an obstetrician, Akimoto Seiji, the head of a women's hospital, described the reproductive life cycle of women in an article entitled "The Sexual Capacity of Japanese Women." Ōzawa Kenji, a medical doctor, declared chastity, women's participation in the workforce outside the home, and birth control the three most pressing "sexual problems" of the years to come. Among the other contributors to this special issue of *Sexuality* were a director of a girls' high school, a journalist from the newspaper *Nagoya Nippō*, a "scholar of race improvement," and a few others whose expertise was not specified (*Sei* April 1920).

The collection of comments by more than forty contemporaries on what Ōzawa termed the three "sexual problems concerning women" is perhaps the most fascinating part of this issue on female sexuality (*Sei* April 1920:79–91). Editor Akiyama and most of the contributors were members of the Japanese Society of Sexology (Nihon Seigakkai), a small group based in Tokyo (not to be confused with another organization with the same name founded in the postwar era and carried by people with a quite different agenda, to which I shall return in chapter 5). The list of official supporters of the first Japanese Society of Sexology and the journal *Sexuality* was long and included a wide range of men and a few women. Among them were medical doctors, scientists like Ishikawa Chiyomatsu, journalists such as Shimada Saburō, educators, mostly from teachers' colleges and high schools, and literary critics (*Sei* April 1920: 154–155).

Another Tokyo-based group of sexologists, the Sex Study Society (Sei no Kenkyūkai), under the leadership of Kitano Hiromi, began to publish *Sex Research (Sei no Kenkyū)* in December 1919. The goals of the group, noted in almost every issue of the journal, were similar to those of other groups of sexologists: "Our goal is to carry out various kinds of sex research and disseminate all of this knowledge. In order to realize this goal we will take the following steps: First, we will publish *Sex Research*. Second, we will publish major Eastern and Western works on sex. Third, we will collect books and other materials related to sex. Fourth, we will hold group meetings from time to time. And fifth, we will act as serious [*majime*] advisors of people who suffer from various kinds of sexual problems" (*Sei no Kenkyū* December 1919).

The editor of *Sex Research* strove to attract three kinds of members to the group: supporters who worked for the group, special supporters who paid a monthly membership of 50 sen, and regular members who paid a monthly fee of 25 sen (*Sei no Kenkyū* December 1919). Like Yamamoto Senji and Yasuda Tokutarō, Kitano was attracted mostly to Germanic sexology. In the first issue of his journal he briefly reviewed the history of sexology and mentioned several German, Austrian, and Swiss sexologists, such as Iwan Bloch, Magnus Hirschfeld, Albert Moll, Richard von Krafft-Ebing, Auguste Forel, and Albert Eulenburg, and praised the German sexological journals *Journal of Sexology (Zeitschrift für Sexualwissenschaft), Sexual Problems (Sexualprobleme),* and *New Generation (Neue Generation).* Kitano also noted that the existence of the American *Rational Sex Series* proved that the necessity for sex research had been acknowledged in the United States as well.[22] Claiming that sex research had gained approval in Japan, he accurately stated that nonetheless there were still few researchers who actually carried it out (Kitano 1919:4).

In the following issues Kitano continued his historiography of Western sexology and introduced a great number of other, mostly European, authors' works. He chose the Japanese neologism *seiyokugaku* as the translation of the German *Sexualwissenschaft,* and most of the contributors to his journal focused on what Yamamoto and Yasuda would reject as studies of "abnormal" or "perverse" sexuality (Kitano 1919:4). This tendency toward the "abnormal" was articulated in special issues on prostitution and frequent advertisements for books on prostitution based both on Kitano's ten-plus years of research and Nakamura Kokyō's journal entitled *Perverse Psyche (Hentai Shinri).*

A writer and medical doctor, Nakamura was engaged in the introduction of psychoanalysis and European psychology to Japan. He was the chairman of the Japanese Medico-Psychological Society (Nihon Seishin Igakkai) and in addition served as a criminological advisor to the Tokyo police. In 1917 he became the editor of the popular psychiatric journal *Perverse Psyche,* to which Kitano also frequently contributed.

The expertise of most other authors of *Sex Research* was not identified, except for those of the gynecologist Habuto Eiji and the amateur Edo historian Mitamura Engyō.

Sex Research also printed extracts of Sigmund Freud's *Three Essays on the Theory of Sexuality* (1962 [1905]:88–126), the chapter on neo-Malthusianism in Iwan Bloch's *Das Sexualleben unserer Zeit,* (1919 [1906]:715–730), and extracts from several works of other European sexologists. Despite Kitano's connections to the police, who were in charge of protecting public peace and morals and were thus in charge of censorship, *Sex Research* was censored frequently, and at times entire issues were prohibited from being distributed.[23]

A frequent contributor to *Sex Research* and Kitano's friend, Habuto Eiji eventually founded his own journal entitled *Sexual Desire and Humankind (Seiyoku to Jinsei)* at the beginning of the 1920s. Habuto was a graduate of the Medical Department at the University of Tokyo and practiced as a gynecologist in a small clinic in the vicinity of the University of Tokyo's campus in Nezu, the playground of many literati and medical doctors, including Natsume Sōseki, Mori Ōgai, and Ōta Tenrei, during the early twentieth century. His first main work, entitled *Perverse Sexual Desire (Hentai seiyokuron,* 1915) and co-authored with Sawada Junjirō, was based on Richard von Krafft-Ebing's *Psychopathia Sexualis* (1886). During the next fifteen years, he wrote numerous popular books and articles, in which he preached furiously about the pathology of homosexuality and the mental and physical harmfulness of masturbation. When he committed suicide in 1929, the author of an obituary in *Popular Medicine* noted without a hint of irony that Habuto had died from the consequences of neurasthenia, which Habuto himself—like many other contemporaries—had considered a result of masturbation (Yokoyama T. 1929). Habuto addressed a wide range of themes in *Sexual Desire and Humankind.* Issues that focused on a particular theme included, for example, one on sexual love (January 1921), one on systems of prostitution (February 1921), an issue on female sexual desire (March 1921), and one on sexual desire in literature and art (April 1921). The pool of contributors to *Sexual Desire and Humankind,* like those to other sexological journals, included medical doctors, journalists, and occasionally university professors and directors of hospitals and health advice offices. In addition, advertisements for Habuto's numerous popular book publications filled a considerable number of pages in his journal. His books also were advertised in other sexological journals and in women's and popular health magazines.

Sexual Theory (Seiron; see figure 8), published by yet another small group of sexologists, the Society of Sexual Theory (Seironsha), was of a slightly different character than *Sexuality* and *Sexual Desire and Humankind.* Besides the dominant Habuto Eiji, contributors included a few medical doctors and other men and two women with law degrees. However, the majority of the contributors were not identified by profession. Like *Sexuality, Sex Research,* and other sexological journals, *Sexual Theory* contained equal portions of sexological information and supposedly entertaining, sometimes grotesque, stories. In the May 1928 issue, for example, the criminal law that declared abortion illegal was questioned and the laws and the problems involved were discussed in a factual manner. A certain medical doctor, Kawatani Masao, compared the legal situation concerning abortion in Japan to that in Russia and Germany in order to justify and promote a more liberal abortion law. Another medical doctor described case studies of sexual ailments and how they had been healed. Among these were the case of a twenty-one-year-old student at a professional school who had suffered from nocturnal emission, that of a thirty-five-year-old electrical technician who was plagued by premature ejaculation, and that of a forty-seven-year-old politician who was haunted by impotence.

In contrast to these articles, which evoked the language of social scientific research, Tanaka Chiune, whose expertise was not clarified, told several versions of the same legend about "perverse marriages" *(hentai kon).* One version of the story ran like this: "A certain man lived alone. He became lonely and eventually played with one of his own pigs. The pig brought forth many young, all of which looked like humans" (Tanaka C. 1928:48). In the essay, Tanaka did not draw any conclusions from these stories, nor did he make any explicit judgments. From his introduction, however, it is clear that he considered Japan and the Japanese to be beyond such "perverse" stories or perhaps even such behavior. At the beginning of his essay, he pointed out that these stories did not originate in "mainland Japan" but in Taiwan, Korea, China, and India (Tanaka C. 1928:48).

By 1925, Yamamoto, disillusioned by the unfavorable response to his efforts to promote education and research on sex and fired from Dōshisha and Kyoto Universities, had turned to the education of laborers. As a representative of the Labor Farmer Party he became increasingly engaged in politics and founded *Birth Control Review,* which was renamed *Sex and Society* after a few issues. Targeting a lay audience rather than scholars, all texts in *Sex and Society* were printed with the phonetic

Figure 8. *Sexual Theory* (*Seiron*, April 1928) distinguished itself from the beginning with its entertaining spoofs of most other
sexological magazines. Erotic stories as well as contributions
on prostitution and questions on abortion were printed.

syllable writing systems *hiragana* and *katakana* next to uncommon Chinese characters in order to facilitate legibility, and the journal was sold
at the price of 20 sen—cheaper than any of the women's and general-
interest magazines that cost between 30 and 40 sen (*Sanji Chōsetsu
Hyōron* 1925a). The texts of Yamamoto's sex education lectures ran

in almost every single issue (i.e., Yamamoto Senji 1925a–p, 1926c, 1927a–d). His translations of sexological works were also a central feature of the journal.

Ōta Tenrei's *Research in Sexology (Seikagaku Kenkyū)* was the last journal founded before the outbreak of full-blown war with China in 1937, when censorship set out to sweep the journals and their authors into oblivion. I shall examine censorship and other developments destructive to the sexological project, including the power of pronatal propaganda, "racial hygiene," and the tightening of the economic situation, in chapter 5. Here, I wish to introduce Ōta Tenrei (1900–1985) as one of the medical doctors-cum-sexologists who underwent a transformation from researcher to popularizer of sexological findings. He also is of particular interest in the colonization of sex as a proponent of sex education and sex research who continued his activities in the postwar era, which I will revisit in chapter 5.

Ōta graduated from Kyoto Medical University in 1925. He opened his gynecological practice in a poor neighborhood in Kyoto and was soon stamped as a "socialist doctor." He spent many years researching the female cycle in his own laboratory, and eventually developed a new means of contraception—an intrauterine device (IUD), or "spiral"— which he introduced in 1932. As he noted in his memoirs, his colleagues in the medical profession, particularly those from Tokyo, were rather critical of his invention, which he had described in several articles for professional journals. At the beginning of the 1930s, it was uncommon for a respectable physician to engage in the development of contraceptive methods. Nevertheless, several hundred doctors based mainly in Taiwan and Korea tested the Ōta–Ring. Because of his research, Ōta was in close contact with Ishimoto Shizue, Yasuda Tokutarō, Abe Isoo, and Yamamoto Senji, all leading activists in the birth control movement. In contrast to other sexologists, Ōta did not engage in popularizing his findings and inventions beyond the boundaries of his own journal and other scholarly publications.[24]

CULTIVATING THE SEXOLOGICAL FIELD

On trains one sees people reading books exclusively
on sexual questions, the psychology of love, and sex
research. Many magazines write continuously about
sexual topics only to capture the curiosity of youth and

to increase the number of copies sold. Nowadays there
are even specialized journals dealing entirely with these
topics.

Fujo Shinbun 19 June 1921

These observations by the editor of the *Women's Newspaper (Fujo Shinbun)* may have been an exaggeration. They hint accurately, however, at
the growing market for publications about sex, which marked the establishment of a sexology whose aim was to bring scientific knowledge
about sex not only to children and youth but also to the wider public.
To some contemporaries, "sex education" seemed to be the most popular expression used during the 1920s (*Hentai Shinri* 1921; see also Furukawa 1993:114), and by the 1930s, medical reference books for home
use included extensive sections on masturbation, menstruation, pregnancy, and recommendations for the treatment of venereal diseases
(Araki 1931; Arai 1934).

All sexological journals began with the goal of increasing the body of
knowledge on sex and distributing this knowledge to a wide audience.
However, these journals differed considerably in how these goals were
pursued and in the means used. Some were scholarly in both style and
language and thus unintelligible for readers with less than higher education. Others made an effort to be comprehensible and also attractive
to a less educated readership. However, the contents of the journals and
their authors' professional expertise or lack thereof were not the only
indicators of their scholarliness or popularity. As a rule, the use of *furi-
gana* next to almost all of the Chinese characters indicated that a broader
audience was targeted. Three-color covers and illustrations were used as
a means to attract an audience beyond scholarly readers.

Most of the sexological journals adhered to the laws applicable to the
commercial print media market, as indicated by the kinds of advertisements found among the pages of the sexological journals, which ranged
from self-advertising announcements to mainstream product advertising
that could be found in any contemporary magazine. The journals advertised for other sexological journals, announced books by their authors,
and printed advertisements for the clinics of those doctors who either
appeared as authors or answered letters in advice columns.

In his journal *Perverse Psyche*, Nakamura Kokyō advertised the first
edition of the monthly *Sex Research*, published by Kitano Hiromi (*Hentai Shinri* April 1920: back cover). The advertisement, printed in nearly
all of the subsequent issues, explicitly recommended it as reading in the

"psychology of love" *(ren'ai shinri)* for educators, theologians, literary scholars, teachers, and parents, and thereby all people who were entrusted with raising children. The publishers and authors attempted to publicize not only their own research results, but also the names and work of "other great scientists" in the field *(Sei no Kenkyū* April 1921: inside cover). *Sexuality* printed full-page advertisements for the works *Sexual Hygiene and Prevention (Seiteki eisei oyobi yobō)* and *Pathology of Sexual Desire (Shikijōkyō),* both written by Sawada Junjirō, who was characterized as *the* authority on sexology *(Sei* February 1923: advertising section). In the case of *Sexual Desire and Humankind (Seiyoku to Jinsei),* the great number of personal letters that Habuto Eiji received motivated him to set up an advice column in his journal. Most of the sexological journals also contained tear-out forms that could be filled in and sent to the journal's editorial offices. The content of the advice columns, with titles like "Solutions to Sexual Agony" ("Seiteki hanmon kaiketsusho") in *Sexual Desire and Humankind* or "Questions and Answers on Hygiene" ("Eisei mondō") in *Popular Medicine,* echoed the issues that were discussed in the journal's articles. They offered the counselor the possibility of giving concrete instructions for concrete problems in the form of a staged dialogue. By the end of the 1920s, sexuality had become the crucial subject of a choreographed communication between readers and experts in both sexological journals and other magazines.[25]

Next to self-promoting announcements, advertisements for medical and hygiene treatments and devices were most common. The first issue of *Birth Control Review,* for example, praised a great variety of products ranging from an anti-tobacco addiction medicine, to a skin tonic named Beautiful Face Water (Bigansui) that promised to remove pimples, to biscuits containing calcium *(Sanji Chōsetsu Hyōron* February 1925). In later issues, advertisements for German medical treatments were added. A cream named Sana Geox supposedly killed vaginal and urethral bacteria *(Sanji Chōsetsu Hyōron* March 1925, April 1925). Supūman, available in two varieties, one especially for gonorrhea patients, was praised as a suppository "approved by the German government" and served the same purpose *(Sanji Chōsetsu Hyōron* April 1925, *Tsūzoku Igaku* May 1926). Even *Sex Research* advertised medical treatment for venereal diseases, although no other aesthetic means were used to make the journal more appealing to non-professional readers *(Sei no Kenkyū* April 1919). A pharmacy advertisement claimed that Menzē Suponchi, made of silk, would prevent venereal disease during menstruation and announced that condoms made of fish skin were available at the same pharmacy (*Sanji Chōsetsu Hyōron* June 1925). However, some journals, such as *Sex and Society*, also printed full-page advertisements for the major department stores Mitsukoshi, Daimaru, and Takashimaya, advertisements which could be found in other magazines and newspapers and thus perhaps added to the respectability of the sexology journals.

Intellectuals involved in the social reform movements of the 1920s were wary of institutions, which were available only to a small circle of the intellectual elite. In an effort to reach the general public they voiced their ideas and theories in media that were available through mail order and from publishing houses and, after 1925, on the radio (Marshall 1992:95; Silverberg 1998:33).[26] The widespread use of magazines and newspapers was one of the most important strategies sexologists and other Taishō intellectuals used to increase their visibility and introduce their ideas to a wider audience. Whereas earlier proponents and opponents of diverse policies published their views primarily in scholarly journals that were accessible and intelligible to only a small circle of readers, the intellectuals of the Taishō era took advantage of the rapidly developing popular media market. Now, the views of university professors and other intellectuals were published by widespread media, especially when those views deviated from common sense (Marshall 1992: 95–97). Thus, knowledge and the means of exchanging information across great distances were no longer the exclusive possessions of a small elite but gradually became the property of a large number of educated citizens.

Sexologists might have had much less success at creating their field, and the influence of their ideas and theories might not have been so great, if not for their presence in women's magazines, general-readership magazines, and newspapers, which attracted a larger readership than any of the sexological journals ever could have. Crucial for these activities were specialized journals such as *Purity* and popular health journals such as *Popular Medicine* and *Popular Hygiene (Tsūzoku Eisei)*. Equally important was the support of other papers, especially the *Asahi Shinbun*, women's magazines like *Women's Review (Fujin Kōron)*, general mass-circulation magazines such as *The Sun (Taiyō)*, and popular psychiatric and criminal-psychological journals such as *Perverse Psyche*. All of these contributed to intensifying sexual discourse and furthered the multiplication of sexological writings by offering sexologists the opportunity to voice their concerns, present their knowledge, and advertise their more specialized publications.

In one of many examples in general-interest magazines, *The Sun* advertised a book edited by a medical doctor entitled *Sexual Problems (Seiyoku mondai)*. In nine chapters, the "scientifically based results of several years of research" on the "sexual desire in humans, society, marriage, love, literature, morals, religion, education, and hygiene" were presented to a wide audience. The advertisement promised that "fleshy words" had been avoided and praised the book as mandatory reading for all who "dealt directly with children" and therefore "with the development of the race." These readers were specified as educators, theologians, business people, parents, and siblings (*Taiyō* 3 September 1913: advertising section).

The almost symbiotic relationship of the sexologists to the more progressive print media was instrumental for the successful establishment of sexological journals that contained articles on sexual hygiene, pathology and the history of sexual life, educational series, erotic stories, and advice columns. Japanese sexologists, like their European colleagues, found letters to the editors to be an important instrument for legitimizing their science and themselves as authorities on sexual issues. In Austria, Richard von Krafft-Ebing had encouraged homosexuals to tell him their stories, which had led to a flood of letters. He took most of the biographical contributions in his work *Psychopathia sexualis* from these letters (Hauser 1994:211). Similarly, Sawada Junjirō's 1922 treatise "Actual Contraception and the Possibilities of Limiting Births" ("Jissaiteki hinin to sanji seigenhō") contained a tear-out sheet for readers' questions. He personally answered more than 350 questions each year after the publication of his first book in 1918, which addressed female hygiene before, during, and after pregnancy (Kawamura K. 1996:152).

In the same issue, the Chūō Yakuin Pharmacy promised free delivery of a brochure providing information on sexual neurasthenia, unsatisfactory genital development and functional impairments, uterine and venereal diseases, as well as menstrual complaints—and pimples, freckles, and tuberculosis (*Taiyō* 3 September 1913: advertisement section). *Women's Review* printed detailed advertisements for Habuto Eiji's book *Sexual Hygiene (Sei no eisei)*, on sale for 1.70 yen, which was about "youth and sexual neurasthenia, masturbation among girls and boys, ejaculation and impotence, methods to satisfy sexual desire, sexual hygiene for newlyweds, venereal diseases, and more." Habuto's older works—*General Sexology (Ippan seiyokugaku)*, *Studies on Femininity (Fujinsei no kenkyū)*, and *Sexual Desire and Modern Currents of Thought (Seiyoku to kindai shichō)*—were advertised constantly in women's magazines, and some had appeared in their fifteenth edition by as early as 1921. Women's magazines like *The Housewife's Companion (Shufu no Tomo)* and *Women's Review (Fujin Kōron)* also sent their subscribers medical reference books and household hygiene manuals that contained large sections on sex and sexuality.

Many scholars from various disciplines, employees in health and police departments, women's rights activists, and journalists whose work was widely advertised and whose ideas were debated in broadening circles of educated readers wrote in several of these journals and magazines themselves. Yamamoto, for example, promoted sex education and research in his own magazine *Sex and Society,* as well as in *Perverse Psyche* and *Popular Medicine.* Habuto saw himself as a defender of normalcy and as such wrote contributions for *Sexual Theory, Popular Medicine,* and *Women's Review,* in addition to his own magazine. At the end of the 1920s he turned toward a mass audience and wrote innumerable sex advice books. Abe Isoo promoted his ideas on prostitution, birth control, and eugenics in *Purity, Women's Review, Perverse Psyche,* and *Popular Medicine.*

Sexologists employed a number of strategies to promote their goal of establishing a new field of research and education. One set of these strategies involved careful definition of the boundaries of what they claimed as their field. Sexologists frequently distanced themselves from women's magazines but they never attacked the more sophisticated "high-class women's magazines" *(kōkyū fujin zasshi),* such as *Women's Review* or *Women's Newspaper,* which were read almost as frequently by men as by women of the educated classes. Rather, they criticized rival illustrated magazines whose popularity, in their opinion, was based mostly on confession stories. Sexologists may have envied these magazines for their commercial success but they made a point of differentiating their journals from them. They shook their heads over article titles such as "My Confession: I Threw Myself Away to a Murderer," or "My Confession: I Became the Slave of a Lady-killer," which may have helped increase these papers' circulation. Sexologists frequently accused print media of dishonest motives when they reported on sex scandals or when authors they considered incompetent voiced their views, but they wrote articles on sexual issues for the very same magazines in order to reach the greatest possible audience. Although they invited a variety of people to contribute to their sexological journals, they sometimes devalued authors' articles by remarking that they disagreed with their views.

The public attention directed at sexual issues also drew in other social reformers who, for various reasons, became involved in an ever more complex series of debates that colonized more and more social problems, drawing them under the umbrella of the sexual issue. The debates about sex research and sex education, prostitution and venereal disease, masturbation and homosexuality continued, but another matter best exemplified the willingness of various groups within Japanese society to put research results into practice and turn visions into legal measures: birth control, the subject of the next chapter.

CHAPTER 4

Claiming the Fetus

In the April 1935 issue of *Popular Medicine (Tsūzoku Igaku)*, a half-page advertisement offered a total of thirty-six different products for contraception and the prevention of infection with venereal disease (see figure 9). Ranging from several categories of "condoms for men and women" *(danjo sakku)* to pessaries, silk sponges, and disinfectant creams, these products were marketed toward both sexes as "tools of birth control" *(sanji seigen yōgu)*, "specialized rare articles and medicine for men and women" *(danjo senyō chinki chinryaku)*, and "friends of familial harmony" *(katei wagō no tomo)*. An illustration in the upper middle part of the advertisement hinted at the pharmacy's potential clientele. A man dressed in a modern business suit is taking off his shoes at the entrance to what seems to be his own house. A traditionally dressed woman greets her husband upon his return from work, requesting that he use the condoms she gives to him. The wife says, "I bought something that will make you blush. Please use it." "Yes, yes," replies the husband *(Tsūzoku Igaku* April 1935:175).

It is not entirely clear whether she wants her husband to use the condoms with her and expects him to blush because of the suggestive nature of such a gesture, whether she assumes that he will have sex with somebody else and she expects him to blush because of the embarrassment of acknowledging that. In any case, the subject of their conversation is birth control–cum–prevention of venereal disease, as some of the prod-

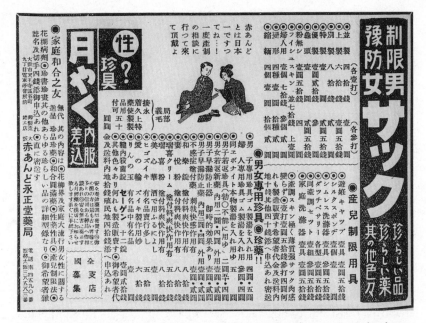

Figure 9. Advertisements for birth control devices placed next to articles for the prevention of (venereal) diseases hint at their availability even during the late 1930s, when, in the name of pronatalism and militarism, attempts at limiting family size were persistently denounced and criminalized (*Tsūzoku Igaku* April 1935:175). Used with the kind permission of the Kyōto Ika Daigaku Library.

ucts advertised were intended for birth control, others for the prevention of an infection with a venereal disease, and yet others for both.

Three condoms were advertised for the price of 1 to 3 yen, depending on their quality; a pessary for 1.50 yen. The price of other products ranged between 1 and 3 yen. Customers in mainland Japan could order any of these products by mail from a pharmacy in Osaka for an additional fee of 10 sen. From other places under Japan's colonial rule, one could order them for four times that price. The advertisement texts also emphasized that the products were safe to use. As the illustration in the advertisement indicates, most of the contraceptives featured were not affordable to the working class, farmers, or even the less well off middle class. The illustration also accurately underlines the well-established conviction that women were responsible for hygiene and health matters in the home and—by implication—for matters concerning the domestication of sex.

In several other respects, however, the advertisement is surprising. First, by 1935, attempts at birth control by healthy, well-off couples ran counter to pronatalist national policies that aimed at increasing the number of births and shunned attempts at limiting them. Second, the use of devices like the contraceptive needle *(hinin pin)* featured in the advertisement was illegal. And third, the journal *Popular Medicine,* like other journals and magazines that addressed issues of sex and procreation, had been frequently censored over the previous ten years for taking a pro–birth control stance. By intertwining the purposes of disease prevention and contraception, the creators of the advertisement skillfully subscribed to the health regime's goals and at the same time incorporated means of birth control, perhaps the most contested issue at the crossroads of debate about the creation and popularization of sexual knowledge, social order, women's rights, and empire building.

In contrast to the debate about the "sexual issue" that had taken place in the *Yomiuri Shinbun* seventeen years earlier, Japan's birth control movement and the public controversies that accompanied it did not involve a relatively homogeneous set of participating doctors and pedagogues, but were staged in highly heterogeneous forums and were characterized by great complexity. All participants progressively shaped the movement, albeit to varying degrees. By engaging in the movement, they defined its contested content and brought in several "worlds of relevance" (Limoges 1993) that unfolded in the space the controversy began to claim.[1] In this process, as sexual issues seeped into ever broader public realms, debates and controversies gradually drifted away from the seemingly disinterested utterances of claims to the truth about sex—attempted by the early sex researchers described in chapter 3—and toward decisions about lawmaking, for reasons made urgent by a combination of economic and political crises as well as imperialist ambitions.

In the early 1930s, the total population of mainland Japan had reached 67 million.[2] The educated classes were convinced that an increase in national prosperity alone, vigorously advocated since the early days of the Meiji era, would no longer suffice to contain the enormous annual population growth of one million inhabitants (BSOPM 1980: 11–13). The rapid population growth of 15 in 1,000 per year was perceived to be a national problem. Throughout the early decades of the twentieth century this growth was framed as a set of issues that addressed sexual knowledge and practice in diverse ways. For imperialist and militarist ideologues, the population increase was proof of a prosperous empire, potent and willing to fight future wars not only thanks to healthy and well-trained male subjects, but also to a supply of off-spring provided by unlimitedly fertile women. As a way to deal fruitfully with overpopulation, they proposed emigration into Japan's colonies and other neighboring Asian countries, which also further facilitated imperialistic goals. Tens of thousands of Japanese realized that the options for domestic avenues of advance were shrinking, and they came to see emigration as a way to seek their fortune elsewhere. "Go! Go abroad! Abroad! Go!" exhorted one writer in 1911, when Korea, in particular, was the place to go (see Duus 1995:321). Even popular songs addressed the waves of emigration resulting from the "population problem" *(jinkō mondai)*, with lines such as "Because I go, you go too. Away from crowded Japan. Beyond the sea lies China" (see Miyamoto 1965: 43). Leading ideologues began to welcome rapid population growth propagated by popular slogans such as "give birth and multiply" *(umeyo, fuyaseyo)* in order to spur Japanese migration and somehow to "naturally facilitate Japan's expansion into East Asia" (Hashimoto Kingorō, reprinted in Tsunoda, de Bary, and Keene 1964:289).[3]

For certain women's groups, the population problem provided a setting for the redefinition of women's roles, status, and rights in society. They realized the political capital of their wombs, the expansive part of their bodies that would—if fully functional—improve their status as imperial subjects and by the same token further the expansion of the empire. As I will discuss below, there was by no means unity among feminists, members of other women's groups, and social reformers on this point, but many came to believe that one could not be had without achieving the other. At a time when women were refused political rights, the idea of lending their bodies to larger political goals and thus aligning the uterus with the empire was too alluring. Some feminists believed in the virtue and power of women's sexual self-discipline and morals in order to both curb overpopulation and improve men's moral standards and, by implication, the moral state of society. Others declared that preventing or terminating a pregnancy was a woman's exclusive right and the decision to do so should rest with her alone.

Emphasizing the ignorance of female farmers and workers as well as the hardships of their lives, socialists demanded the legalization of abortive and contraceptive means of birth control, particularly for peasants and workers. They viewed the population growth rate as worrisome and a precursor to class and international conflict. Socialists also rejected Japan's emigration policies as bourgeois and declared imperialism and war their most probable implications (Katō T. 1925b; Katsura 1926; Sugiyama M. 1925; Taniguchi 1925; Yoshida S. 1925). Some of them joined sexologists in their rejection of the conventional view that sex was inevitably guided by and restricted to the goal of procreation, and they promoted research and education on matters of conception and pregnancy.

In their efforts to popularize sexual knowledge, sexologists allied themselves with women's groups, socialists, and other social reformers. Advocating sexual enlightenment and reform of the laws concerning pregnancy, birth, abortion, and contraception, they founded the Tokyo-based Japanese Birth Control Study Society in 1922 and the Osaka Birth Control Study Society in 1923. These two groups successfully sought allies among a wide range of social groups, including tenant and labor unions, several units of the health administration, and the police and the legislative body of the Japanese government. Throughout the 1920s, however, friction within the birth control movement prevented it from becoming an effective political force. When representatives from both groups eventually managed to write up petitions for the legalization of birth control in 1929 and 1932, the radical demands voiced during the early 1920s had long since been eliminated.

INVENTING "CHILD MURDER"

During the early Meiji era, a series of regulations that gradually criminalized abortion, infanticide, and eventually every other means of birth control marked an incremental break with policies and attitudes toward conception, pregnancy, and abortion in Tokugawa Japan when, according to sex researcher Tanaka Kōichi (1927), "nobody had thought of abortion as reprehensible." In premodern Japan, infanticide had been associated with the Buddhist doctrine of the transmigration of souls, according to which infants under the age of seven belonged to the gods. Infanticide therefore was not homicide but an act that returned the child to the other world. Moreover, because the first four months were not clearly included in the concept of pregnancy, abortions in the early months were not perceived of as such. Abortions were permitted in an advanced state of pregnancy as well, however, and abortion *(datai)* and infanticide *(mabiki)* were commonly thought of as one concept (Ochiai 1999a–b).

In 1868, the central government decreed the first nationwide Law Regulating the Sale of Drugs and the Practice of Abortion Techniques by Midwives (Sanba no baiyaku sewa oyobi dataitō no torishimari hō). In

1880, the "crime of abortion" *(datai no tsumi)* was established in the new criminal laws and was carried over unchanged as Articles 212 to 216 of the new Criminal Code, which was enacted in 1907. Several other regulations were later implemented, including the Ordinance Regulating Harmful Contraceptive Devices (Yūgai hininyō kigu torishimari kisoku) in 1930 and its amended version in 1936.

According to Article 212, a pregnant woman who had procured an abortion would be punished with imprisonment of up to one year. A person who was not a medical or health professional and who performed an abortion for a pregnant woman at her request was considered a co-offender and punished with penal servitude of up to two years. If the woman was killed or injured as a result of the abortion, imprisonment could be extended to five years (Article 213; see Sebald 1936:165–166; *Sei to Shakai* October 1925:25). Physicians, midwives, chemists, and druggists who performed an abortion with a pregnant woman's consent risked imprisonment of up to five years. If the woman was injured or killed, they awaited imprisonment of up to seven years (Article 214; see Sebald 1936:166–167).

With the implementation of the Midwife Regulations (Sanba kisoku) in 1899, midwives and doctors who had commonly performed abortions were replaced by a younger generation of doctors and midwives trained in Western medicine. The government began to strictly control the use of drugs and obstetric devices, organized rural midwives into associations, and subjected them to official supervision. Another powerful means of curbing abortion was the control of harmful drugs. Vaginal suppositories also became more difficult to obtain. Finally, it became the responsibility of midwives to notify the police of miscarriages or stillbirths that occurred after the third month of pregnancy. Within the new medical system that made the police not only the guardians of public order but also the supervisors of health and hygiene, pregnant women who were beyond their first trimester were subjected to police surveillance (Tama 1994:7; see also Steger 1994). A fisherwoman from Kyūshū recalled a related incident from her youth: "In my grandmother's days [toward the end of the nineteenth century] there were fewer children per family, on average, because the women practiced infanticide and carried out abortions on themselves. My mother heard of a woman who, after killing her baby, was immediately interrogated by the police. For this reason, my mother decided not to kill her last born, my little sister" (see Bernstein 1976:29–31).

Despite the harsh punishment for abortions and the increasing number of regulations controlling abortifacients and those in health professions, thousands of women put themselves at risk and somehow managed to have back-alley abortions. Fujikawa Yū noted that in 1919, for example, more than 600 women per year were subject to punishment for illegal abortions (Fujikawa Y. 1919c).[4]

The punishment for perpetrators of infanticide was potentially more severe. The cases of "child murderers" documented by the Ministry of Justice showed that they were usually first offenders between eighteen and twenty-five years of age. Annual crime rates showed a female perpetrator share of less than 10 percent in all categories of crime. The share of women in the "homicide" category, however, was significantly higher (17 percent of all homicides in 1925), and statistics were reversed in the "child homicide" category, with 90 percent of the recorded homicides committed by women (Nihon teikoku shihōshō 1925:362–387).[5] The two motives most commonly cited by female offenders were "specific events" and "poverty" (Nihon teikoku shihōshō 1925:362–387; Fuwa 1933:275). Considering that for other cases of homicide the Criminal Code foresaw the death penalty, a life sentence, or, at the very least, three to fifteen years' imprisonment, the prison sentences of one to two years for infanticide were relatively short and perhaps can be understood as an indication that despite the introduction of modern views on reproductive health, in legal practice more traditional views of human life persisted. However, both laws and legal practice came under fire when representatives of progressive currents demanded the liberation not only of the female sex but of sexual practice altogether.

RECLAIMING THE FETUS

The "woman problem" debate of 1910 brought forth divergent arguments about how women should respond to the "population problem," the role and ideology of motherhood, and women's social status vis-à-vis men. Feminists ranging from maternity ideologues Hiratsuka Raichō and Yamada Waka to socialist Yamakawa Kikue voiced their views about women's sexual desire and motherhood. In this debate, some feminists envisaged abortive and contraceptive means of birth control as tools for the liberation of women; others saw them as instruments of patriarchal oppression. Still others suggested women should utilize their uterus as a politically potent organ. The uterus and women's ability to conceive and bear children became a tool not only for taming and morally improving men but also—within the framework of imperialist pronatal body politics—the chief instrument for furthering the empire.

For lack of effective and affordable means of birth control, "the limitation of births" *(sanji seigen)* initially was debated primarily in terms of the right to terminate a pregnancy *(ninshin chūsetsu no jiyū)*, and only in a few instances in terms of contraception. In the June 1915 issue of the feminist periodical *Bluestocking (Seitō)*, Yasuda Satsuki claimed the right to abortion by maintaining that the fetus was part of the woman's body. Ignoring the limited availability of safe and legal abortions, Yasuda stated that it was purely a woman's own decision whether she chose to carry a fetus or to terminate the pregnancy. She told the readers of *Bluestocking* to follow their own dictates, even in violation of the law, and counseled women to have abortions if motherhood was going to be difficult (Yasuda S. 1915; see also Sievers 1983:183–184).

The "problem of birth control" *(sanji seigen no mondai)* came up frequently at the meetings of "new women" and began to preoccupy many of them, including Okada Sachiko, the poet Yosano Akiko, and Hiratsuka Raichō. Referring to Malthusian theories, Okada Sachiko argued that according to modern morals, to indulge in sexual intercourse and reproduce in an uncontrolled manner was one of the most serious crimes. Speaking of her own experience as a mother of ten, Yosano Akiko also felt that parents did no service to their children if they had too many and could not provide for their basic needs and proper education (see Hiratsuka 1983 [1916]:238).

Hiratsuka Raichō, a Japan Women's College graduate, prominent feminist, and cofounder of *Bluestocking,* propagated contraceptive methods and the legalization of abortion from the perspective of a "good wife and wise mother" *(ryōsai kenbo)*. In her view, unlimited reproduction out of "instinctual love" *(honnōteki ai)* was a crime against the responsibility of parents to provide for their offspring's livelihood and happiness and to secure the "future of the race" *(shuzoku no shōrai)*. In contrast to Western countries such as France, Sweden, Russia, Germany, the United States, and England, Hiratsuka pointed out, Japan's birth rate was not yet falling and the mortality rate among infants continued to remain high (Hiratsuka 1983 [1916]:242). Almost a year later, in another article on contraceptive methods, Hiratsuka further explicated her views on the population problem. She suggested diversifying the debate on contraception and declared it a public issue that needed to be tackled from the perspective of the "woman's problem," examined as an economic problem, and analyzed from the viewpoint of "improvement of the race" *(shuzoku kairyō).*

On the one hand, Hiratsuka opposed the view, held by more conservative public women, that contraception was "unnatural" and should thus remain branded as an intolerable practice. On the other hand, she remained unconvinced that women should—due to their individual professions and their public life as scholars, writers, novelists, or musicians—be able to avoid pregnancy, as suggested by Yosano Akiko. Inviting the state's interference in reproductive matters, Hiratsuka wrote that the "poor and ignorant lower classes" had no sense of responsibility and thus gave birth to countless children who would in turn also be poor and ignorant and, in the worst cases, spread "criminal seeds" *(zaiaku no shushi).* The Japanese state, as Hiratsuka saw it, had no working policy in place to prevent alcoholics, epileptics, victims of leprosy, syphilitics, and the insane from reproducing. Thus, for the sake of children, the maturing of the race, and the development of the state and society, she argued, children should be more highly cherished (Hiratsuka 1983 [1916]:337 and 1918).

Criticizing Hiratsuka's stance on birth control as bourgeois, socialist feminist Yamakawa Kikue pointed out the gap between rich and poor women. She held that birth control would be the individual woman's only solution to poverty until the bigger social problem, capitalism, was resolved. In contrast to Hiratsuka's appeal to simply value children more highly, Yamakawa encouraged working-class women to refrain from having children altogether until they actually could be worshipped—as Hiratsuka had demanded—and provided with the best of lives. Raving against the bourgeois concern of how birth control should best be administered were it to be made available to proletarian women at all, she pointed out that the struggle of proletarian women was to direct the wealth they produced back toward themselves. For them, birth control was one important means of reaching this goal. Yamakawa urged her female comrades at the forefront of the proletarian movement, just like activist proletarian women in the West, to remain single and childless (Yamakawa 1925:19–21).

Unimpressed by criticism, from Yamakawa and other socialists, of her class-biased position, Hiratsuka became the fiercest propagator of the advantages of bringing fewer children into the world and providing a better upbringing for them *(sukunaku umite ōku kyōiku seyo),* rather than accepting the current birth and infant mortality rates. She urged

her readers to be aware that giving birth to children who were unable to
live ordinary lives was a great crime against society and the Japanese
race, and she demanded that rather than increasing the number of children, more emphasis should be put on the quality of their lives (Hiratsuka 1983 [1916]:337). She too directed the attention of readers toward
birth control movements in "civilized countries" *(bunmeikoku)*, which
were informed by ideas of race improvement, eugenics, and other new
knowledge, and led by eugenicists, physicians, social reformers, and
other propagators of new morals. Enthused as she was about the potential of birth control for social reform and improvement, she nonetheless
remained concerned about the dissemination of methods and thoughts
on birth control in Japan. By no means, she insisted, should they serve
as devices to enable people to disregard their childbearing responsibilities and indulge in sex merely for their own pleasure. Instead, women
should strive to raise the "public value" *(kōteki na kachi)* of reproduction, contribute to the improvement of the social status of women as
mothers, and strengthen the voice of women in population policy (Hiratsuka 1983 [1916]:336–337).

Hiratsuka and many male and female contemporaries believed that a
"deep wish to have children" was at the root of women's sexual desire
(see also Sakai 1924a–b, 1925a–g, 1926a–g). Given this conviction, it
is not surprising that Hiratsuka found temporary abstinence and *coitus
interruptus*, which she saw as the "control and training of *men*'s sexual
desire" (emphasis added), as the only tolerable birth control methods.
In her view, women were meant to discipline themselves sexually as
"chaste wives" in order to differentiate themselves from mistresses and
prostitutes, at least in the eyes of men. By irresponsibly indulging in
purely physical sexual pleasures, Hiratsuka warned, women risked their
husbands' respect, and in turn husbands might consider them to be
merely one of the two vices most common to men and most disruptive
of an ideal society: alcohol and women *(sake to onna)* (Hiratsuka 1983
[1916]:339). Maintaining a belief in the capacity of human beings to
tame their desires, Hiratsuka encouraged women to "pull up their husbands to their own high level of love." If they did so, limiting the number of children would come about in a morally adequate and natural
manner. Hiratsuka was aware how difficult it would be for women
to achieve this goal alone. Hence in one of her *Bluestocking* essays she
again appealed to the Japanese government to implement a law that
would prohibit "certain types of individuals" from marrying and force
sterilization on them (Hiratsuka 1983 [1916]:340; see also Chūma

1921; *Josei Dōmei* 1921; Garon 1993a). I shall revisit this thread in chapter 5; here I wish to examine other feminists' attempts at politicizing the uterus.

Yamada Waka, another maternity ideologist, welcomed Hiratsuka's demands for government protection for mothers and children but vigorously disagreed with her on birth control matters. One of the most prominent maternity ideologues of the Taishō and early Shōwa eras, Yamada pointed out in her tirade against birth control that "nature" had always taken care of population problems, either by epidemic or by war (Yamada 1922:379).[6] In 1922, Yamada wrote at length about her position on birth control and contraception in *The Social Significance of the Family (Katei no shakaiteki igi).* Propaganda for birth control and contraception, she noted, hindered the "psychological growth" that enabled men and women to become responsible partners and parents. She maintained that birth control underlined and legitimated the animalistic side of humans and ignored the necessity of using the mind to control sexual desire (Yamada 1922:373). Like Hiratsuka, Yamada was concerned that the legalization of birth control and contraception would make the free and uncontrolled satisfaction of (male) sexual desire seem acceptable and would undermine the importance of "psychological love" *(seishinteki ai),* which she and most of her contemporaries typically associated with women's emotional apparatus. As men lacked a sense of responsibility, in her opinion, the legalization of birth control and contraception would enable them to indulge in their sexual desire at the cost of women's psychological love (Yamada 1922:374).

That this psychological love that Yamada exclusively attributed to women could be enhanced by sexual pleasure was unimaginable for Yamada. For her, birth control could not possibly entail the liberation of women from the burdens of bearing one child after another, as Yamakawa insisted, but would turn them into victims trapped by uncontrolled male desire once sexual intercourse lost the inevitable outcome of pregnancy. Here, Yamada reiterated the convictions of Meiji health administrators, according to whom men were essentially driven by their desires. To wives, she ascribed the noble role of taming their husbands with love and persistence. Taking one's fate into one's own hands was not on Yamada's agenda, and she doubted that other women felt like doing that either.

Yamada acknowledged that there were unhappy women who suffered from lack of love in their relationships. She also admitted that there might be plenty of women who would rather not have children but had no choice. In her view, however, the legalization of birth control would lead to a four-, five-, or even tenfold increase in the number of these women. Moreover, she insisted that the number of women in Japan striving for equality with men was by no means the majority. Yamada opposed the birth control activists' dictum that it was better for the woman in question, her family, and the state to have fewer and healthier children than to have many weak ones who would die early. Even Hiratsuka's preoccupation with the quality of the race could not win Yamada's agreement. The main problem of the day, she wrote, was not the quality of children but the quality of parents. Oblivious to the economic hardships of the underprivileged classes, Yamada insisted that parents who were able to raise two or three children properly would be able to raise seven or eight. If the parents were not good parents, however, it did not matter how many children they had (Yamada 1922:375; see also Yamada 1915, 1919a–c). In 1922, when activists for birth control and contraception first began to organize, Yamada declared that birth control propaganda must be suppressed because it was an instrument that undermined humanity and a tool of "racial suicide" (*jinshu-teki jissatsu*) (Yamada 1922:381).

Despite Yamada's knowledge of the heartbreaking situations in which women frequently found themselves, she remained adamant in her position when she began to serve as a counselor for a woman's column in the *Tōkyō Asahi Shinbun* roughly ten years later. On 31 March 1932, Yamada appealed to a woman who had become pregnant as a consequence of rape that she must by all means bear the child because women were "the pillars for the continuation of the race" (see Ishizaki 1992: 102–103). Published in the newspaper, her advice set off a storm of indignation among her contemporaries. Prominent liberal democrat Yoshino Sakuzō used the opportunity to question the abortion law. "Laws that do not make people happy," he suggested, "lack authority. It is necessary to abandon laws that punish people and instead create laws that make them happy" (quoted in Ishizaki 1992:103). The medical doctor Kawasaki Natsu was similarly appalled by Yamada's position: "This young woman must by all means have an abortion. Regardless of her condition, considering today's unemployment, an abortion is safer and better for a woman than the hardship of an unwanted pregnancy carried to term because of this law. . . . The legislation of abortion must be reconsidered" (quoted in Ishizaki 1992:103).[7]

When Yamada's letter appeared in the column, propagators of the legalization of birth control were about to lose their fight, and the inva-

sion of Manchuria had proved their worst fears to be accurate—that
"overpopulation" and the criminalized status of abortion and contraceptives would bring about war.

PREVIEWING WAR

Most birth control advocates in Japan, who were commonly associated
with various farm and labor unions, agreed that the country's rapid
population growth harbored many dangers for social and international
peace (Abe 1927a; Oguri 1926). In 1925, Kagawa Toyohiko, founder of
the Salvation Army and cofounder of the Japanese Farmers' Union,
which aimed at the coordination of tenant protests and the improvement
of the welfare and status of farmers, suggested that "scientific birth control" *(kagakuteki sanji chōsetsu)* was the only means of preventing war.
He maintained that wars often had been caused by economic circumstances, which in turn had been brought about by a "population problem." A common solution advocated by the Japanese state was the
search for new territories that could be exploited and for markets
opened by emigrating populations. These activities, he warned, would
inevitably provoke a war (Kagawa 1925:34).

   It was perhaps this scenario more than any other that made some sexologists put their attempts at establishing sexology as a field of research
and teaching on the back burner and join forces with socialists, pacifists,
and feminists—among whom were midwives, doctors, pharmacists,
university professors, teachers, farmers, workers, and bureaucrats. They
brought forth various arguments for the legalization of birth control and
abortion whose political implications ranged from the pacifist utilization of birth control means to curb the population problem to eugenic
motives for improving the quality of the imperial body. In this way, both
pronatalists and birth control activists linked the individual female
body—and more precisely, the functionality of the uterus—to the empire. Some activists set their claims for sexual enlightenment and liberation in opposition to Japan's increasing militarism and imperialism.
Most radically, they promoted a liberation of sex from its ties to reproduction, of the working class from poverty, and of women from their
roles as childbearing machines and from the pronatalism that deprived
them and their families of all means of controlling family size. These
new configurations of birth control advocates also revisited the arguments that had been brought forward by the participants in the "woman's problem" debate. They hoped that birth control would serve as

a pretext for the protection of maternal health and the improvement of women's status as mothers, eliminate (the necessity of) abortions, and provide the true foundation for the improvement of the race. Thus, debates about birth control were situated at an imaginary intersection of ideas about the liberation of sexual desire, individual and women's rights, childbearing as individual choice or social duty, and the meanings and significance of maternity, race improvement, and empire building.

In his article entitled "The Population Problem in the Peasantry," Inamura Ryūichi described the sight of hardworking women farmers, torn between the demanding farm work and the burden of bearing and raising several children. Society, he lamented, expected these women to bear numerous children despite their inability to care for them sufficiently. Farmers' children remained uneducated and yet women farmers believed it a crime not to have many children. The ideologues of "conservative thought" *(hoshu shisō)* and imperialism *(teikokushugi),* Inamura pointed out, wanted to expand the race outside of Japan's borders. Railing against these ideologues, Inamura demanded that the farmers' unions protest the employment of farmers for militarist ends and as instruments of invasion (Inamura 1925:24; see also *Sei to Shakai* 1926b:43). Attacking the government's encouragement of the emigration of workers, Inamura stated that there was no gain in working in Japan's colonies, as pay was low and opportunities for advancement were scarce. Not emigration, he suggested, but birth control would solve the population problem (Inamura 1925:26; see also Katsura 1926).

Economics professor Abe Isoo also was convinced that Japan's colonial policy was disastrous. Emphasizing that migrant workers did not leave Japan out of a lack of patriotism but because they could not earn a living, he pointed out that Japanese workers could not compete with cheaper indigenous laborers in Taiwan, Manshū, or Korea. Rather than oppose Japan's imperialist activities, however, he insisted that the flow of migrant workers from Korea to Japan *(waga naichi,* or "our homeland")* had to be stopped in order to avoid food shortages. Food shortages inevitably would increase the number of abortions and infanticides. To deter this, industrial reform should be accompanied by birth control measures (Abe 1926b).

Abe only indirectly criticized the government's expansionist policies, ridiculing the dominant ideology that aimed at increasing Japan's potency to successfully fight future wars through a "multiplication of the heads." He spoke contemptuously of the many people who still believed, "as in the era of Oda [and] Toyotomi," that the strength of a nation lay in the size of its population (Abe 1926b).[8] The only true policies for increasing wealth and military prowess, he argued, would not be realized by multiplying the sheer numbers of people, but by improving the physical and mental capabilities of these people.

ORGANIZING FAMILY LIMITATION

It was not until Margaret Sanger's first visit to Japan that these diverse groups of social reformers organized what became a birth control movement. In July 1922, Ishimoto Shizue (1897–2002) founded the Japanese Birth Control Study Society (Nihon Sanji Chōsetsu Kenkyūkai) in Tokyo. It was headed by Abe Isoo, and soon to join were the labor leader Suzuki Bunji, the well-known medical doctor Kaji Tokijirō and the socialist feminist Yamakawa Kikue (*Yomiuri Shinbun* 1922c). In 1923, Yamamoto followed suit with the Osaka Birth Control Study Society (Ōsaka Sanji Seigen Kenkyūkai).[9]

While Ishimoto oversaw the tedious work of translating Sanger's unofficial lectures in Tokyo, Yamamoto served as translator at several of Sanger's unofficial lectures in the Kansai region, and in May of 1922 translated her text *Family Limitation* into Japanese as *Critique of Sanger's Family Limitation Methods (Sangā joshi kazoku seigenhō hihan)* (Yamamoto Senji 1922c; Ishimoto 1935:227–232). The explanations of several methods of contraception, ranging from rinsing lotions for cleansing the vagina after intercourse to the condom, pessary, and sponge, were illustrated and the means of birth control discussed (Yamamoto Senji 1922c). The word "critique" in the Japanese title must be interpreted not only in the literal sense but also as one of several strategies to circumvent censorship. Two warnings leaped to the eye of anyone who picked up the booklet. "This small booklet on scientific research and critique is not to be distributed to people other than medical and pharmaceutical specialists" and "Reproduction without permission is prohibited" were printed on one cover, "Confidential" on the other. These signaled to the authorities that the booklet was not produced to disseminate knowledge on birth control to the masses (Yamamoto Senji 1922c: covers).

As opposed to Ishimoto, who raved about "the invasion of 'Sangerism'" (Ishimoto 1935:220), Yamamoto was warier of Sanger's promotion of birth control. In the introduction to his translation *Critique of Sanger's Family Limitation Methods,* Yamamoto noted that the book was useful for lectures and for those who were knowledgeable in medical and pharmaceutical matters, but it was not always correct "from a biologist's perspective" (Yamamoto Senji 1922c:6). Throughout the text, he added warnings to Sanger's claims that certain methods were safe. Moreover, the main part of the Japanese booklet consisted of a general critique of Sanger's text, peppered with references to publications of German sexologists with whom, he implied, Sanger was unfamiliar. Yamamoto also discussed the obstacles that contraceptive methods faced in Japan: reliable contraceptive methods were unavailable; the dissemination of knowledge about contraceptive methods was illegal; and the general public's demands for knowledge about contraceptive methods were thoroughly suppressed (Yamamoto Senji 1922c:81).

When Margaret Sanger visited Japan in March 1922, her ambiguous reputation traveled with her. Reminiscing about the "black ship" of Commodore Perry in 1852, the press referred to the steamer on which she arrived as the "black ship of Taishō" (see Yamamoto Senji 1922c:4). Sanger's visit to Japan was given widespread attention, as evidenced by several hundred newspaper articles and interviews (Watanabe Katsumasa 1978; Johnson 1987:68–70). As early as January 1922, newspapers reported on the attempt of the Japanese authorities to hinder Sanger's entry into the country. In February, the *Tōkyō Asahi Shinbun* was outraged at the Japanese government's refusal to provide Sanger with a visa (*Tōkyō Asahi Shinbun* 1922a). The *Tōkyō Asahi Shinbun* also explained the most important reason for birth control outlined in Sanger's brochure *Family Limitation*. The bottom line of Sanger's message, the *Tōkyō Asahi Shinbun* wrote, was to bear and raise fewer healthy children instead of many who suffered (*Tōkyō Asahi Shinbun* 1922b). Three weeks later, the same newspaper reported on the restrictions on Sanger's activities that were to prevent her from giving public lectures (*Tōkyō Asahi Shinbun* 1922b).

Worried about the impact of birth control as a force disruptive to the social and political order, the authorities suggested that the willingness of the educated middle and upper classes to reproduce would be put at risk. As they were considered morally and intellectually superior, their reproduction seemed especially desirable.[10] Moreover, the dissemination of the means of and knowledge about birth control among members of the working class was perceived as a threat to the social order because proponents of birth control promised no less than the liberation of women if they were only given correct knowledge and means of birth control. Sanger wrote, again and again, that once empowered with "scientific birth control methods, the mother no longer considers herself a slave. She is glad to be standing on her own two feet. She feels herself mistress of her own life, and no longer the inert, helpless, hopeless victim of circumstances" (Sanger 1929:527). Sanger told her audience in Japan that the difference between a "sexually ignorant woman" and a woman who is able to practice birth control was as striking as the difference between a free man and a slave. Mothers who were liberated from "the relentless pressure of involuntary motherhood" through the exercise of their own intelligence and foresight almost automatically became more interested in life, the future, raising their children, and the affairs of the community at large (Sanger 1929:527). One of the crucial ways to reach this fortunate state was through "true education" about the methods of birth control, which would only be successful if "men, women and children had the possibility to recognize the consequences of their behavior" (Sanger 1929:526–529).

Before her journey to Japan, Margaret Sanger had visited Europe to learn about birth control there. Upon her return to the United States in 1916, she set up the first birth control clinic in Brooklyn, New York. Officials immediately closed the clinic and imprisoned Sanger for thirty days for her efforts to familiarize women with contraceptive methods. Her magazine *The Woman Rebel* was banned after the seventh issue. Sanger fled to England before she could be convicted for the dissemination of information about contraceptive methods. Sanger's family and friends had distributed her booklet *Family Limitation,* and subsequently Sanger's husband was imprisoned for a month because he refused to reveal her whereabouts.[11] Upon her return to New York in 1920, Sanger met with Ishimoto Shizue. Eventually Ishimoto arranged for an invitation from the magazine *Kaizō,* one of the progressive magazines of the time, for Sanger, then president of the American Birth Control League, to visit Japan (see Johnson 1987:20, 182).

After lengthy negotiations, Sanger was allowed to step onto Japanese soil but was instructed to restrict her lectures to professional circles. Upon arrival, she was received by hundreds of people. The police immediately confiscated her brochure *Family Limitation.* As Sanger was prohibited from making public appearances, Ishimoto offered her house for discussions with other women. Sanger also lectured for the Kyoto Medical Association and other physicians' and pharmacists' organizations (*Tōkyō Asahi Shinbun* 1922c–d; *Ōsaka Asahi Shinbun* 1922; see also M. Beard 1953:173). The government had announced that it would not tolerate gatherings where "the limitation of births in the Japanese empire is propagated" (see Sasaki 1979:689), but apparently the attempts to repress Sanger's activities backfired. Ishimoto noted in her memoir that Sanger was "a stronger magnet than she ever could have been if allowed to go about undisturbed making speeches on birth control." Far more had been accomplished, she maintained, by the agitation growing out of the police prohibition than ever could have come through simple lectures on the subject (Ishimoto 1935:226–227).

Sanger spoke about the means and methods of birth control on more than a dozen occasions. While she respected the condition laid down for her entry in her address at the public meeting called by the magazine *Kaizō,* she had plenty of opportunities to express her views on birth control at private meetings with Ishimoto and other women who became important proponents of birth control in Tokyo, with sex researcher and educator Yamamoto Senji and his circle in Osaka, and with bacteriologist Kitazato Shibasaburō and other prominent figures in science and politics (M. Beard 1953:170; Sasaki 1979:689). A few years later, Abe Isoo was convinced that Margaret Sanger was more famous than any other American or British citizen in Japan, and Ishimoto wrote in her memoir that "no woman, foreign or native, had ever been so well received by Japanese men as was Mrs. Sanger" (Ishimoto 1935:228; Johnson 1987:74).

Shortly after Sanger's departure and despite the declaration of controlled dissemination on the cover of the booklet *Critique of Sanger's Family Limitation Methods,* Yamamoto had 2,000 copies of his translation printed and distributed to university professors and physicians (see Sasaki 1979:691–692). Subsequently, the booklet did not remain in the hands of "specialists." Several left-wing members of the Osaka unions, including Noda Ritsuta, Noda Kimiko (Noda's wife), Mitamura Shirō, and Kutsumi Fusako (Mitamura's wife) heard about it and obtained permission from Yamamoto to print another 2,000 copies, which they distributed among the members of the labor movement (Sasaki 1979: 691–692). In September 1922, the newspaper *Japan and the Japanese (Nihon oyobi Nihonjin)* printed an article entitled "One Example of the Harm Caused by the Secretive Way in Which We Deal with Sexuality," based on Yamamoto's translation of Sanger's booklet (Yamamoto Senji 1922d). In the autumn of 1922, labor union members Noda Ritsuta, Noda Kimiko, Mitamura Shirō, and Kutsumi Fusako visited Yamamoto in Kyoto and talked about the future direction of the propagation of birth control in Japan. In turn, they invited Yamamoto to Osaka to lecture at the Sōdōmei Labor School, which they had founded. In January

1923 they met again in Osaka to create the Osaka Birth Control Study
Society (Ōsaka Sanji Seigen Kenkyūkai). Since unions were not recognized at the time, employees were fired for being union members, and
since it also was illegal even to discuss birth control, Kutsumi and Mitamura went undercover and used Noda Ritsuta's house as the society's
office.[12] Noda Kimiko served as the president and Abe Isoo and medical
doctor Majima Yutaka joined the group (Kutsumi in Hane 1988:152;
Sanji Chōsetsu Hyōron April 1925: advertisement section).

Representing the left wing of the birth control movement vis-à-vis the
bourgeois wing in Tokyo, differences surfaced quickly along the lines of
political convictions, class alignment, and gender. Ishimoto Shizue, Kaji
Tokijirō, Hiratsuka Raichō and others shared a position with strong
eugenic leanings that foreshadowed the eugenic policies of the late 1930s
and early 1940s, which I shall discuss in chapter 5. The study prospectus of the Tokyo-based Japanese Birth Control Study Society, drafted
in July 1922, emphasized the necessity of eugenic regulations for birth
control, explained social problems by addressing the "biological" or
"genetic" predisposition of the people concerned, and approved qualitative and negative birth control based on "social hygiene" (shakai eisei). With respect to the rapid rate of population growth, the Japanese
Birth Control Study Society acknowledged that "the noble spirit of humanism" had served to avoid "wasteful conflict between the nations,"
and the progress of science had decreased the ravages of diseases by revealing their causes.

The text also warned that "in time there would be appalling shortages of the necessary materials for human existence" if the birth rate
continued to rise, even if advanced scientific knowledge promoted public welfare. This development, the paper proposed, not only would cause
severe competition inside the nation, but also would become the "source
of international entanglement." Its most distressing aspect, the authors
of the prospectus noted, was apparent in individual lives. "Uncontrolled
pregnancies" robbed mothers of health and raised infant mortality
rates, overburdened the family economy, and prevented a decent education of children. Late marriage, an increase in the number of illegitimate
children, infanticide, abortion, and other "social immoralities and tragedies" were identified as additional consequences of "uncontrolled pregnancies." Finally, the society declared it "absolutely necessary to avoid
any pregnancy when either parent has a disease that should not be transmitted to the offspring." Moreover, it claimed, the correct practice of
birth control principles should cease to be considered an act of immor-

ality and instead should be reevaluated as an act in harmony with social morality (Ishimoto 1935:230).

In contrast, Yamamoto Senji, Kutsumi Fusako, Tsuchida Kyōson, Mitamura Shirō, Yamakawa Kikue, and a few others at the left end of the spectrum of birth control advocacy insisted that poverty could be eliminated only through reform of the economic system. They attacked the moderates for promoting the all-too-simple neo-Malthusian equation that if more people were able to practice birth control, fewer would suffer from poverty. They also spoke out against state interference in birth control matters and insisted that decisions about the uses of birth control methods should remain with women, uninfluenced by governmental regulations. Through birth control methods, women would and should be enabled to decide independently against another pregnancy and the birth of another child (Kutsumi 1925; Tsuchida 1925; Unnō 1925a–b; see also Fujime 1986:87).

Relations between the Tokyo group's initiator Ishimoto and the Osaka group's leader Yamamoto remained rather distanced throughout the 1920s. Ishimoto mentioned Yamamoto only once in her memoirs, stating that his understanding of birth control principles was not entirely the same as Sanger's. As a Marxist, she wrote, he "frankly opposed the neo-Malthusian doctrine, and his attitude carried weight in New Japan at that time, since Marx was a great master there." She felt, however, that Yamamoto never fully explained the inconsistency between Malthusianism and Marxism (Ishimoto 1935:231–232). Identifying herself as a feminist, Ishimoto had been drawn to the birth control movement by her sympathy for the plight of poor families and her desire to elevate the status of women. Ishimoto was aware that she and her aristocratic friends were viewed as "ladies of leisure toying with plants in a hothouse," and pointed out that in reality they were "really serious and eager to comprehend the problems of the day no less than to heighten our cultural charm" (Ishimoto 1935:232). Like Hiratsuka and other middle- and upper-class women more than ten years earlier, she hoped that birth control would eventually strengthen motherhood and the family (Tipton 1997:351).

Yamamoto in turn hardly ever commented on Ishimoto's role in the movement and sometimes mentioned only her husband's name, even though Ishimoto Shizue was far more engaged in the Tokyo group. He associated her with those members of the aristocracy who turned to social reform out of pity for the poor rather than out of a desire to empower them and change power relations substantially. Even to his death,

Yamamoto rejected what he considered Ishimoto's bourgeois stance on birth control. Yamamoto also remained reserved with respect to Ishimoto's activities, as he felt that Ishimoto's Christian humanism appealed mainly to the bourgeoisie and the aristocracy. It should be forbidden, he demanded, for the bourgeois classes to propagate birth control in order to "improve the quality of the genes" and to declare it the "people's duty" (Yamamoto Senji 1922c:88). Ishimoto was certainly not a socialist or a revolutionary, even though she was accused of just that by the authorities because of her engagement in the struggle for birth control, but she was one of the few upper-class women who continued—or rather renewed—her birth control activities in the postwar era. I shall describe her stance on birth control and eugenics after World War II in the next chapter; here it should suffice to mention that today it is Ishimoto, rather than the politically more radical Yamamoto, who is celebrated as the primary pioneer of birth control in Japan. Although he was not against eugenic reasoning per se, Yamamoto dedicated himself primarily to the empowerment of uneducated laborers through knowledge, and in his opinion they needed to "know about a woman's cycle in order to protect themselves properly" (Yamamoto Senji 1927a).

Perhaps due to its engagement on behalf of and entanglement with labor unions, the Osaka group was far more successful in recruiting members. While the society in Tokyo published only one issue of its journal, *Small Family (Shokazoku)*, and other activities remained highly individualized, by the spring of 1923, more than a thousand people had joined the society in Osaka. Officially, only people who had at least five children at the time of the application could obtain membership (Kutsumi in Hane 1988:152; Ōta T. 1976:146–147; Sasaki 1979:693–694). Nonetheless, the society attempted to interest a great number and variety of people in the organization. The society invited "childless couples"—so read the recruitment material—because birth control should be practiced both by childless couples who did not want children and by couples who were blessed with children. "Couples with too many children" were especially welcome because birth control was useful for women who were weakened by giving birth too often. The society also targeted "single men and women," reasoning that many single men postponed marriage only for economic reasons.

Very few ever challenged the gendered order of Japanese society, according to which all women were "equipped with maternal instincts" *(honnōteki ni bosei o sonaete iru)*. Following this reasoning, women were predestined to make society a safer place for children. Addressing "male and female taxpayers," appeals to join the society pointed out that a "large portion of taxes was spent on the care of the physically weak and the disabled," and the society promised help in preventing the birth of mentally handicapped children and criminals. The society also hoped that "idealists" who agreed that motherhood had been turned into something all too sacrosanct would be interested in a membership. "Politicians" were urged to become members because the population had a vital interest in birth control matters, and "statesmen" were addressed because birth control was crucial to preventing war. And finally, "everybody" was declared eligible to join because the birth of children was everybody's responsibility and birth control was necessary to appropriately respond to this responsibility (*Sanji Chōsetsu Hyōron* 1925b:6 and 10).

In the course of its fourteen-year existence, more than 6,000 members from Japan proper, Taiwan, Manshū, Karafuto, and the South Seas joined the society in Osaka. It was clear from the membership application forms that many applicants were residents of back-street tenements and other poor people (Kutsumi in Hane 1988:152).[13] The Birth Control Study Society failed to document their cases systematically, but it did register the number of requests for information and help and recorded the applicants' age, sex, and place of residence (Katsura 1926). According to these notes, the vast majority of inquiries came from men (more than 5,000), while women sent about 1,300 inquiries (*Sanji Chōsetsu Hyōron* 1925e:41).

In numerous outreach efforts, tens of thousands of copies of Yamamoto's *Critique of Sanger's Family Limitation Methods* were printed and distributed among the audience at activists' lectures on sex education and birth control. Society members held numerous educational lectures within the organizational framework of the labor movement and offered personal counseling to workers (Okuda 1925; *Sanji Chōsetsu Hyōron* 1925e; Ishimoto 1935:234). In order to facilitate access to birth control information, the Birth Control Study Society founded branch offices in Kyoto, Kōbe, Nagoya, Okayama, Hiroshima, and Sakai, all of which also served as birth control consultation offices. Counselors were available at all of the branches (*Sanji Chōsetsu Hyōron* 1925e:41), and posters and pamphlets addressed potential members in the following manner: "For poor people who do not have children! For people whose health has been weakened or who are ill! Do not hesitate to come in. We will advise you in a friendly manner. . . . If you are from the countryside, please send us a letter and enclose an envelope and a 3-sen stamp for our

reply. This counseling office is not a private business. It is a public counseling office where well-known people will advise you" *(Sei to Shakai*
February 1926c:52).

The Heimin Hospital in Tokyo housed the Central Counseling Office
for Birth Control (Chūō Sanji Chōsetsu Sōdanjo), which welcomed
people who were in need of advice on birth control. Its representatives
and counselors were Abe Isoo, Kaji Tokijirō, Yamamoto Senji, Suzuki
Bunji, Shimanaka Yūzō, and Tsuchida Kyōson *(Sei to Shakai* February 1926:52). Various other organizations also set up counseling centers for birth control, and their number rapidly increased during the latter half of the 1920s and the early 1930s *(Sei no Kenkyū* 1919c). *Popular
Medicine,* for example, printed an advertisement for the counseling center in Osaka, announcing that people who were in dire straits because
they had too many children and those who should not have any children
because of their physical condition could order informational material
about "true, serious birth control" for 2 sen *(Tsūzoku Igaku* March
1927:96).

The Federation of Kansai Women (Kansai Fujin Rengōkai) in Osaka
founded the Japanese Union for Birth Control (Nihon Sanji Seigen Kyōkai) and set up a eugenic counseling center *(yūseiji sōdansho)*. There,
Ōku Mumeo, a companion of Hiratsuka Raichō and one of the first female Diet members after World War II, opened the office with the slogan "To bear or not to bear is a woman's liberty" *(umu mo umanai mo
onna no jiyū)*. In 1934, Ishimoto Shizue founded yet another counseling
center for birth control on a "purely scientific and non-commercial
basis" modeled on that of Margaret Sanger's clinic in New York. The
main service consisted of biweekly consultations with a doctor she was
friendly with. In addition to numerous visits by women who had traveled from afar, more than 700 written requests reached the clinic in its
first two months. Fifty patients were advised personally and Ishimoto
began to document cases (see Johnson 1987:92).

According to Ishimoto's notes, the main motive of women who
sought advice about birth control was the inability to offer their children
a good upbringing. Counseling centers were used mainly by married
women, workers from disadvantaged classes, and mothers who already
had two or three children and who saw a further child as an economic
burden that would threaten their very existence (Ishimoto 1935:372–
373). Yamamoto also noted that the number of women in the counseling
centers was particularly high toward the end of the year, when money
was tight, and continually emphasized the lack of knowledge and the

desperate situation of poor couples with many children. Yamamoto and other birth control activists described case after case in their publications (Koiwa 1925). One exemplary story of a couple desperate for advice on birth control was printed at the outset of a debate among three activists in the *Taiwan Nichinichi Shinbun* from 31 July 1925: "There are nine people in our household. We have eaten almost all of this year's food. We are still young, have four children and will probably have two or three more unless you instruct us about contraception methods" (quoted in Yamamoto, Yasuda, and Katsura 1925).

Poverty was most often cited as the core problem in the plight of proletarian women who contacted the birth control offices by mail. Their lack of health care and proper nutrition was rooted in their poverty as well as in the hard work they did for their families and in the factories. Frequent births only added to an already disadvantaged existence. Arguing that birth control was more necessary for proletarian women than for anybody else, the politically more radical activists emphasized that liberation from their plight could come about only through class conflict (Kanda 1925:46–48). The reports of the birth control branch offices typically described the economic situation of workers who sought advice on contraception as harsh and almost unbearable. One letter explained, "I earn 50 yen and my wife earns 10 yen. That makes for a hard life in a three-person household. Thus, birth control is of vital importance to us" (Okuda 1925:26). Another letter read, "We have four children and my husband makes about 62 yen a month. Our environment is rather unhygienic and the care for my children is insufficient. I cannot understand the bourgeois position that birth control is morally objectionable. Please advise me" (Okuda 1925:26). Defending contraception against the moral reservations of the "petty bourgeoisie," activists maintained that birth control was "the last resort of the poor and weak." To counter opposition to the legalization of birth control methods, they maintained that it was "entirely unrelated to the aristocracy and the wealthy" and should not remain prohibited just because "a few aristocrats took advantage of it" (Koike Shirō 1925).

However, middle-class women and men were also among those seeking counseling. A significant number of middle-class women reported that they took up work because they had run away from their husbands or their husbands had abandoned them and they saw themselves incapable of raising another child. Men who were looking for a spouse and hoped for appropriate advice on how to find one also came to these counseling centers. It is unclear to what extent they succeeded as, according to Yamamoto's recollections, few women who were in financial difficulty due to a divorce took up the advice to remarry. After the disappointment with one man, most preferred to raise their children alone (Yamamoto Senji 1926a).

When Yamamoto, together with some of the other founding members of the birth control movement, began to publish the journal *Birth Control Review (Sanji Chōsetsu Hyōron)* in February 1925, he had long since redeemed the promise he and Yasuda Tokutarō had given to Margaret Sanger upon her departure. She had urged them to fight with her "for the sake of the world's working class and world peace" (Sasaki 1979:689). The board of *Birth Control Review* included some of the most outspoken activists in the movement and reflected the increasing cooperation between the two groups in Tokyo and Osaka. In addition to Yamamoto Senji, Yasuda Tokutarō and Abe Isoo were on the board. Other members included medical doctors: Kinoshita Tōsaku as well as Kaji Tokijirō and Katō Tokiya, who were hospital directors of the Tokyo People's Hospital (Tōkyō Heimin Byōin) and the Osaka People's Hospital (Ōsaka Heimin Byōin), respectively. Majima Yutaka served as a head physician in the Social Affairs Office (Shakai-kyoku) of the Tokyo city government. Suzuki Bunji provided an important link to the labor union. Fujizawa Atsushi was the Osaka branch leader of the Harmonization Society (Kyōchōkai), and Unno Kōtoku was a professor at Ryūtani University (*Sanji Chōsetsu Hyōron* May 1925:60).[14]

The Osaka-based Birth Control Study Society aimed at "constructive birth control" *(kensetsuteki sanji chōsetsu)* and "race improvement" *(jinshū kōjō)* and published a seven-point agenda. Its first point was that children swayed the health and happiness of families and society. The responsibility and duty of parents was "to cooperate and guide these children with sufficient knowledge and farsightedness through matters of strength and weakness, wisdom and folly, ups and downs." Evoking "life in an era of science," the manifesto urged readers that "knowledge of various sciences, namely biology and the rapidly advancing sciences of genetics, eugenics, and sexology," had to be made fruitful for humankind in order to liberate the populace from "useless menaces and mistaken superstitions." According to the society, individual life was not to "run counter to the great principles of society, and knowledge about birth control must not be lacking in our families' everyday lives" (Yamamoto Senji 1925a). On the Birth Control Study Society's agenda, "knowledge of birth control" was defined in a twofold manner. It meant "giving the desired child to the lonely, childless wife" and also "giving the mother who is exhausted from continuous pregnancies a rest." Indeed, the physical burden of frequent pregnancies was not a trivial matter. As Mitamura Shirō reported, even "physically strong and healthy women" eventually suffered from giving birth too frequently and were often additionally burdened by their children's early death. He recalled a "physically strong couple" who had come to see him for advice on contraception. They had wed in 1920 and had had a new baby almost every year thereafter. Their first boy had been a miscarriage but in 1922 the woman gave birth to a girl who was then (in 1925) four years old. Another boy, born in 1924, died in infancy. A second girl died in 1925, shortly after her birth. How could he, Mitamura (1925) seemed to plead, not help this woman?

For many left-leaning advocates of birth control, their engagement remained tightly intertwined with what they called the "liberation of sex." Unnō Kōtoku (1925a), for example, wholeheartedly agreed with Yamamoto (1925c) about the "liberation of sex" when he wrote that the happiness of the individual (and of the populace) was of primary importance. He also expressed his hope that pronatalist ideology *(umeyo, fuyaseyo)* and "other superstitious beliefs" would soon disappear (Unnō 1925a). Ignoring that Malthus had first formulated his "Essay on the Principle of Population" (1798) as a polemic against the socialists in England who believed that the transformation of ownership would lead to social harmony, Unnō pointed out to the readers of *Sex and Society* that modern life was more complex than it had been during Malthus' time (1766–1834). In contrast to Malthus' Law of Nature, which according to Malthus' suggestions could be overcome only by abstinence, Unnō advised his audience to acknowledge that sexual desire had an impact on marriage, the happiness, health, and beauty of a couple, their children's occupations, and in fact all of cultural life. The use of contraceptive devices (which Malthus had opposed) would enable individual women and families to take control of all of these factors (Unnō 1925a).

If the "liberation of sex" for Unnō meant the empowerment of individuals to make decisions on family size, other advocates of birth control embraced the new possibilities of engaging in the pleasures of sex without worrying about conception at all. Quite radically for the mid-1920s, Tsuchida Kyōson proposed understanding sexual intercourse and the production of children as two separate matters. Just as his sexologist comrades did, he attributed an overwhelming importance for human life to the overall "sexual reality," rather than only to certain sexual problems. He insisted that sex was important not simply because it caused problems but because it had a powerful impact on a human being's entire life. "We have all kinds of desires," he assured his audience, "but none are as strong as our sexual desires and fantasies" (Tsuchida 1926:7). He also wrote that children were one goal of love but not the only one. Equating sexual intercourse with producing children, he proposed, would mean perceiving the two people involved as mere machines. Hence, birth control methods had to be employed correctly to ensure the parents' happiness and the child's health. Tsuchida proclaimed the slogan "multiply and procreate" as a plea for quality— quality of life for parents as well as children—which was of course detrimental to how pronatalist ideology was understood and promoted by the state (Tsuchida 1925:4–5).

Another core item on the Osaka group's agenda concerned desirable techniques of birth control. The birth control they fought for was defined by the manifesto as "hindering the unification of egg and sperm." Hence, birth control was considered a "tool based on life and biology in order to escape mere chance." The seventh and last regulation explicitly rejected the various family limitation measures taken after conception, such as infanticide and abortion, as "cruel and inhumane." In order to avoid these "criminal practices," the Osaka group's agenda emphasized that it was "necessary to instruct male and female youth in correct sex education" (*Sanji Chōsetsu Hyōron* 1925a). In their writings, the members of the Birth Control Study Society and the authors of *Birth Control Review* agreed that contraception was the only way to abolish back-alley abortions. Contraception would put a stop to doctors who "misused their art." It would not only impoverish physicians willing to perform abortions but it also would make abortions themselves unnecessary (Yamamoto Senji 1926a). In their roles as writers and public lecturers, most crusaders for birth control drew a clear line between the practices of infanticide and abortion and contraception. In their role as practitioners, however, they did not.

Rather than questioning the "immorality of the techniques that terminate life," as had Yasuda Satsuki roughly ten years prior to the foundation of the society, most of them restricted themselves to promoting contraception as a means of preventing rather than terminating pregnancy (Abe 1925:1). In numerous essays on the necessity of birth control, Yamamoto thundered against abortions, which, according to newspaper reports, increased during the latter half of the 1920s, a period fraught with economic difficulty at the onset of the worldwide depression. Yamamoto remembered one of these reports as follows:

On 19 May 1926, the police discovered that the military physician Kimura Yasuo had performed abortions in his clinic Kunai in Osaka for several dozen women from prefectures all over Japan—Fukuoka, Okayama, and Fukui. There may have been more women involved whose place of residence remained unknown. The abortions were done by surgery. About ten buried fetuses were discovered in the garden of the clinic. As if that were not bad enough, it also was discovered that another two or three physicians at reputable hospitals had performed abortions for coffeehouse employees as well. (Yamamoto Senji 1926a)

When confronted with desperate women, not all advocates of birth control were as adamantly opposed to abortion as Yamamoto, but they did consider it the last resort of an involuntarily pregnant woman (Katō T. 1925a). Providers of safe, if illegal, abortions reminded the skeptics among birth control activists that pregnant women seeking to terminate the pregnancy could easily fall into the hands of charlatans. Other skeptics observed in dismay how people took advantage of women who were pregnant with unwanted children. In one reported case, a man had put an advertisement for a questionable abortive medication in a newspaper. When pregnant women came to him complaining that the medication had not worked as promised in the advertisement, he performed high-priced abortions and later attempted to blackmail his victims. The police estimated the number of victims at more than one hundred (Tama 1994:8). A pharmacy in Osaka offered an abortive device and made the price relative to the month of pregnancy. A woman in her first month was charged 10 yen, in her second month 20 yen, and so on. In another town, a man sold an "abortion cream" for 10 yen. By the time women realized that the cream was useless, he had disappeared (Katsura 1926).

Hence, those members of the movement who were capable of doing so also helped women who did not fulfill the requirements for terminating a pregnancy legally. Majima Yutaka, for example, who had learned of the latest abortion techniques while visiting Switzerland and England, founded a sex education counseling center *(seikyōiku sōdansho)* where he provided women with counseling about methods of birth control. Every day he examined and advised dozens of mostly working-class patients. Many women, however, first came to him when they were already pregnant and abortion appeared to be the only solution to their dilemma. In his autobiography, Majima noted that he and other doctors sometimes deliberately made incorrect diagnoses so that they could perform abortions in order to help these women (*Sei to Shakai* January 1926:69; see also Ishizaki 1992:103, 192). Eventually, Majima was arrested after he had carried out an abortion on a woman at the request of her well-to-do partner. Suggesting that abortion was a crime that was carried out only for upper-class women, newspapers referred to Majima and his friends as an "abortion club" *(datai kurabu)*. They did not mention, however, that Majima also had performed abortions on poor women to his own financial disadvantage (see Tama 1994:9). Other members of the birth control movement also frequently dealt with women who were desperate to get an abortion. Shibahara Urako, for example, a midwife activist in Osaka, was engaged in the dissemination of hygiene concepts, social education, and the improvement of living conditions in fishing villages. Trained as a nurse and midwife, she agitated for birth control primarily among the working class and provided abortions for involuntarily pregnant women, for which she was repeatedly arrested (Fujime 1993:93, 1999).

PREVENTING CONCEPTION

Insights into the worrisome situation of involuntarily pregnant women constantly reminded birth control activists of how crucial the dissemination of sexual knowledge was, how desperately many women were searching for means of birth control and abortion, and thus how necessary the development of safe birth control devices and the reform of abortion laws were. Although birth control activists vigorously advocated contraception, the law and the lack of knowledge, especially among workers and farmers, were not the only reasons contraception was not practiced more broadly. Women and men who were willing to practice contraception had very few safe options and still fewer affordable ones.

The methods most commonly recommended by birth control activists were temporary abstinence and *coitus interruptus. Coitus interruptus,* or the Onan Method (Onanfū), was classified as a "constructive birth control method" (Yamamoto Senji 1925a) that "prevented pregnancy" (Tsuchida 1925) and was thus a "cultured method" *(bunmeijin toshite no mottomo rikō na yarikata)* (Mitamura S. 1925). For fear of censorship, the authors of both *Birth Control Review* and *Sex and Society* avoided describing specific methods but explained that readers should search in the Bible for the section on Onan (Yamamoto Senji 1925h:39; Abe 1929).[15]

Another method the birth control advocates approved was developed by Ogino Kyūsaku, who initially did not engage in the popularization of sexual knowledge and birth control. A medical doctor, Ogino developed a timetable for ovulation that complemented the calculations of the female cycle by the Austrian physician Hermann Knaus. He published his findings in the *Journal of the Japanese Association of Gynecologists (Nippon Fujinka Gakkai Zasshi)* in 1924 and was rewarded for outstanding research by the same professional association. Despite this prize, Ogino received mixed medical reviews from his colleagues in Japan.[16] His theory, however, quickly moved outside medical journals and circulated through midwifery journals, sexological journals, women's magazines, and other popular print media. Ogino began in 1932 to publish his findings of a contraceptive method based on his scientific research and thereafter wrote works in Japanese, German, and English for a general audience (see, e.g., Ogino K. 1930).

By that time, the Ogino Periodical Abstinence Method *(Ogino-shiki shūki kinyoku hininhō)*—commonly referred to as the Safe Period Method *(Anzenkihō)*—had already caught the attention of birth control advocates who recommended it but also cautioned that it failed if women were not adequately informed. It is unlikely that many were. Yamamoto estimated that the failure rate ranged between 10 percent among educated women and 70 percent among women who came to birth control counseling centers (Yamamoto Senji 1925f). In addition, neither physicians nor midwives received sufficient training and their textbooks contained no information on this or any other contraceptive method. Hence in most cases they were unable to advise women accordingly (Katō T. 1925b; see also Rousseau 1998).

Since the beginning of the twentieth century, condoms *(danshi sakku)* and diaphragms *(shikyū sakku),* when advertised in general-interest magazines, commonly had been described not as contraceptives, but as devices to prevent venereal diseases and other pathological impairments of the womb. In the text of an advertisement in *The Sun,* for example, a certain Dr. Akimoto, head of a gynecological clinic, assured readers that the diaphragm was the ideal preventative device for venereal and other diseases in women. Its contraceptive potential remained unmentioned *(Taiyō* 3 September 1913: advertisement section). As shown at the beginning of this chapter, during the 1920s and early 1930s, condoms, diaphragms, and other contraceptive devices typically appeared together with other means of protection against venereal diseases. While the use of condoms in the military was clearly and exclusively driven by the wish

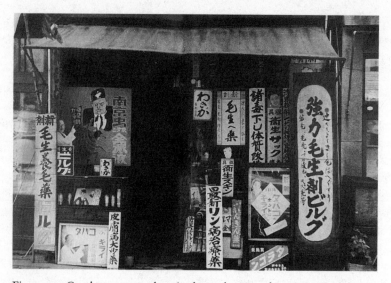

Figure 10. Condoms were advertised openly even after 1937. Rather
than being sold exclusively as contraceptives, they were promoted as
protective devices against venereal diseases under the name "hygiene
sack" *(eisei sakku)*. These advertisement boards were photographed by
Kuwabara Kineo in 1937 at the entrance of a pharmacy in the Ueno
district of Tokyo. From Kuwabara Kineo's *Tōkyō 1934–1993* (Tokyo:
Shinchōsha). Used with the kind permission of Shinchōsha.

to prevent infection with venereal disease, their use was very different in
civilian society, where the possibilities of birth control added to the at-
tractiveness of these devices.

In counseling centers for birth control, condoms could be bought for
20 or 30 sen, roughly a third of the price on the free market. Diaphragms were distributed by counseling centers for 30 or 40 sen,
whereas in pharmacies they cost almost five times as much (Kutsumi in
Hane 1988:152) (see figure 10). Even if contraceptives remained a luxury to many and agitation for sex education and birth control was monitored and often suppressed by the authorities, they eventually did reach
remote regions of Japan. Ella Wiswell documented the case of a young
woman who moved from Suyemura to a city in 1935. One day she sent
a packet of condoms to her parents in Suyemura. In the enclosed letter
she wrote, "Use these! You have too many children" (Smith and Wiswell
1982:89).

Another kind of intrauterine contraceptive device was developed by
medical doctor and founder of the journal *Sexological Research* Ōta
Tenrei and introduced in 1932 *(Ōta-shiki hinin ringu)*. Similar to the

Contraceptive Needle that had been banned in 1930, this new model faced its own problems. One was the cost. As a gold and gold-plated instrument, it was exorbitantly expensive at 10 yen and was clearly unaffordable for those who needed it most (Katsura 1926). In addition, it had to be inserted by a capable doctor to ensure that it worked and did not injure the woman internally. Often neither was the case. Women became pregnant despite using it and many suffered from uterine infections or even became infertile (Takeuchi 1934:404; see also Shimazaki 1991:96). In 1936, the Ordinance Regulating Harmful Contraceptive Devices of 1930 was amended to include Ōta's instrument on the grounds that it was dangerous to women's health.[17] Other provisions restricted the use of devices injected or inserted into the uterus as well as contraceptive devices that were determined to be threatening to a woman's health. Condoms were not covered by this provision but—after 1937—that did not keep the authorities from pursuing those who distributed them (Shimazaki 1991:96; Rousseau 1998:214–218).

REMODELING THE LAW

By 1929, the powerful emergence of eugenic and genetic concepts had begun to decisively influence the direction of the birth control movement. Most of those who initially had hoped for the liberation of the masses and had focused on economic reform and individual freedom of choice slowly moved toward a more state-centered position that prioritized the national body rather than individual liberty. The seductive prospect of modeling the imperial populace according to eugenic rules, and the frustratingly small successes of the birth control movement in terms of contraception, inspired a number of activists to take up even Hiratsuka's 1917 proposal to force sterilization on people who were diagnosed with "genetic diseases." They proposed that preventing "genetically defective" people from reproducing was of primary importance for these people's "own protection and the protection of the entire society." They classified conditions as diverse as tuberculosis, syphilis, diabetes, hemophilia, epilepsy, hysteria, mental illness, chronic alcoholism, "habitual criminality," and "idiocy" as "genetic defects" (Abe 1927a, 1929; Sugiyama N. 1928).

Abe Isoo considered the marriage prohibition for the "genetically burdened" enacted in many Western countries an inadequate solution because it did not keep them from reproducing. He elaborated that for wealthy capitalists, the birth of handicapped children might not present a material problem, but such children could present an existential threat to lower-class families. Among the "genetically burdened" persons he listed were alcoholics, those suffering from tuberculosis and leprosy, and "genetically burdened criminals." The solution he offered was routine sterilization of persons when they came to the hospital to receive treatment for these conditions (Abe 1927a). Once a savior of the underprivileged as the founder of Japan's first socialist party and a crusader for the abolition of prostitution, Abe previously had found it "immoral" for young women to be forced into prostitution by their own families in order to save the parents from financial ruin (Abe 1911a–b, 1915). Abe had argued that the victimization of several tens of thousands of women who were sold into prostitution by their families merely to uphold social customs had to be stopped and had insisted that peace lay in the realization of birth control (Abe 1911c, 1925, 1927a). At the end of the 1920s, however, he began to support mandatory sterilization because he considered "genetically diseased" descendants too great a burden on society (Abe 1927a), and by the end of World War II he had turned into an advocate for early marriage (Abe 1944).

Unno Kōtoku, another author of articles in *Sex and Society* and activist in the birth control movement, deemed it difficult to "give people with bad genes the right to have a child," but he insisted against the new voices for positive eugenics that a newborn child by all means had "the right to live." He agreed with Abe that people with "bad genes" *(identeki na akushitsusha)*, the mentally ill *(seishin byōsha)*, "idiots" *(hakuchi teinōsha)*, criminals, and the handicapped were all "anti-social" *(hanshakaiteki)* and a nuisance to society, but claimed that they had the right to live because they had been born. In contrast to Abe's confident call for the sterilization of certain "types" of people, Unno aimed at reminding his audience that "far too little was known about genetics to make any connections between the progress of a society and the genetic quality of its people" (Unno 1925b:16–17).

Other birth control activists increasingly pushed for the massive involvement of the state in birth control matters. In the last issue of *Sex and Society,* before it was discontinued for financial reasons, Kaji Tokijirō's appeal to the state to provide the legal and institutional framework for his concept ran sharply counter to the stance of its founder and editor, Yamamoto Senji. Yamamoto had always emphasized that use of the various means and methods of birth control should be based on individual choice rather than on state enforcement. In contrast, Kaji Tokijirō, an advisor in the Central Advice Office for Birth Control in Tokyo, appealed to the state to make birth control part of its business *(kokka jigyō),* to support research on birth control methods, and to encourage the population to practice these methods. Kaji's proposal for the "building of customs" in order "to manage sexual duties" called for the massive involvement of the state in the production of "good-quality children" (Kaji 1926a:13–16). The first step in that direction would be a strict contraception law forcing people who suffered from infectious and genetic diseases to practice birth control, as, in his view, contraception should not be a matter of individual choice. Kaji declared the promotion of early marriage the second important step. He urged the readers of *Sex and Society* to stop considering marriage sacrosanct, as "we do not consider eating rice a sacrosanct affair either." If people got married at a young age, as he recommended, more marriages might end in divorce, but he viewed a rising divorce rate as preferable to the many problems an unmarried life entailed (Kaji 1926a).

Lamenting the consequences of the late marriages of men around the age of thirty and women around the age of twenty-five, Kaji maintained that all these middle-aged men and women experienced difficulties marrying and consequently engaged in a variety of "unnatural practices." Among these, he noted, was masturbation, of which one could not be sure that it was not injurious to the body and the mind. He acknowledged that homosexuality *(dōseiai oyobi nanshoku)* might well be an age-old custom, common among both female prostitutes and *daimyō,* but insisted that contemporary homosexual behavior emerged from unfavorably delayed marriages and people being single—and hence was problematic.

Illegitimate children and abortion, in Kaji's view, were another result of the vast numbers who remained unmarried. Often illegitimate infants were abandoned, and women who had had an abortion suffered from severe health problems, died, or killed themselves. Even if things did not escalate that far, Kaji argued, to remain unmarried until middle age would bring about hysteria, neurasthenia, and suicide in women and sex crimes and murder in men (Kaji 1926a:11, 1926b). Kaji's solution to this scenario was simple. If birth control was legal and possible, young and middle-aged couples could postpone pregnancy until they felt economically secure. Instead of having children immediately after marriage, couples would be able to spend time together and find out whether they wanted to stay together. Thus, the divorce rate would decrease and there would be fewer single women with children. Couples who did not want children would not have to have them and those who were physically weak or suffered from "genetic defects" would not have children either (Kaji 1926a:12).

In 1929, members of both birth control groups, the Osaka Birth Control Study Society and the Japanese Birth Control Study Society in Tokyo, wrote up a Petition for the Public Recognition of Birth Control (Sanji seigen kōninan) that compromised on the more radical demands of previous years. They emphasized that birth control was desirable not only from the perspective of the proletariat, but from the perspective of all representatives of the "new people" *(kakuha shinnin daigishi)*—i.e., those who had the welfare of society in mind, favored social reforms, and understood the social and political significance of sexual knowledge. Based on the assumption that abortion up to the third month was relatively safe for the pregnant woman, the Petition for the Public Recognition of Birth Control demanded its legalization within this time frame. The petition also proposed the introduction of a fine instead of imprisonment for people who carried out an abortion at a later stage of pregnancy. Along with the relaxation of the maternal protection criteria and thus a broader interpretation of the "mother's weak constitution" as the basis for a legal abortion, it suggested that practice should be restricted to physicians who would be the only specialists able to diagnose the previously mentioned indications (Ishizaki 1992:100).

The first petition was never presented to the Lower House. Yamamoto Senji, who should have presented it, was stabbed to death by a right-wing radical on 5 March 1929, after an assembly where he had spoken out against Japan's China politics. However, in January 1931, Abe Isoo, Ishimoto Shizue, Hiratsuka Raichō, Majima Yutaka, and a few other activists founded the Japanese Birth Control Federation (Nihon Sanji Chōsetsu Renmei) as an umbrella organization for all birth control branch offices. They drafted a new petition for the legalization of abortion and contraceptives based on three sets of indicators. The medical indicator aimed at the "pure protection of the mother" *(jun bosei hogo)* and affected all women for whom a full-term pregnancy or giving birth would be life-threatening. Among these potentially life-threatening diseases were tuberculosis, severe liver, heart, and blood diseases, severe disabilities, diseases of the reproductive organs, and mental disorders. The doctor also would be allowed to prescribe contraceptives in the case of serious illnesses associated with pregnancy, nervous ailments, and brain disease and certain eye and ear diseases. As in the first petition, they also proposed to initiate scientific research on birth control methods and to place into the hands of doctors expensive contraceptives that until then had been distributed by laypersons working in advice centers (see Ishizaki 1992:102).

The eugenic indicator initially was useful only as a basis for contraception and was intended primarily to prevent women with genetic diseases, who represented a "burden to their family and the state," from reproducing. Another eugenically motivated proposition was to advise blood relatives against marrying one another. If it were not possible to prevent that, then birth control for both partners should be used in order to prevent the birth of disabled children *(fugusha)*.

The socioeconomic indicator left doctors with the greatest leeway for issuing a certificate, as the findings merely had to attest to the fact that a further birth would endanger the financial existence of the family and would be the source of poverty and crime. The petition once again emphasized that only physicians should be qualified to certify the existence of one of the three indicators, as well as to carry out abortions. If "impure motives" were involved, however, then an abortion should be considered a "dangerous crime" (Honda 1931:32–35). Eventually, the Japanese Women's Birth Control Federation (Nihon Sanji Chōsetsu Fujin Renmei), successor to the Japanese Birth Control Federation (Nihon Sanji Chōsetsu Renmei), brought forth this second petition for the reform of the abortion law in August of 1932.

In the first year of the establishment of Manchukuo, the Home Department again rejected the petition. The movement lost its momentum and began to disintegrate; it eventually collapsed in 1937, when even publications on birth control were banned. The increasing militarization of Japanese society during these years and especially the outbreak of a full-blown war with China in 1937 had brought new challenges to the sexological project, eventually thrusting it into oblivion. Rather, as I shall describe in the next chapter, several forces contributed to its disappearance from public space.

CHAPTER 5

Breeding the Japanese "Race"

We are like a great crowd of people packed into a small and
narrow room, and there are only three doors through which
we might escape, namely emigration, advance into world
markets, and expansion of territory. The first door, emigration, has been barred to us by the anti-Japanese immigration
policies of other countries. The second door, advance into
world markets, is being pushed shut by tariff barriers and the
abrogation of commercial treaties. . . . It is quite natural that
Japan should rush upon the last remaining door.

             Hashimoto Kingorō, "Seinen ni uttau"

The increasing militarization of Japanese society during the 1930s and
early 1940s, addressed by ideologues like Hashimoto Kingorō (Tsunoda, de Bary, and Keene 1964:289), brought new challenges to the sexological project. The disintegration of sexology, however, was not simply the effect of suppression by the state, nor did it happen in one blow.
Rather, sexologists faced numerous difficulties (e.g., a paper shortage)
that affected them in the same ways it did authors and publishers of
other kinds of publications or social reformers and activists more generally. Some challenges, however, were perhaps specific to the sexological project. One of them was censorship and other means of suppression, which drove some sexologists into bankruptcy or underground
and simply silenced others. The authorities responsible for the preservation of social order and morals became increasingly involved in the blatant suppression of activities that challenged this order, be it the labor
movement or sexological utterances. Censorship equated the sexological project with pornography, or writing that aimed at the stimulation
of uncontrolled erotic pleasure rather than the creation of knowledge.

As more and more political activities were branded as communist and therefore destructive to the state, sexological publications, instructions on birth control, attempts at appeasing those who deemed masturbation injurious, and representations of the incitement of erotic desire and pleasure all were classified as "disruptive to morals" or simply "obscene."

The emergence of "racial hygiene" challenged the fragile position of sexologists within the realm of science. The forceful emergence of eugenic and racial hygienist thought represented a competing program that, by co-opting the rhetorical figures of the sexological project, such as "the demands of the masses," marginalized a sexology that had positioned itself as a tool of liberation. Racial hygienists emerged as the new experts ready to provide the imperialist state with the instruments for manufacturing a flawless, superior race, ready and able to push the Japanese empire to new heights. Finally, a turn to pronatalist-imperialist propaganda in popular media robbed the sexologists of their hard-earned foothold in the public arena.

THE SUBVERSIVE POWER OF SEXUAL KNOWLEDGE

During the second half of the 1930s the censorship of sexological publications, the confiscation of contraceptives, the frequent imprisonment of leading proponents of sex education and birth control, and the prohibition of all other activities brought to a standstill the efforts of sexologists and other birth control activists. Financial problems resulting from frequent censorship and the confiscation of published issues had forced many publishers to discontinue their journals (Oshikane 1977: 185–201), and by 1938, sexological journals had been completely swept out of public sight.

Two sets of legislation—both of which affected the activities of the sexologists—provided the hazy boundaries of the censors' range of actions, which varied from active social policies to open suppression. Publications, public lectures, and other activities of sexologists were classified as violations of legislation that aimed specifically at regulating either public order or morals. One set of legislation was to ensure the maintenance of "public order." Its most significant manifestations were the Peace Police Law of 1900, the Peace Preservation Law of 1925, and the increasingly strict regulations implemented after 1937. Eventually, these regulations were applied not only to communists, socialists, and sexologists but also to other groups that were viewed as a thorn in the sides of the authorities (Mitchell 1973). The Peace Preservation Law comple-

mented the Peace Police Law (Chian keisatsu hō), which had targeted
primarily "anti-government" groups.[1] Passed at the same time as general
male suffrage, the Peace Preservation Law was meant to serve mainly as
the legal base for strict procedures against communists and other persons who had "organized an association with the object of revolutionizing the national constitution" (Sebald 1936:259).[2]

The other set of legislation was concerned with the careful establishment and preservation of "public morals" and with increasing vigor targeted publications and activities that were deemed "obscene," "vulgar,"
or, more generally, destructive to public morality. A number of decrees
within the legislation for the preservation of public morals regulated the
publication of texts and images in "books and periodicals that violated
customs and morals" (fūzoku kairan no shuppanbutsu oyobi shinbun-
shi).[3] This last set of regulations was also modified frequently in order
to adapt to new types of publications. Accordingly, new categories of
public moral violations continuously emerged from the censors' reports.
The legislation eventually covered almost all representations of sex, with
the exception of those that defined reproduction as the exclusive purpose of sex and unambiguously emphasized that sex belonged within the
confines of marriage (Akama 1927; Naimushō keihokyoku 1976a:193).
In the case of publication, violations of regulations on customs and
morals (fūzoku kairan) were covered by the term fūzoku kinshi, which
included a broad range of so-called immoralities. These labels were of
course neither clear-cut nor unmistakable.

Officers of the Special Higher Police served as censors who controlled
the production and distribution of publications, including information
on sex, which was deemed injurious to public morals. The guardians of
mores and social order in the police insinuated that the sexologists'
agenda not only was morally questionable but that their engagement for
sex education and enlightenment threatened the social order. Propagators of sex education, sex research, and birth control viewed overpopulation and the poor living conditions of the disadvantaged classes as a
precursor to war; their educational campaigns were classified as politically "dangerous" and were persecuted according to the regulations of
the Peace Preservation Law. Because they questioned state policies, sex
researchers and other popularizers of sexual knowledge put their professional reputations on the line and continually ran the risk of conflict
with the authorities. Yamamoto Senji, who devoted himself to the sexual enlightenment of the working class in particular and who was accused of subversive activities in connection with his involvement in the

proletarian movement, eventually paid with his life. Attacks against Yamamoto were to be expected at the end of the 1920s, when he dedicated himself ever more to the proletarian movement and frequently spoke out against the Peace Preservation Law. Despite warnings from friends, however, he rejected their suggestion to employ a bodyguard. After ten years of activities as a sex researcher and educator, he was fatally stabbed by a right-wing extremist in 1929 after giving a speech against Japan's involvement in China. Although they could never prove it, communist comrades were convinced that the murder had been "carefully planned by the Tanaka government" (Katayama Sen 1929, quoted in Beckmann and Okubo 1969:173; see also Taniguchi 1960:257).[4]

Just as the censors defined who would be counted as a communist, they also decided who and what was to be considered "immoral" or "obscene." In doing so, they were not interested in the fine differentiations sexologists had made within the large body of writings on sex. The censors' choice of incriminated publications ignored the boundaries between "obscene" sexual writing and instructive, scholarly texts that had been drawn with so much care by Yamamoto and other sexologists. Throughout the early twentieth century, in fact, sexologists had made frequent and explicit efforts to dissociate themselves from the commercial interests of popular magazines that packaged sexual issues in sensationalist stories intended to increase the magazines' sales.

Many sexologists attempted to draw clear-cut lines between their own agenda and the overly sensational or lighthearted articles in popular media. Yamamoto and other sexologists strictly opposed the practice of leaving sexual issues in the hands of dubious print media, "obscene magazines," and "certain women's magazines," which—in Yamamoto's opinion—took up sexual perversions or sex scandals mainly for "dirty motives" *(fujun na dōki)* (Yamamoto Senji 1921:513, 1924b). Others, however, hoped that readers tempted to buy a magazine because of sensational "true stories," such as, for example, the attempted suicide of a female homosexual, also would embrace the more matter-of-fact information provided in some sexological journals and other works.[5] Moreover, some sexologists, such as Habuto Eiji, for example, increasingly embraced new commercial opportunities that were opened up by the expanding print media market.

Nonetheless, just as frequently, sexologists were unsuccessful in entirely escaping the accusation of obscenity. Colleagues from established academic disciplines doubted the respectability of the sexologists' intentions and voiced the concern that sex research sullied the purity of science. Japanese sexologists shared this problem with their European and American colleagues. Havelock Ellis, for example, believed that a medical degree behind an author's name served as justification for investigating such a topic, assuring readers that the author was not concerned with prurient interest but rather with helping them cope with problems. To add to this aura of respectability, most Western treatises on sex printed in the first half of the twentieth century carried a warning that they were intended for a medical and professional audience, not for the general public. However, suspicions remained. When an English edition of Ellis's work on sexual inversion first appeared, an American reviewer stated that Ellis was inclined to fill his book with the "pornographic imaginings of perverted minds rather than cold facts." Similarly, when William Masters confided that he wanted to do research on human sexuality, he was given three pieces of advice: first, he should establish a scientific reputation in some other scientific field before starting any sex research; second, he should secure the sponsorship of a major medical school or university; and third, he should be at least forty years of age and preferably married (Bullough 1997:236–238).

Although some sexologists in Japan fulfilled these criteria, censors were not easily impressed with these superficial signs of respectability. With increasing frequency, sexological articles were denounced as pornography and censored for moral reasons. Sexological lectures were interrupted or prohibited from the outset and classified as a threat to both the social order and public morals. The censors frequently collapsed the labels "revolutionary"—or disruptive of the social order, anti-state, anti-military, or anti-war—and "obscene"—or disruptive of mores, pornographic, or vulgar. The definition of utterances and writings injurious to public morals remained vague and allowed for largely arbitrary enforcement by the Special Higher Police.

One judge described morally objectionable publications as writing that "arouses a sense of disgust, which depicts ugly, vulgar matters—especially fornication and adultery—too concretely or in such a way as to provoke or encourage them, or to express sympathy or admiration for them" (Judge Imamura, quoted in J. Rubin 1984:88). When printed on the cover of a journal or magazine, the line "Reproduction of all articles in this paper is forbidden" *(Honshi no kiji wa subete tensai o kinzu)* or simply the words "Reproduction ban" *(tensaikin)* constituted an existential threat, particularly to smaller papers.

Especially after the Japanese invasion of Manchuria in September 1931 and the establishment of the puppet state Manchukuo in 1932, the guardians of public morals suspected threats to the social order and morals in a vast number of areas. Among these were the approval of the "liberation of women," the "liberation of the family," and the "critique of marriage." Another set of problematic activities and thought included the mere "thematization of sexual desire," the dissemination of "theories about pregnancy," and what was classified as "neo-Malthusian assertions." Although the censorship authorities acknowledged that some of the authors of texts on these themes approved of the official pronatal population policy, they classified most of them as "frivolous concessions" *(fuhaku na mono)* to the zeitgeist (Naimushō keihokyoku 1976a:224).

Whereas the activities of sexologists and other social reformers were tolerated or hardly recognized during peacetime, they became subject to rigid oppression in times of social unrest and instability—i.e., during the 1920s, especially after the Kantō earthquake of 1923, annually on May 1 (International Workers Day), and during the war in the 1930s and 1940s. By 1937, when the last remaining sexological journal was discontinued and the militarization of Japanese society had become ever more blatant, sexologists had dealt with an abundance of hurdles that the Japanese administration had placed in their way. As discussed in chapters 3 and 4, they did not rely only on the printed word for the mediation of sexual knowledge. Sexologists also made a considerable effort to reach out to groups that did not read their books and journals by giving lectures at meetings of the professional associations of doctors, pharmacists, and teachers, and union meetings, as well as in factories, schools, and universities. After 1925, they also spoke on radio programs and made use of every available opportunity to present their agenda (Nogami 1932). Wherever sexologists had sought and found support for their sexological program, they also encountered resistance of various kinds. Every public lecture in the course of nearly two decades was, depending on the audience in question, threatened by police intervention. As long as they presented their ideas in professional circles, they were relatively safe from state repression—although frequently reprimanded. However, serious threats were made to the continuation of their publications, the security of their academic careers, their freedom, and their lives, especially when they appealed to the general public in their writing and lectures. Their endeavors allowed sexual knowledge to reach ever-greater groups in Japanese society, thus increasingly provoking the authorities' attention.

In 1931, the censorship authorities in the Home Department noted with concern that the number of censored books and magazines had multiplied during the previous years. They acknowledged the general increase of publications and of the numbers of readers but also pointed out that the production of "sexual desire books" *(seiyokuhon)* was mainly responsible for that development (Naimushō keihokyoku 1981:316). Censorship could lead to the confiscation of a book or the discontinuation of a journal, and frequent censorship was a threat especially for the sexological journals, which were—in the documentation of violations against public morals and social order—categorized as "sexual desire journals" *(seiyoku zasshi)*.

Sometimes the censors demanded only the replacement of the cover, but more often whole issues were censored because of particular articles such as, for example, "Women's Sexual Awareness and Men" or "Condom Nonsense" *(Sei* May 1929 and May 1932). The police's justification of the confiscation of sexological journals varied only slightly. They acknowledged that *Sexuality,* for example, frequently had discussed the dangers of venereal diseases, but they claimed that the many "obscene" articles violated the sense of "proper morals" (Naimushō keihokyoku 1976b:214–215).

Generally, censorship practices varied according to the type of publication, the readership, the circulation numbers, and influence of the social climate at a given point in time, and the distribution and extent of the incriminating content. Typically, political journals faced more restraint than academic ones and those with a broader readership were more prone to censorship than those that targeted a specialized audience. Of ten newspaper and magazine categories examined by the censors between 1929 and 1931, literary magazines and "sexual desire journals" were most frequently censored. Viewed as an expression of a psychologically confused time, one that commonly was referred to as an era of heightened eroticism and the prevalence of the grotesque and nonsensical *(ero guro nansensu),* journals that focused on sexual issues were particularly endangered.

Several sexological journals directed at an educated lay audience were discontinued as a result of censorship, while only one academic journal was censored during those years. Within a few years, censorship cases totaled 102. Thirty of these cases affected "sexual desire journals."[6] Repeated prohibitions to reproduce and distribute certain issues led to the end of the journal *Sexuality.* When Akiyama Yoshio, the editor of *Sexuality,* gave up the production of the journal, it had been censored seventeen times within a few years. Originally approved as a "professional journal" by the authorities, *Sexuality* had to deal repeatedly with censorship and confiscation that targeted literary contributions, such as sexual tales, in particular, but also stories about personal sexual experiences and scholarly essays. Yamamoto Senji designed his journal *Sex and Society* as a forum for the publication of the results of sex research and other instructive articles in order to educate the masses. His engagement for sex education and sex research and his involvement in both the birth control movement and the labor movement, however, made him a target of censorship and frequent police observation on both moral and political grounds.

Magazines and journals directed at youth and laborers seem to have been observed most closely, but newspapers and magazines with high circulation numbers were checked especially carefully, while those of smaller, sometimes more radical groups possibly were overlooked (Kasza 1988:33–35). Moreover, the popularity of the publisher or author and the circulation numbers played an important role in being targeted by censors. Yamamoto Senji and Abe Isoo, for example, were public men, well known from their articles in daily papers. Hence, their activities were observed more carefully.

During the early 1930s, newspapers and magazines that generally were considered reputable were censored or confiscated if they contained articles with dubious sexual content. Articles that were perceived as violations of the censorship regulations were prohibited from being printed, and sometimes entire editions of a book or periodical could be affected by a printing ban (Kasza 1988:172–174). *Women's Review* had to remove an article entitled "Advice on Life from a Thousand and One Nights" (*Fujin Kōron* November 1933), and *Popular Medicine* had to withdraw "Story of an Unsuccessful Wedding Night" (*Tsūzoku Igaku* January 1934). Similarly, *Research in Sexology,* founded in 1936 by Ōta Tenrei, had to be discontinued after scarcely one year in existence when it changed its course from that of a scholarly journal to one that targeted an educated lay audience and no longer addressed an exclusively academic readership. In the first three editions of *Research in Sexology,* the results of the sex surveys carried out by Yamamoto and Yasuda were printed anonymously as a "Collection of Material on Sex Education" (*Seikyōiku shiryōshū*). The often-recurring word "masturbation" prompted the prohibition of the journal. *Research in Sexology* was the last sexological journal to disappear under the pressure of legislative control (Yasuda I. 1955:284).

The censors increasingly sharpened their instruments and by the mid-

1930s, four categories of periodicals, in addition to ordinary news-papers, were examined. These four categories included "sexual desire journals," entertainment magazines, mass-circulation magazines, and women's magazines. Ōta Tenrei described new means of contraception, Sawada Junjirō introduced new sex research, and Kikuchi Kan contem-plated love and marriage. All of them faced censorship at some time or another (Naimushō keihokyoku 1976b:192–196). The subtle and sometimes not-so-subtle differences between prescriptions for healing venereal diseases, essays about sexuality and puberty, adaptations of *The Thousand and One Nights,* and modified versions of *The Decameron* or the *Kama Sutra* mattered less and less to the censors, who were on the lookout for incriminating material that violated what they saw as good public morals (Naimushō keihokyoku 1976a:284–304).

Prior to 1938, censorship was neither consistent nor foolproof. In ad-dition to the criteria described above, individual judgments must have played a major role in what was censored and what was not. Miyatake Gaikotsu (1867–1955), journalist and prominent satirist, printed parts of two different sketches of female nudes in his *Humor Newspaper (Kok-kei Shinbun),* and in the accompanying text ridiculed the arbitrariness of the censorship authorities. Besides individual differences in the cen-sors' judgments, Miyatake suggested, censorship depended on how much a newspaper's or magazine's general orientation bothered the au-thorities: "Take pleasure in the unholy nudes *(fushinsei naru rataiga)* in number 113, the present edition. The nudes, which appeared in the *Ōsaka Shinpō,* a paper with special ties to the Home Department, were not subjected to a fine. However, when the *Kokkei Shinbun* does not scatter their nudes [throughout the magazine, rather than reproducing them as one complete image], they are fined. What irony!" (*Kokkei Shin-bun* 20 April 1906: editorial).

Publishers and presses, however, knew how to apply certain strate-gies to escape censorship, and the officials in the Home Department alerted their officers to "secret publications" of incriminated material and other tricks that publishers used to circumvent the censors' verdict. They held back certain articles and did not present them at preview meetings. They changed the titles of problematic articles slightly or printed the same essays with different titles. Some publishers also took on the risk of even higher fines and printed articles that had been cen-sored. Others repealed the censored articles but nonetheless described those articles that had been censored from the last edition in the next edition of their magazine. *Women's Review,* for example, frequently re-

sponded to censorship by printing critical statements on censorship policy in the subsequent issue of the magazine (Shimanaka 1921), and it is
likely that magazine editors used the label "scandalous" of a censored
article to their own commercial advantage in order to increase sales
figures.

When the conflict with China escalated, the censorship regulations
were tightened again. Previously, publishers of newspapers and magazines were not given direct guidelines for publications, but were provided with commentaries about very specific events. Whereas until 1938
incriminated publications or parts of publications commonly were censored after their publication, now entire texts prepared for publication
had to be presented to the censors for approval. These obligatory pre-
views marked the transformation from direct to indirect censorship,
paving the way for the self-censorship of broadcasting corporations and
other media (J. Rubin 1984; Kasza 1988). The new guidelines of 1938
prescribed a more rigid censorship of women's and "entertainment magazines" *(goraku zasshi),* and more than ever before affected novels classified as "vulgar." Among the works censored, novels that described the
extramarital love affairs of married women, negated the ideal of premarital female chastity, or dealt with lovers' suicide pacts were high on
the list (see also Robertson 1999). Others included confessions related
to sexual desire and similar provocative articles related to sexual matters, which were declared to have a "bad influence on women's upbringing." Typical examples of stories prone to censorship were vivid descriptions of "The Misfortune of the Inability to Experience Sexual
Satisfaction," the "Difference between Virgins and Non-virgins" and
"Secret Hygiene Instructions for Newlyweds," as well as articles about
sexual hygiene in which venereal diseases or contraceptive methods
were mentioned.

RACIAL HYGIENE

Closely tied to prewar and wartime censorship was the increasing cur-
rency of racial hygienic thought that forcefully contradicted the claims
of some sexologists, feminists, and other social reformers who had promoted the legalization of contraception and birth control and the view
that sexuality should be considered an individual, private matter that
should not be controlled by the state. The escalating conflict with China
and its effects contributed to a political climate that advanced a population policy based on a set of claims that were rooted in social medicine,

social biology, biometrics, and genetics, and furthered the disintegration of the sexological project. Sexologists had been concerned with the education of the wider public and assumed that "correct" sexual knowledge would also lead to "correct" sexual behavior. The Japanese administration, however, under the auspices of first the Home Department and after 1937 the Ministry of Health and Welfare, pushed for state-controlled pronatalist population policies at the onset of what promised to be a long war that would demand enormous manpower. These policies, which were established at the end of the 1930s and remained an important part of population policies since, came to include elements of both negative and positive eugenics under the name "racial hygiene" *(minzoku eisei)*.

From 1924 on, several eugenics organizations were founded that generated a number of debates on theories of heredity. Only one organization, however, was successful at formulating concrete policies: the Japanese Association of Racial Hygiene (Nihon Minzoku Eisei Kyōkai), founded by Nagai Hisomu in 1930. In an attempt to design a set of concrete population policies, the members of the association declared that racial hygiene policies would solve the problems that had been addressed throughout the Taishō and early Shōwa eras as sexual and/or social issues by sexologists and other social reformers. In Nagai's view, sex and reproduction were exclusively intended to serve the "improvement of the race" *(jinshu kaizen)*.[7] In order to clearly differentiate the association's project from elements of eugenic thought discussed since the late nineteenth century under the guise of improvement of the national body, Nagai and other members of the group abandoned the term "eugenics" *(yūseigaku)*, which had been used by a diverse group of reformers, and created a new name, "racial hygiene" *(minzoku eiseigaku)*, an adaptation of the German *Rassenhygiene* (Suzuki Z. 1983:148; see also Otsubo and Bartholomew 1998:556).[8]

An audience of more than 1,000, including professionals from medicine, education, and politics, the home minister and the minister of education, the director of the Academy of Science and several Shintō priests, attended the first meeting in Hibiya, Tokyo. The association's mission statement dismissed "neo-Malthusian Sangerism" as a "worldwide plague" that undermined the "biological vitality of the cultured races." It appealed to responsible representatives of racial hygiene, social medicine, cultural history, and social politics on behalf of the future of the Japanese people. The declaration also emphasized that Japan must not remain outside this worldwide trend of "neo-Malthusian Sangerism" and promoted the appropriation of birth control that had been so "urgently demanded by a great number of people" in order to improve the Japanese race. The Japanese Association of Racial Hygiene had been set up, the statement concluded, in order to fulfill these wishes (see Suzuki Z. 1983:145).

Borrowing from diverse sources—including an earlier petition of the Japanese Women's Alliance for Birth Control, which I discussed in chapter 4, as well as national-socialist legislation and language—Nagai proposed several measures. He deemed it necessary to sterilize "inferior persons" *(rettōsha)* and people with hereditary diseases in order to physically and mentally improve the Japanese race, and he promoted the enactment of a sterilization law. The association also proposed the promotion of "eugenic marriages" *(yūsei kekkon)* through marriage consultation offices in order to advance the proper "breeding of the Japanese race" *(Nihon minzoku no zōshoku)* —under the control of eugenicists. The prohibition of every means and method of birth control that depended on the individual woman's desire to prevent contraception and birth complemented the set of policies that worked to tighten the criminalization of contraception and abortion beyond the boundaries of racial hygienist reasoning.

Following Nagai's recommendation, a package of regulations against harmful contraceptives *(Yūgai hinin kigu torishimari)* was implemented, and contraceptives found in the possession of birth control activists were confiscated (Fujime 1986:91). Doctors, midwives, and other professionals (and nonprofessionals) who were accused of violating the abortion law were arrested and imprisoned. In 1933, midwife Shibahara Urako was arrested; she was politically aligned with socialists and communists and indicted for assisting in fifteen different abortions, for which she was punished with a one-year sentence (Fujime 1993).[9] In 1934, the police interrogated Majima Yutaka (Ishizaki 1992:104). And in December 1937, Ishimoto was arrested for her "communist activities," her propagation of birth control, and her critique of the Japanese aggression in China. After her release two weeks later, she was placed under house arrest and forbidden to participate in any type of public activity (see M. Beard 1953:167–173).

At another meeting, the members of the Association of Racial Hygiene debated a set of five policies to further its goals: the promotion of racial hygienist thought; the execution of racial hygienic surveys and the establishment of a state-sponsored research institute; the establishment of measures for the prevention of the "poisoning of the race"; the promotion of the reproduction of healthy people according to racial hygienist criteria; and the establishment of measures such as isolation, eugenic marriage, abortion, castration, and sterilization in order to enhance genetic health and eradicate "bad genes." All of these goals were to be implemented and executed under the control of the Association of Racial Hygiene (Matsubara 2000:177–178; Suzuki Z. 1983:159).

In 1934 and repeatedly throughout the remainder of the 1930s, Nagai and other eugenicists submitted drafts of a sterilization law to the Bureau of Hygiene in the Home Department. However, their proposals continued to provoke substantial criticism and to meet with rejection. Geneticists like Komai Taku, for example, insisted that from the viewpoint of population genetics, sterilization would be entirely worthless. Other geneticists warned that research in genetics was not advanced enough for political and legal application. Psychiatrists objected to the enactment of the law, insisting that it would encourage prejudice against the mentally ill. Social reformers on the Left remained unconvinced that people with "bad bodies" or "bad minds" were useless or even harmful to society. After all, some pointed out, many of the most successful Japanese poets and artists shared a weak constitution. Critics of eugenic policies warned that it would prompt the extinction of exceptional people with special talents such as scientists, religious leaders, and artists, because racial hygienist measures were based on an overly simplistic concept of the human. They argued that these exceptionally gifted, albeit physically weak, people did not produce many children anyway and few started a family at all (Matsubara 1998:191).

Representatives of the Left also were wary of the law because it tackled in a biological manner what they perceived to be problems of economic inequity. Yasuda Tokutarō, Yamamoto Senji's former comrade, for example, protested the principles of the sterilization law because he viewed crime and mental illness as typical deplorable conditions of capitalist societies. In his view, these conditions could be eliminated not by improving the "human material" through racial hygiene policies but only by socioeconomic reforms. Unintentionally playing into the hands of the association, which sought scientific recognition and political influence, Yasuda shared another argument with a more cautious group of geneticists. Genetic research, Yasuda declared, had yet to be developed well enough to be transformed into policies. This lack of scientific evidence for the likelihood of inheriting "inferior dispositions" was acknowledged even to some extent by those who demanded policies based on racial hygienist concepts. Nagai and other members of the Association of Racial Hygiene pushed for a state-sponsored eugenics research institute similar to the Swedish eugenics laboratory he had visited in Uppsala.[10] Thus Yasuda's latter concern was in a way shared—if for different reasons—by the leaders of the association, who called for the establishment of a research institute for racial hygiene, the dissemination of racial hygienic knowledge, and influence in policy matters. Other opponents of the law attacked racial hygienists from yet another perspective, insisting that the Japanese people were so unique they could not be treated like animals or other peoples (Suzuki Z. 1983:162).

Contested as it was, racial hygiene gained considerable ground, and in November 1938, the Eugenics Section in the Ministry of Health and Welfare installed a Racial Hygiene Study Group (Minzoku Eisei Kenkyūkai). The study group began under the newly created term *minzoku yūsei* to debate policies for both increasing the reproduction of "superior healthy" *(yūryō kenzen)* people and preventing the reproduction of people classified as "inferior" *(retsuakusha* or *rettōsha)*. The Eugenics Section's tasks covered issues of racial hygiene, mental diseases, "chronic intoxication," including alcoholism, and chronic diseases, including beriberi and cancer, venereal diseases, and leprosy *(Japan Times and Mail* 1937, 1938; Matsubara 2000:176–177).

The vice president of the Association of Racial Hygiene, Koya Yoshio, supported Nagai in transforming the goals of the association into political measures. A professor of medicine at the Institute of Hygiene of the Kanazawa Medical University, Koya had begun to publish the bilingual periodical *Racial Biological Research (Minzoku Eiseigaku Kenkyū—Rassenbiologische Untersuchungen)* in 1936. The journal printed exclusively results of biometrical, sociobiological, and physioanthropological studies, which were carried out by Koya and his collaborators at the Institute of Hygiene. Typical contributions dealt with the analysis of fertility according to social class, the heredity of physical traits, racial biological studies of the rural versus the urban population in Japan, and the physical condition of Japan's schoolchildren.[11]

In 1939, two years after the founding of the association, Koya began to take on various functions in different departments of the Ministry of Health and Welfare. Like Nagai, Koya sympathized with Germany's national-socialist politics. Under his leadership, the Association of Racial Hygiene developed an increasingly intimate relationship with the Ministry of Health and Welfare, foreshadowing the almost complete "colonial ruling apparatus" over sex and sexuality and introducing processes of co-option that were perfected in the immediate postwar era. At the association's annual conferences between 1940 and 1942, more than a third of the participants came from various departments of the ministry. Meetings and conferences initially had been held at universities. From 1943 on, however, the twelfth and subsequent conferences took place in the Ministry of Health and Welfare's own research institute. An increasing number of ministerial officials published articles in the association's periodical, and eventually they wrote all contributions (Oguma 1995:251–253).

Several other attempts at pushing through a bill for the eugenic protection of the Japanese race (Nihon minzoku yūsei hogo hōan) also failed until eventually, in 1940, the National Eugenic Law (Kokumin Yūseihō) was passed with the support of the Bureau of Prevention (Yobōkyoku) in the Ministry of Health and Welfare (established in 1938) and put into effect in July 1941.[12] The sterilization law was modeled after the first German racial hygienist law of 14 July 1933, the Law on Preventing Hereditarily Ill Progeny (Gesetz zur Verhütung erbkranken Nachwuchses), which in turn, as Stefan Kühl (1994:23) has argued, had grown out of earlier American models. Members of the Prussian Health Council drew on a Swiss law as well as on existing sterilization laws in twenty-four states of the United States. In Germany, however, the law went far beyond the American statutes. Physicians were required to report all "unfit" people to the hundreds of hereditary health courts established to adjudicate the German procreational future. Within three years, German authorities sterilized some 225,000 people, ten times the number treated in the previous thirty years in the United States (Kevles 1985:116–117) and four hundred times the number of Japanese sterilizations until the end of World War II (Kōseishō imukyoku 1955:828).

The Japanese sterilization law allowed the government to order the sterilization of people with hereditary illnesses, but, in contrast to the situation in Germany, the health and welfare minister agreed not to enforce compulsory sterilization, although the compulsory sterilization clause was not deleted from the bill. The five subcategories of illnesses included hereditary mental illness, hereditary mental deficiency, severe and malignant hereditary personality disorder, severe and malignant hereditary physical ailment, and severe hereditary deformity (Matsubara 1998:191; Ōta T. 1976:319; Oguma 1995:249–250).[13] Between 1941 and 1947, 538 people (217 men and 321 women) were sterilized for eugenic reasons (Kōseishō imukyoku 1955:828).

In his account of the law's history, Ōta Tenrei noted that this radical population control policy was enforced to a fairly limited extent because after 1941 most men were on the front, and men who had remained at home were either too old or too young for reproduction (Ōta T. 1976: 159). However, considering that the majority of sterilizations during the first half of the 1940s were carried out on women and—after 1948, when the National Eugenic Law was modified and renamed the Eugenic Protection Law—sterilizations were performed almost exclusively on women (Koya 1957), Ōta's explanation is unsatisfactory. There were indeed other reasons for the limited application of the sterilization policy in Japan. Perhaps most importantly, the law ran counter to other population policies already in place. In order to achieve the strategic militarist goals of the pronatalist state, the population was to be increased by one-third, to 100 million persons, somewhat diminishing support for sterilization as a eugenic strategy. Thus enforcement of compulsory sterilization was prevented in part because of policymakers' lack of enthusiasm (Robertson 2001).

Another reason may have been the low numbers of institutionalized mentally ill and mentally retarded, who were the main targets of the law. As the most common measure was detention at the patient's home, most of them were out of psychiatric and governmental control. Moreover, after Japan's attack on Pearl Harbor in December 1941 and particularly after the devastating battle of Midway in June 1942, the war situation must have further undermined the efforts of propagators of racial hygienist policies (Matsubara 1998:191–192, 2000:179–180). The significance of the law, then, lay not in its efficiency but in its embeddedness in an entire set of measures that were based on the five propositions the Association of Racial Hygiene in the Ministry of Health and Welfare had worked out. These measures reinforced the central effect of the National Eugenic Law—not only to prevent people with certain diseases from reproducing but also to entice healthy people to reproduce frequently and to prevent them from practicing birth control and having abortions.

A system that was to promote and advise people on eugenically sound marriages had been put in place by the early 1930s. State-sponsored consultation offices for eugenic marriages (yūsei kekkon sōdansho) had been established in order to encourage members of the younger generation to marry a partner with a sound genetic makeup as early as possible. Designed to increase women's desire to bear children, another element of the policy was introduced in 1939. Families with more than ten children were given awards similar to the German Mutterkreuz, and mother-child health care policies were introduced. By August 1939, the award had been given to 23,000 families, and in 1940 alone, 10,336 families were honored. In 1942, another 2,200 families received the award. By April 1941, the Japanese government had begun to award a prize of 20 yen, a good third of many households' monthly income, for every newborn (Enjoji 1942; Wada 1993:172; Kato Toshinobu 1978:7). Despite these efforts, the net population increase in mainland Japan fell from 1.07 million in 1940 and 1.12 million in 1941 to 504,000 in 1944.[14]

In 1941, the National Eugenic Federation (Kokumin Yūsei Renmei) was established and provided with a budget that facilitated the printing of an instructive pamphlet, *Explanatory Diagram of National Eugenics*. In addition to the provisions of the law, restrictions on marriage between people with hereditary and venereal diseases also were considered but not established, due to persisting doubts among professionals about their usefulness. In 1942, the Ministry of Health and Welfare merged its National Research Institute of Population Problems (Jinkō Mondai Kenkyūjo, established in 1939) with its Welfare Division in an attempt to better research racial hygienics, psychiatry, eugenics, and eugenic policies (Matsubara 2000:178–179).

VIRILE WARRIORS, FERTILE WOMBS

Throughout the 1930s and early 1940s, the demands of the imperialist state that were powerfully expressed in pronatalist and racial hygienist population policy were echoed in popular media. Underlining the official policy of population growth and territorial expansion, popular media linked economic success to reproductive capabilities and military prowess to sexual potency. By doing so, they suggested a congruence between the empire's expansive capabilities, women's reproductive capacity, and men's sexual potency. The rigor of imperialist aggression and propaganda was curiously reflected in the propagation and marketing of products that had long been available but were now advertised as remedies that improved sexual and reproductive functioning and enhanced the health and physical fitness as well as the fighting spirit of Japanese men (*Tsūzoku Igaku* July 1942:80). In certain ways, medical advertising and imperialist propaganda refashioned the early Meiji cry for the defense of the nation through the defense of men's bodies. In a twofold move of the remilitarization of sexuality and the sexualization of war, early Shōwa ideologues as well as marketing professionals aligned (female) reproductivity and (male) sexual energy with practices of invasion, aggression, and war.

Advertisements for a great variety of hormone products began to occupy the pages of professional and nonprofessional journals and newspapers and gradually pushed aside those for contraceptives and other means of individually manageable birth control methods. The rise of pharmaceutical companies, which were interested in marketing hormonal extracts, was widely celebrated in the Japanese media and seemed to emulate Japan's militarist effort during the 1930s and early 1940s.[15] This commercialization and commodification of pronatalist ideology through potency-enhancing drugs further challenged the sexological project in ways different from both censorship and racial hygiene. Representations of commodified pronatalist ideology disrupted the authority on sexual knowledge that sexologists had claimed for themselves. Sexologists who strove to achieve what they called the "liberation of sex" from both traditional, nonscientific beliefs and state control were increasingly perceived as a threat to the colonialist and militarist state, but they also lost ground in the public arena that they had so aggressively pursued since the Taishō era.

Addressing the necessity of medically enhanced sexual potency and reproductive activity, articles and advertisements for hormone medication and "aphrodisiacs of perpetual youth" *(furō kyōseiyaku)* occupied the pages of newspapers and periodicals throughout the 1930s and early 1940s. Family and household magazines, midwifery and obstetrics-gynecology journals, and women's, popular medical, and general-interest magazines fed anxieties that the reproductive apparatus of Japanese women might be impaired, resulting in hysteria, frigidity, or infertility. Similarly, they fueled anxieties that Japanese men's genitalia might not be fully developed and that their sexual potency might be challenged by nonreproductive sexual practices, delayed marriage, and overwork. While "frigidity" was portrayed as an exclusively female problem, "hysteria" was imagined as a condition that could haunt men or women. Hence, some of these hormone extracts were recommended for consumption by both sexes.

In the imagination of medical doctors, women's circulating blood and hormones became "chemical messengers" of femininity (Rousseau 1998:259), whereas "male hormones" were marketed to improve male physical strength and heal mental fatigue as well as treat a long list of other ailments, including impotence, the decline of sexual potency, senility, loss of stamina, hysteria, and neurasthenia. In 1922, the news-

paper *Japan and the Japanese (Nihon oyobi Nihonjin)* began to run
a one-page advertisement for the hormonal product Tokkapin (*Nihon
oyobi Nihonjin* 1 May 1922: advertisement section). It appeared frequently throughout the 1920s, and other magazines and newspapers
began to advertise the same product and to print advertisements for similar hormone treatments. Pharmacies profited from selling dubious devices and hormone products named Rēben (*Tsūzoku igaku* September
1925), Oikarubin Gotō (*Tsūzoku igaku* September 1925), Tokkapin
(*Tsūzoku igaku* January 1927), Komuhorumon (*Tsūzoku igaku* March
1929), and Andorosuchin (*Tsūzoku igaku* February 1937), all of which
supposedly cured the ailments mentioned above.[16]

In its 1927 January issue, *Popular Medicine* began to run an illustrated version of the advertisement for Tokkapin (see figure 11), which
reflected some of the themes central to the times. In the illustration, a
young man with elongated legs stands in a Superman-like pose while
holding up a packet of the product. Wearing a Western-style business
suit and a bow tie, he stands on a whole pile of Tokkapin packets.
Through his legs and behind him, the readers of *Popular Medicine* had
a glimpse of the smoking chimney of a factory, in front of which a few
rickshaw men were on their way to meet customers. The young, successful, male, white-collar worker in the advertisement apparently was
able—in addition to all of his professional achievements—to strengthen
the functions of his genitalia and increase his energy in general simply
by taking Tokkapin (*Tsūzoku Igaku* January 1927). Two years later,
in its October issue, the same magazine praised healing methods for
neurasthenia, which had become an umbrella term for all of the afore-
mentioned disturbances of male (sexual) potency.[17] In 1942, the imag-
ery of hormone products that targeted a male clientele had shifted from
the faceless businessman to the warrior sporting a headband that featured the Japanese national flag, an image similar to the suicide pilot de-
pictions of the last years of World War II (*Tsūzoku Igaku* July 1942:80).
Advertisements for hormone extracts for the treatment of "sexual defects" and the "incomplete development of the genitalia" claimed that
injections and other complicated methods of treatment finally had become unnecessary. Instead, it was announced, the medical world welcomed and praised new methods of treatment for sexual neurasthenia,
the unsatisfactory development of the sexual organs, atrichia, frigidity,
apathy, and other disorders. Samples of the products could be ordered
by sending 2 sen in postage stamps to the Japanese Society for Popular

Figure 11. Advertisement featuring a man on Tokkapin tablets from the January 1927 issue of *Popular Medicine*. Used with the kind permission of the Kyōto Ika Daigaku Library.

Medicine (Nihon Tsūzoku Igakkai) in Osaka, which published *Popular Medicine* (*Tsūzoku Igaku* October 1933:156).

Some pharmacies advertised hormone products directly. A certain Shisandō Pharmacy in Tokyo, for example, sold hormone tablets that supposedly healed premature ejaculation, nocturnal emissions, frigidity, a decline in sexual desire, and a number of other disorders. Experts who were identified as medical doctors explained the "scientific" methods used in the production of the medications. They pointed out that the substance for the tablets was extracted scientifically from the genital glands of healthy bulls, and claimed that the results of recent research in internal medicine showed the efficiency of the hormone in the treatment of sexual neurasthenia. Others claimed that the treatment was successful for improving an unsatisfactory sex life.

In numerous similar advertisements, physicians described the successful treatment of (typically married) men who felt incapable of having a satisfactory sex life. The advertisements' texts commonly pointed out that the medication did not cause dependency, and one can imagine that those who could afford it might have taken more than the recommended number of tablets, eventually spending a small fortune. The products were sold at exorbitantly high prices and hormone treatment was a luxury for most customers. At a time when the monthly income of a middle-class household was 60–70 yen and many worker households had to scrape by with less than 50 yen (Okuda 1925; Ishimoto 1935; Shinohara 1967), the monthly supply of hormone tablets cost between 4.5 and 7 yen (*Tsūzoku Igaku* August 1933:124, January 1938:114).

Hormone products that supposedly enhanced sexual potency and physical strength and that cured sexual malfunctions commonly targeted a male clientele. While sexual intercourse between men and women was rarely mentioned explicitly, many advertisements featured a woman's face or other parts of a woman's body, suggesting why nocturnal emission, premature ejaculation, neurasthenic ailments, or impotence should be cured. Images of female body parts, a suggestively lifted skirt, provocatively crossed bare legs, or a woman's smiling face represented an imaginary sexual counterpart. These images also reinforced the twofold message implicit in the texts, namely that nonreproductive sex was a waste of energy, and that men's sexual desire was to be shared with women (see figures 12, 13, and 14).

The market for hormone-based products that targeted women may have been even larger than that for products for men. By the mid-1930s, hormone-based cosmetic products such as tonics and creams *(horumon keishōsui)* promising to rejuvenate female facial skin hit the advertisement sections of women's magazines (see, e.g., *Shinjoen* March 1937: 99; *Fujin Kōron* March 1935:32 and advertisement section). However, magazines frequently also advertised medication for menstrual irregularity, infertility, hysteria, and frigidity, among other female physical

Figure 12. Androstin (Andorosuchin in Japanese) was just one of many hormone products that were advertised in magazines and newspapers from the late 1920s onward. This advertisement is from the March 1937 issue of *Popular Medicine*. Used with the kind permission of the Kyōto Ika Daigaku Library.

Figure 13. Advertisement for Chireorupin from the December 1933 issue of *Popular Medicine*. The text advertises Chireorupin as a treatment for sexual neurasthenia, premature ejaculation, nocturnal emissions, and a number of other sexual problems. Used with the kind permission of the Kyōto Ika Daigaku Library.

impairments. In these magazines at least, medical doctors were preoccupied with married women's sexual functioning almost exclusively in the context of ensuring their reproductive capabilities, thus reinforcing earlier claims of the uterus as a vehicle of empire building. Medical encyclopedias for home use perhaps best represent this attitude. Such encyclopedias were frequently distributed to the middle- and upper-class readers of women's magazines. Supplements to the widely read magazine *Women's Club (Fujin Kurabu)* included the *Hygiene Reader for Women* and the *Medical Household Encyclopedia for Nursing and*

Figure 14. Advertisement for Bunpirēshon from the April 1937 issue of *Popular Medicine*. Among other things, the advertisement promises that Bunpirēshon will cure "premature ejaculation caused by neurasthenia that has resulted from masturbation during youth." Used with the kind permission of the Kyōto Ika Daigaku Library.

Healing in 1933 and 1937, respectively. In 1937, the *Hygiene Reader for Daughters, Wives, and Mothers* was distributed to the readers of the *Housewife's Companion (Shufu no Tomo)*. And in 1934, *Women's Club* subscribers received such a book with the June issue, a supplement of more than 400 pages entitled *Household Medical Encyclopedia for Nursing and Healing Methods (Kango to ryōhō: Katei iten)*.[18]

The authors of the encyclopedia were medical doctors, some of whom served as consultants to advice columns in popular medical journals and household magazines. The encyclopedia contained sections on all kinds of medical fields and health problems, which included but were not limited to pediatrics, the cerebral nerve system, dermatology, urology, obstetrics and gynecology, nursing at home, hygiene for girls, and hygiene in matrimony.[19] In the section on hygiene in matrimony *(kekkon eisei)*, a husband's excessive sexual desire was discussed as a problem wives might have to deal with. Takeuchi Shigeyo, a prominent and politically influential medical doctor and eugenicist, outlined several scenarios.[20] As most women married late, Takeuchi suggested, unbalanced sexual needs might be less common than they had been previously. However, if it turned out that a wife was simply too small physically for her husband, she could not be helped but might have to introduce a mistress to him. Takeuchi emphasized that both partners should share their sexual satisfaction and that a woman should not accept her husband's pleasure while not feeling any herself. Takeuchi also alerted her readers to worry about suffering from frigidity if a lack of sexual pleasure on their side became permanent. Frigidity would be diagnosed if the woman had not felt any sexual pleasure from the very beginning of her relationship or if she had become ill and ceased to have sexual feelings (Takeuchi S. 1934:401).

Takeuchi noted that among the causes of frigidity were anatomical problems, uterine infections, less than fully developed sexual organs, and severe nervous diseases. The pain caused by these ailments would psychologically influence the relationship between husband and wife, eventually resulting in the wife's frigidity. If the husband regularly reached climax before his wife did, this condition also was to be diagnosed as a form of the wife's frigidity. In any of these cases, frigidity would harm the relationship; therefore Takeuchi urged readers of the encyclopedia to see a doctor immediately if they suffered from any of these symptoms. Sexual satisfaction was considered important for both partners, not for pleasure's sake, but because it was believed to have if not a decisive, at least a positive impact on conception and reproduction.

Hence, the enhancement of physical strength and in particular of male virility and female sexual functioning would guarantee successful marital relations, leading to frequent pregnancies and births and, by implication, a prosperous, powerful empire (Takeuchi S. 1934:401–402).[21]

ENDURING LEGACIES OF THE
COLONIAL RULING APPARATUS OF SEX

The aggressively pronatalist tone was quickly dropped from the pages of popular medical journals and other publications after the end of World War II, but strains of eugenic thinking about the human body, health, and sexuality were reinforced during the 1950 and 1960s and have proved relatively resilient to radical changes ever since. Despite important legal changes made after World War II, eugenic thought and practice continued to govern decisions by physicians and potential parents. The wartime sterilization legislation and other pronatalist efforts were partly abolished and the law was renamed the Eugenic Protection Law (Yūsei hogo hō) in 1948.[22] Women were no longer "coerced to bear children" *(shussan o kyōyō)*, but sterilizations still could be performed by order of a physician even if the concerned person and/or her or his partner disagreed with the physician's verdict (Date 1951b:42; Muramatsu 1955, 1960). Other components, such as discouraging the transmission of "bad genes" to offspring, remained intact as well.

According to Article 14 of the revised law, a woman seeking an abortion qualified if she or her spouse had a mental illness, mental deficiency, psychopathic disorder, hereditary physical ailment, or hereditary deformity; if a blood relative within the fourth degree of consanguinity to the woman in question or that woman's spouse had a hereditary mental illness, hereditary mental deficiency, hereditary psychopathic disorder, hereditary physical ailment, or hereditary physical deformity; if either spouse suffered from leprosy; if the continuation of pregnancy or childbirth was likely to seriously harm the mother's health, directly or indirectly (i.e., by reducing her economic status); and if pregnancy resulted from rape due to assault, coercion, or an inability to offer resistance or refusal (Norgren 1998:61–62, 2001:149).

Eugenic concepts also reappeared in popular household literature of the 1950s. According to instructive hygiene literature of the 1950s such as the *Hygiene Encyclopedia for Daughters, Wives, and Mothers (Musume to tsuma to haha no eisei hyakka zenshū)*, for example, the ideal woman had to fulfill four criteria. She was supposed to be "healthy, equipped with a well-developed body, free of bad genes, and able to raise children and manage a household" (Date 1951b:28).[23] Echoing wartime notions of "eugenic marriages," a medical doctor explained in the same encyclopedia that "it was known that maternal genes were more influential than paternal ones for the development of a child. Bluntly put," he explained that "this is because at the beginning the maternal body and the child are one. Genes can be carriers of diseases—most importantly, mental diseases, but of all kinds of other diseases as well. They are difficult to detect but if many relatives [of a potential spouse] suffer from certain diseases one had better reconsider marrying this person" (Date 1951b:30).

Between 1949 and 1959 the numbers of sterilizations soared, reaching 340,580. Of those sterilizations, 97 percent were performed on women (Koya 1961:136). The data on sterilizations were collected by several state institutions and analyzed by, among others, Koya Yoshio, one of the leaders of the Association of Racial Hygiene during World War II. Now engaging in research on family planning, Koya continued his career as a professor of public health at Nihon University and began a new one as president of the Family Planning Federation of Japan.[24]

His data clearly indicated that far from being abandoned, eugenic legislation and thought were tremendously powerful in the immediate postwar period, in a sense completing rather than obstructing that strain of the colonization of sex. He was careful, however, to point out in 1957 that only about 5 percent of sterilizations were carried out for "eugenic reasons," whereas roughly half were performed for "medical reasons" (a threat to the woman's life), and the other half for "health reasons" (the risk of a decrease in the woman's health). Moreover, he suggested that many more sterilizations might have occurred illegally and estimated that the actual number of sterilizations may have exceeded a million (Koya 1957).[25]

In the early 1970s, organizations of people with disabilities began to openly criticize the eugenic legislation as national-socialist, but it was not until the 1990s that a revision movement finally succeeded. A portion of the law was altered and in 1996 it was renamed the Maternal Body Protection Law (Botai hogōhō).[26] Sterilization now can be performed only with a woman's consent and the consent of her spouse, if there is one; and instead of being governed primarily by a national health policy, decisions about sterilizations are now largely individualized (Norgren 1998:74; Matsubara 2000:231). As Matsubara Yōko's ongoing research attests, eugenic thinking and practice, among physicians who perform sterilizations and abortions as well as among potential parents who agree to them, have been firmly established.

Censorship proved similarly resilient to abrupt changes. It was not only carried on by the occupation forces but also by those who managed to continue their careers in the postwar era by sanitizing their murky personal prewar and wartime history. Omnipresent to his death in 1956, Nagai Hisomu (1954:23) declared in *Marital Life (Fūfu Seikatsu)* that love was important for a marriage and that sexual love had to be "properly practiced and properly enjoyed." Forgotten seemed the days when he had preached that producing offspring was the primary purpose of marriage and had promoted the rapid growth of the Japanese population and the sterilization of people classified as "unfit." It goes without saying, then, that in 1952, when Nagai founded the Japanese Association for Sexology (Nihon Seigakkai), the earlier sex research he had opposed as harmful to "true science" and the sex researchers he had denounced as charlatans were utterly ignored (Akagawa 1999:281). In 1950, Nagai and Andō Kakuichi had translated into Japanese the book *Sexual Behavior in the Human Male* (1938) by Alfred Kinsey, Wardell B. Pomeroy, and Clyde E. Martin, and had established themselves as Japan's experts of sexology without a past (Shinozaki 1954a:168).[27]

As early as 1954, Shinozaki Nobuo claimed that occupation-era censorship had firmly driven sexologists into the realm of popular journals. "In the past," Shinozaki explained, "we attempted to publish our work in scholarly journals but were denied access. One cannot help the fact that because sex research focuses on the relations of men and women, an air of eroticism will always surround it . . . . However, our discussions are not only about 'married life' but are closely tied to social and psychological aspects as well" (Shinozaki 1954a:169). The author of the first major sex survey of married couples, *The Sex Life of the Japanese (Nihonjin no seiseikatsu,* 1953), and a public health policy official in the Ministry of Health and Social Welfare, Shinozaki was one of many postwar sexologists who valued and represented links between individual sexologists and state agencies. He had first entered the University of Tokyo to study mathematics and anthropology in 1935 and had graduated in 1941. In 1943, he was employed by the Ministry of Social Welfare and in 1946 transferred to the Institute of Population Problems in the same ministry.

Shinozaki began a series of state-sponsored, large-scale sex surveys of married couples that still dominate sex research carried out by state agencies today, but he also founded a Study Group of Sexual Problems

(Shinozaki 1954a), provided marriage counseling (Shinozaki 1954b), wrote factual articles in household encyclopedias and women's magazines about abortion, contraception, and eugenic policies (Shinozaki and Moriyama 1952), and continued his studies of population and family planning problems until his retirement (Shinozaki 1978). In contrast to prewar sexologists who saw the state as enemy of a "liberated sexuality," this postwar generation of administrators of sex set out "to free Japan of the militarist suppression" of sex in order to allow research and education on sexual matters (see, e.g., Kaneko 1955:67–94). Yamamoto Sugi (1954:231) and Kanzaki Suzushi are other examples of the type of sex expert who authored articles on sexual matters in women's and household magazines. Yamamoto Sugi was a medical doctor, a representative of the Council for Purity Education in the Ministry of Education, and president of the Japanese Motherhood Federation (Nihon Bosei Renmeikai). Kanzaki served the Japanese state as a member of the Council for the Social Welfare of Children in the Ministry of Health and Welfare.[28] Several bureaucratic units in the new government quickly set out to ground the new liberties, and the postwar sex surveyors became agents of the state who contributed to containing the new, supposedly liberated sexuality.

In 1947, the Ministry of Education published a first paper on what the authors termed "purity education" *(junketsu kyōiku)*. Two years later, the ministry had established the Council for Purity Education (Junketsu Kyōiku Iinkai) in its Bureau of Social Education, which published a *Basic Outline of Purity Education (Junketsu kyōiku kihon yōkō)*. The Council for Purity Education consisted of twenty-four members, including representatives of the Women's Christian Temperance Union, social critics, university professors, teachers, feminists, medical doctors, and officials from the Ministry of Education and the Ministry of Health and Social Welfare (Akagawa 1999:412, footnote 3). In 1955, the council published the *Draft for the Promotion of Purity Education (Junketsu kyōiku no shian)*. Its core item was the teaching of abstinence before marriage (Saotome et al. 1953). Although this is not explicit in the text, historian Kameyama Michiko (Kameyama 1997 [1984]:241) has suggested that the new purity education was primarily, if not explicitly, directed at girls.

Sex research was taken up again almost immediately after the end of World War II, and new sexological organizations and journals fell back on old techniques of slipping through the network of censorship the occupation forces had established. *Married Life,* for example, a magazine mainly written by the members of a new Study Group for Sexual Problems, printed on its cover that the journal was not supposed to be sold to minors, even though it should have been clear from its title that its approach to sexual matters was strictly confined to wedlock and—from the authors' names—that its agenda was educational rather than entertaining. Among the most prominent contributors to the magazine was Ōta Tenrei, who remained critical of the immediate postwar condemnation of premarital sex, declaring repeatedly that if both partners agreed, premarital sex should be tolerated. Just as he had done numerous times during the 1930s, in *Married Life* he explained the functioning of the Ōta-Ring or spiral, his invention (Ōta T. 1954a). He noted the importance of breast care (Ōta T. 1954b) and was also one of the first sexologists who pursued the transition from a fixation on the uterus to a new interest in female sexual sentiments and their relationship to the clitoris and orgasm (Ōta 1954c, 1955; see also Chichibu 1952; *Fūfu Seikatsu* 1954; Hashizume 1954; Akagawa 1999:317–318, 323).

Changes in sex education were accompanied by an increasing number of large-scale sex research projects. Only three years after Japan's surrender, the zoologist Asayama Shin'ichi began to compile data on the sexual behavior and attitudes of both male and female students. His surveys were explicitly modeled on Yamamoto and Yasuda's questionnaire method of the early 1920s. In an attempt to understand the impact of war on eighteen- to twenty-two-year-old youth, he directed about thirty questions at 693 students from six different high schools for boys and 283 students from five girls' schools in the Kansai area. Asayama's questionnaire included questions on experiences with the other sex, the respondents' current sex life, the first occurrence of sexual feelings, seasonal changes in sexual feelings, changes in sexual feelings in the course of a day, masturbation, nocturnal emission, menstruation, venereal diseases, contraception, homosexuality as sexual fantasy, influence of the war on sex life, sex education, coeducation, and perceptions of an ideal sex life.[29]

A professor at Osaka Municipal University, Asayama was the first Japanese sexologist to survey boys and girls. He found that girls realized their subordinate status most of all in sexual relationships and thus suffered from "men's egoism" *(dansei no egoizumu)* and "society's irrationality" *(shakai no fugōri).* Asayama wished his book to be a source for everyone and particularly for youths themselves, and for educators

Figure 15. The April 1949 issue of the magazine *Marital Sex Life*
(Fūfu no Seiseikatsu) offered guidance on perfect sexual love for married couples and an abundance of erotic stories, now almost exclusively illustrated by figures with Caucasian looks.

and parents and those in charge of social policies. "In order that daughters not be hurt, future wives become happy, and sexuality really liberated, we must make an effort to change our society at large," Asayama
wrote. Even these major changes, however, would not suffice. He declared similarly important the improvement of the economic situation of

young men and the revolutionizing of the economic structure in order to encourage and enable young men to get married (Asayama 1949:255). Just as Yamamoto and Yasuda almost thirty years earlier, Asayama forcefully promoted the idea of education as the basis for social change and reform and insisted on the social, economic, and political conditionality of sexual behavior. He too continued his research with ever-increasing numbers of respondents. Okada Enji, a researcher at the Yokohama Pedagogical Institute (Yokohama Kyōiku Kenkyūjo), conducted a five-year survey on *Sexual Knowledge during Puberty (Shishunki no seichishiki)* in which he found what he classified as a shocking lack of sexual knowledge among middle and high school students.[30]

In addition to Asayama's, Okada's, and other individual researchers' studies, learned societies ranging from the Japanese Association for Sexology to the Japan Hygiene Statistics Association conducted their own surveys. In 1953, for example, a group of researchers from the Japan Hygiene Statistics Association classified sex education of teenagers as a huge and serious problem (Saotome et al. 1953:30). The group had found that about a fifth of their respondents did not know what the word "sex" meant, while another fifth did not know how children came into being. The lack of sexual knowledge was more glaring among rural youth than urban youth and sex education and sex research seemed more necessary then ever (Saotome et al. 1953:30).[31]

Scarcely ten years after the end of World War II, Shinozaki Nobuo noted that during the previous ten years the first stage of sex research had been overcome and the second step had been made due to the efforts of the Study Group for Sexual Problems (Seimondai Kenkyūkai) (Shinozaki 1954a:168). The Study Group became the mother organization of the Japanese Association for Sexology (Nihon Seigakkai), founded in 1952 by Nagai Hisomu (Shinozaki 1954a:169; see also Akagawa 1999: 281). The goals of the study group included research on sexual issues, the development of measures for achieving a "wholesome" sexual life, sexual morals, and sex education and contributions to the welfare of humanity *(jinrui fukushi)*.

Among the members of the study group were professors from Shōwa Medical University, the Japan College of Economy, Keiō University, the University of Tokyo, Japan University, and the Osaka Municipal University. Non-academic members included the director of the Yoshiwara Hospital, police officials, middle school principals, officials from the Council for Children's Welfare in the Ministry of Health and Welfare, the director of the Institute of Population Problems, an editor of the

Yomiuri Shinbun, and a representative from the Council for Purity Education in the Ministry of Education (Shinozaki 1954a:169).

Through these channels, processes of achieving a "colonial ruling apparatus" of sex and sexuality continued into the immediate postwar era. Perhaps the ties between the administrators of sex and sexuality in the ministries of education and welfare and sexologists in educational and research institutions, have never been as close as in the postwar era. In contrast to Yamamoto Senji, Ōta Tenrei, and other sexologists who had been associated with the Left and had positioned themselves at a distance from direct governmental control, sexologists after World War II explicitly linked the state and citizens' organizations, thus blurring the boundaries between them.

Epilogue

[E]xpectations of sex education tend to be deeply rooted in
moralism and puritanism and bear the danger of retrogress-
ing history. . . . The kind of sex education we envision is
basically directed at wiping out sexual prejudices that have
emerged in Japanese history and at positively establishing
a rich sexuality as "human sexuality" [English in original]
grounded in human life, and at fostering the power to build
fruitful human relations anew. Based on gender equality
guaranteed in the constitution and in educational legislation,
this sex education is also permeated with esteem for science
and humanity.

Council for Education and Research on
"Humans and Sex/Sexuality," manifesto

In Japan, scholarly interest in sexual difference and in sexual practice
and its connection to health and a long life has a history that reaches
back at least to the beginning of the Tokugawa era (see, e.g., Shimizu
1989). Yet the sexual science that arose at the beginning of the twentieth century was more than simply another chapter in that history. It was
distinctive in a number of ways. In the first place, it attempted to be far
more precise and empirical than anything that had preceded it. In addition, it was able to draw on new developments in science and medicine:
obstetrics and gynecology were emerging fields. Sociology, anthropology, psychology, and pedagogy had just been founded. And a new biology had begun to turn away from a classificatory and descriptive natural history to embrace the comprehensive study of the living organism,
whether vegetable, animal, or human.

By the 1950s, most of the elements that had created a sexual science and continued to make sexual knowledge were in place. Vast social
change was to come. Before and since, potentially explosive subjects have

often involved sexual matters—debates about Viagra and the pill, HIV and sex education, or new types of prostitution. But the ways of making sexual knowledge, the attempts at administering sex and sexuality, and the emphasis on a hardly questioned heteronormativity have not been subject to major conceptual changes comparable to those that took place during the first half of the twentieth century. Recent conflicts, in fact, in many ways both reflect and reiterate earlier discursive procedures over sex and sexuality, power, and knowledge. This epilogue serves to highlight those reiterations in order to demonstrate the enduring power of the colonial ruling apparatus of sex.

MALE ANXIETIES

On 27 March 1998, the American Food and Drug Administration approved a new anti-impotence drug named Sildenafil. The pill for erectile dysfunction is to be taken an hour before sex and only once during a twenty-four-hour period. It creates the release of certain chemicals in the penis that cause muscle tissue in the organ to relax, thereby increasing blood flow in the area and allowing an erection to occur when the man is stimulated. Public response was so great that the drug, better known under the trade name Viagra, quickly took control of more than 94 percent of the anti-impotence drug market, resulting in 120,000 prescriptions in its second week alone. Physicians in the United States claimed that no medical breakthrough had generated so much excitement since the approval of the birth control pill. American medical officials predicted that what some called "the most promising impotence treatment ever" would outpace even the antidepressant drug Prozac to become the top-selling prescription drug of all time (Leavy 1998).

Exploring its potential market in Japan, Pfizer, the pharmaceutical company that produces the drug, confirmed that in Japan, just as in the United States, hundreds of thousands of men suffer from impotence. Throughout 1998, however, Pfizer's representatives in Japan remained pessimistic about a quick approval of Viagra, due to Japan's lengthy drug testing procedure. According to Japanese law, a new drug first must be tested on animals as well as clinically tested on Japanese citizens. Once the results have been submitted to the secretive and male-dominated Central Pharmaceutical Affairs Council in the Ministry of Health and Welfare, it typically takes another two years for government screening to be completed (Amaha 1998; Ueda 1998).

The media hype surrounding Viagra in the United States, however, immediately spilled over into Japan. By the fall of 1998, debates about Viagra's implications for male sexual performance in particular and sexual relationships in general had begun to surface in a great number of Japanese general-interest magazines, as well as in specialized publications (see, e.g., *Gendai* 1998).[1] By early 1999, readers' questions about the use of Viagra had become common in sexual advice columns and frequently appeared interspersed with questions about other common problems such as abortion, extramarital relations, "compensated dating," "abnormal sex," and techniques to reach climax (see, e.g., *Gendai* 1999).

Anticipating a delayed approval of the drug, some Japanese men found ways to circumvent the law and acquire the anti-impotence drug almost immediately after Viagra became available for sale in the United States. A Japanese travel agency, for example, put together tours to Hawaii for men who wanted to buy the drug. The participants—typically men in their fifties—needed to get blood tests from a Japanese physician before leaving. The results were faxed to a physician in Hawaii, who then prescribed the drug. The travel agency offered these tours for $640 (90,000 yen), in addition to $600 for the consultation, prescription, and the first bottle of thirty Viagra tablets (Amaha 1998; Henderson 1998).

In addition to these tours, Japanese men who wanted to use Viagra immediately turned to the internet, where black market dealers offered the drug for double or triple the U.S. price (Amaha 1998; Tashiro and Macintyre 1998; Yamauchi K. 1998; *Asahi Shinbun* 2001). Yet another alternative came from a Los Angeles–based doctor who held American and Japanese medical licenses. He set up a branch in Tokyo and visited every few months to deliver a supply of Viagra. (Bringing drugs back to Japan from the United States is legal, but only if they are for personal use [Amaha 1998; Tashiro and Macintyre 1998].) However, by September 1998, an estimated two hundred Japanese drugstores had begun to sell "individually imported" Viagra pills. These pills were sold on the basis of customers' "personal judgment" rather than a medical examination. Subsequently, media reports claimed that one Tokyo-based drugstore alone had sold more than three thousand bottles of thirty pills each within eight weeks. Men who had tried Viagra were quoted as saying that they would never again fall back on the flourishing market for indigenous Japanese health tonics and aphrodisiacs and other "cures" for impotence such as injection therapy and vacuum pumps (Tashiro and Macintyre 1998; Ōshima and Toyama 1998; Eardley 1998).

In Japan, doctors soon became concerned about the uncontrolled distribution and unsupervised use of Viagra (Ueda 1998).[2] The chairman of the Japanese Association for Sexual Functioning (Nihon Sei Kinō Gakkai), for example, acknowledged that impotence was a condition that should be treated, but he also pointed out that Japanese men lacked understanding of the drug and tended to overestimate its power to improve their sexual relationships (Shirai Masafumi, quoted in Ōshima and Toyama 1998). Ten months after its initial introduction in the United States, Viagra was approved in Japan.

The speedy government approval on 27 January 1999, just six months after an application had been submitted to the Central Pharmaceutical Affairs Council, not only surprised Viagra producer Pfizer but also drew widespread protest from various groups that had long fought for the legalization of the contraceptive pill. Ironically, the unusually rapid approval of Viagra eventually prompted an end to the ban on the low-dose contraceptive pill for women on 22 June 1999. Defending their decision, Japanese health officials argued that Viagra's speedy approval was necessary due to the growing health risks posed by unsupervised illegal imports. They also insisted that the two drugs—Viagra and the pill—should not be compared. Viagra is prescribed to treat an ailment, they argued, whereas the low-dose pill is a contraceptive option for healthy women (Watts 1999).

Critics of the Health and Welfare Ministry countered that the approval of oral contraceptives had been delayed due to concerns about morality, sexually transmitted diseases, and health risks—concerns which were all equally applicable to Viagra. Many also noted that Viagra led to 130 deaths worldwide in one year, whereas the low-dose contraceptive pill had been used safely by hundreds of millions of women for decades. The stark contrast in the treatment of an anti-impotence drug for men and the contraceptive pill for women sparked an uproar that prompted women's groups to accuse the government of sexism. In contrast to the pill, Viagra was approved so quickly that guidelines for the sale of the drug were still in the process of being determined (Watts 1999:819).

Since the late 1960s, Japanese health officials indeed had continued to cite fears about the destruction of the nation's sexual morals, the below-replacement-level birth rate, a reduction in condom use at a time when AIDS prevention was considered a top health policy priority, and even environmental harm from hormones.[3] The debate seemed strikingly similar to a much earlier one, when, from the 1920s through the late

1940s, authorities tolerated the sale of potency enhancing drugs but adamantly refused to legalize means of birth control.

The Viagra debate revealed male anxieties that were similar in many ways to those from the past, but it also differed in important respects. Potency enhancing drugs and treatments from the imperialist era had seemed to reinforce the state's military prowess and at the same time had appeared to help in the fight against the perceived degeneration of the Japanese "race" believed to have been caused by industrialization and modernization. The recent dispute about Viagra and erectile dysfunction, however, seemed to highlight a different kind of male anxiety. The debate about Viagra versus the pill was not simply about the threatening decline in male virility or the availability of two different kinds of drugs; it also highlighted the still unbalanced power relations in matters of control over sexuality and reproduction. In Japan (and elsewhere), erections have been presented as understandable and manipulable in and of themselves, separated from person or script or relationship.[4] A discourse of vascular processes—blood flow into the penis, trapping mechanisms in the penis, venous outflow—has taken over. While one expects women to occupy an essential place in the discourse—the need for vaginal penetration being the justification for the entire enterprise— women are only present in terms of universalized vaginal needs; their actual desires and opinions are conveniently invisible (Tiefer 1994: 374).

The immediate success of Viagra and the struggle to legalize the pill reflect several of the larger issues discussed throughout this book. The imbalance between the rapid handling of what was associated with male sexual needs and potency—reminiscent of wartime notions of a virile and militarist manhood—and the hesitant dealing with women's desire to increase their control over their own sexuality and bodies appears surprisingly constant historically, especially considering the major social changes that have taken place between the two instances.

In contrast to Viagra, the pill has had a much more complicated history in Japan. While the low-dose contraceptive pill has remained contested, high- and medium-dose pills have been prescribed legally for menstrual disorders since the 1950s. Many Japanese women—their numbers were estimated in 1996 at 500,000 to 800,000—have misused these "therapeutic" high-dose progestins for purposes of contraception (Maruyama, Raphael, and Djerassi 1996; Henderson 1999a; Hollander 1999). The legalization of the high-dose pill for contraceptive purposes was first discussed in 1965, but it remained illegal because juridical authorities were worried about its impact on female sexual morale. Moreover, among the Japanese public the fear has remained that the pill might cause unwelcome side effects, such as those detected from the use of earlier versions of the pill during the 1960s and 1970s. After repeated failure to achieve approval for the high-dose pill in the 1970s, various women's groups and family planning organizations pushed for legalization of a low-dose pill. In 1986, the Ministry of Health and Welfare created a set of regulations for the legalization of a low-dose pill, which was tested up until 1992.

Despite the fact that no side effects could be proven to occur, the Central Pharmaceutical Affairs Council again renewed the ban on the pill. This time, officials pointed out that condoms have been the contraceptive method used most often and argued that "legalization of the pill may make people believe that the pill can prevent an AIDS infection" (see Marumoto 1995).[5] Indeed, about 75 percent of respondents in surveys on sexual behavior choose condoms as their primary contraception method. Half of them, however, also use *coitus interruptus* (Imamura, Unno, and Ishimaru 1990:670; Inoue und Ehara 1995:69).[6] Moreover, according to the results of studies on the sexual behavior of youth in present-day Japan, contraceptives are used in only about half of the sexual encounters of Japanese youth, which partly explains the increase in teenage pregnancy and abortion in recent years (Hara 1996:80).

Under the pressure of proponents of the pill, the Central Pharmaceutical Affairs Council again began experiments with a low-dose pill in 1996. Finally, the Council agreed to legalize the pill. Pill producers, physicians, clinics, and women continued to wait, however, as removal of the ban was further delayed. While the pill had been available to most women in the rest of the industrialized world for nearly four decades, Japan was the only country in the United Nations with a ban on the pill. Feminist groups and other organizations that had been fighting for the legalization of the pill concluded that physicians lobbied for the continued prohibition of the pill because they made about 1 billion yen per year providing abortions. According to official figures, about 400,000 abortions are performed annually in Japan; however, the Asia-Pacific Center and other experts on reproductive health suggest that this number would have to be tripled or even quadrupled in order to reflect the actual number of abortions per year, which would mean that half of all pregnancies are terminated by an abortion (Maruyama, Raphael, and Djerassi 1996; *Economist* 1997:71).

Other critics argued that family planning is held firmly in the hands of the rubber industry, represented by an influential lobby in the Ministry of Health and Welfare, which would suffer major losses if the pill were legalized. Since the approval of the pill, in fact, condom companies indeed have become anxious about their profits. Anticipating profit loss, Okamoto, the world's largest condom maker, has announced that it will make its product up to 20 percent thinner—even though Japanese condoms are already considered the most "sensitive" in the world (*Newsweek* 1999).

The rapid approval of Viagra also has raised suspicions of a secret nationalist agenda to boost the population, which is aging faster than any other society in the world due to the negative-growth birth rate. "The drug that lets you get pregnant is approved, but the one that would prevent pregnancy is not," lawmaker Fukushima Mizuho told reporters after the approval of Viagra. "The Japanese government is doing everything possible to increase the birth rate" (Fukushima Mizuho, quoted in Watts 1999:819). It may be unlikely that the anti-impotence drug will have a measurable impact on the birth rate, but Japan's declining birth rate has indeed been a topic of concern for the architects of social welfare and health policies. By the end of the 1980s, the birth rate of 1.59 children per woman between the ages of fifteen and forty-nine had begun to alarm politicians and the media. By 2001, the rate had further decreased, to 1.33. The low birth rate usually is explained by three factors: men and women are marrying at a later age; women are older when they have their first child; and the number of women and men who remain unmarried and choose to remain childless is increasing.

This demographic development has been addressed frequently by officials since the latter half of the 1980s, when the aging of its society, and thus the question of the sustainability of its social welfare system, was declared to be one of Japan's most pressing social problems.[7] In March 1990, then–Prime Minister Kaifu said quite blatantly that the stagnating birth rate would cause a number of problems concerning the future of the country. "Looking into the future," he claimed, "we must encourage our youth to have children" (see Arioka 1990). The president of the Federation of Economic Organizations (Keidanren) went a step further, urging Japanese men to spend less time playing golf and Mahjong and instead spend more time attending to their wives (see Arioka 1990). Many officials share this view. Most women, however, see things differently. The vast majority of women consider the process of conceiving, bearing, and raising a child to be a personal matter and do not see any reason why they should adapt their attitude and behavior to the government's concerns (Arioka 1990:52).[8]

How and if the pill will facilitate women's stance and decision-making remains to be seen, as the results of studies conducted during the 1990s on projected pill use vary considerably. While sociologists Ogawa Naohiro and Robert D. Retherford report that their study shows 13 percent of women favor the pill over all other contraceptives (a number which would be only insignificantly lower than the percentage of actual pill users in North America and Northern and Western Europe), biannual national surveys on family planning conducted by the *Mainichi Shinbun* identify only 7 percent of women as potential pill users (Ogawa and Retherford 1991:378; Kitamura K. 1999:44).[9] In the latter study, 54 percent of the respondents said they would not want to use the pill, 35 percent were undecided and 4 percent did not answer the question.

Among those who answered that they would not use the pill, 70 percent were worried about side effects. Others said that they were satisfied with their current method. Almost 33 percent reasoned that by using the pill instead of condoms or withdrawal, women would end up bearing the burden of contraception. They also noted that the pill did not prevent an infection with HIV. About 10 percent felt that taking a pill every day was too cumbersome, and another 10 percent replied that the pelvic examination needed for the pill prescription would be too much trouble (Kitamura K. 1999:44). Among the two main reasons for a positive attitude toward the pill were its high degree of effectiveness and the control it allows women to maintain over contraception. Other welcome aspects include the fact that the pill does not interrupt sexual intercourse; that it prevents women from having to resort to abortion; that it has no major side effects; and that the method already has demonstrated its success in other countries (Kitamura K. 1999:44).

Proponents of the legalization of the low-dose contraceptive pill attribute the ambivalent attitudes of Japanese women to the legal situation prior to 1999 and widespread ignorance about the pill among the Japanese public, including medical professionals and women of reproductive age. As if echoing the birth control activists' claims during the 1920s and 1930s, a Tokyo grassroots group called the Professional Women's Coalition for Sexuality and Health, which has been pushing for the pill's approval, stated that in Japan, doctors and nurses have almost no knowledge about modern contraception methods (Henderson 1999b). Kitamura Kunio, director of the Family Planning Clinic of the Japanese Family Planning Association, also argued that an enormous educational campaign about the low-dose pill would be necessary in order to establish it as an acceptable alternative to other contraceptive methods and abortion (Kitamura K. 1999:44).

This campaign clearly would need to reach not only professional clinics and women's homes, but also the classrooms of the younger generation. High school sex education, or rather "education for the prevention of AIDS" *(eizu yobō kyōiku)*, as it has been called since the late 1980s, has been characterized by an emphasis on reproduction rather than contraception (thus suggesting that the production of children is the main purpose of sex), by an implicit emphasis on heteronormativity (thus neglecting or discouraging homosexuality and other sexualities), and by the language of a potentially dangerous sexuality (suggesting that sex can lead to sexually transmitted diseases and AIDS). Although in 1965 the Ministry of Education replaced "purity education" with "guidance in sexual matters" *(sei ni kan sure shidō)* or "sex education" *(seikyōiku)* in its documents, teachers have continued to describe the main aim of sex as reproduction within the boundaries of marriage.[10] Emphasizing the importance of premarital abstinence, teachers tend to classify sex as socially unacceptable for high school students.[11] Thus, in the classrooms of middle and high schools, contraception is hardly mentioned and abortion is presented as a sometimes unavoidable, if sorrowful, outcome of teenage pregnancy (Kawahara 1996:143–152).[12]

DISTRUST IN NUMBERS

This conservative approach seems rather mismatched with the actual sexual behavior and attitudes toward sex among Japanese youth, which has caused alarm among educators who have begun to detect a continuing trend toward the "increasingly early age at which youth have their first sexual experiences" and the general "disarray of sex" (Hara 1996:80).

Following the individual sex surveys from the immediate postwar period—modeled on the pioneering efforts of prewar sexologists—government agencies, news corporations, and educational organizations began to undertake large-scale surveys of 3,000 to 5,000 Japanese youth.[13] These surveys frequently have been carried out by large newspapers, the prime minister's office, the Japan Broadcasting Corporation, and the Japan Association for Sex Education (founded in 1974 by the Ministry of Education). All of these organizations consider the age at which Japanese youth have their first sexual intercourse to be a crucial marker of changes in sexual behavior and attitudes among members of the younger generation.

About half of the respondents of a 1983 survey carried out by the prime minister's office found premarital coitus acceptable within the boundaries of a "deep love relationship," while more than 20 percent rejected premarital sex regardless of emotional circumstances (Naikaku sōri daijin kanbō kōhōshitsu 1983:568). As for the "preservation of virginity" *(junketsu o tamotsu),* which had been highly valued up to the 1970s, girls in the 1980s did not seem to care as much about it as their parents might have expected them to. A survey among 4,000 female high school students from 1984 revealed that most of them ascribed diminishing importance to the "preservation of virginity" until marriage (Yomiuri shinbun shakaibu 1984:91). Studies conducted during the 1990s show that an increasing number of Japanese and other youth dissociate sex from marriage.

According to comparative surveys on sexual behavior, however, Japan's youth still appear rather conservative compared to youth in Western and Northern Europe and even North America. Well into the 1980s, only about 4 percent of eighteen- to twenty-four-year-olds in Japan had an unconditionally positive attitude toward premarital sex, compared with about 25 percent of their English, Swedish, German, or French counterparts (Nihon hōsō shuppan kyōkai 1986:75). And in 1997, whereas 70–80 percent of the young people in Germany, Great Britain, the Netherlands, Norway, and Sweden and 41 percent in the United States thought there was nothing wrong with sex before marriage, only 15 percent of Japanese youth fully agreed (Widmer, Treas and Newcomb 1998:351).[14]

However, tolerance toward one's own sexual experimentation did not necessarily indicate a similar degree of tolerance toward the behavior of a potential spouse. While a small portion of Japanese male and female youth allowed themselves premarital sexual activities, many of them expected their spouses not to have had sexual experience (Yomiuri shinbun shakaibu 1984:92). Overall, the interpreters of these sex surveys note, the trend toward a pro–premarital sexual attitude is becoming stronger for both boys and girls, is particularly strong among girls, and increases with age among members of both sexes, but there are no extreme changes in the experience rate of junior high school students (Hara 1996:79–80).

Schoolchildren's attitudes have not been the only indicator of changes in sexual attitudes, however. The 1980s saw the beginning of the heyday of large-scale sociological surveys not only on the sexual behavior of youth, but on that of married couples. Most of these surveys were regionally restricted or otherwise fragmented until Ishikawa Hiroyoshi, Saitō Shigeo, and Wagatsuma Hiroshi published their ambitiously titled study *Japanese Sexuality (Nihonjin no sei)* in 1984. In an attempt to carry out a large-scale survey explicitly modeled on the Kinsey Report and to counterbalance sex-related news in popular media with a "scientific survey" (Ishikawa, Saitō, and Wagatsuma 1984: foreword), they distributed more than 16,000 questionnaires and selected 1,549 responses for further analysis. All of the respondents were married couples. No explanation is given for why the study was exclusively directed at married and supposedly heterosexual people, and questions on extramarital sexual relationships explicitly refer to the opposite sex only (Ishikawa, Saitō, and Wagatsuma 1984:11–12). These flaws did not go unnoticed among sociological sex researchers in Japan.

In an attempt to show the diversity of female sexual experience by supplementing quantitative methods with qualitative research in the form of intensive interviewing, sociologists Imamura Naomi, Unno Yūki, and Ishimaru Kumiko published the *More Report (Moa ripōto NOW)* on sexual behavior and attitudes of women in 1990. The volume documented the responses of 1,987 women between the ages of thirteen and sixty-one, of whom 80 percent were in their twenties and a majority were white-collar workers at the time of the survey (Imamura, Unno, and Ishimaru 1990:656–657).[15]

The major part of the 678-page book consists of personal accounts of female sexual experiences. As in virtually all sex surveys of the postwar era in Japan, sexual satisfaction was measured in orgasms, including the age at which the respondents had their first orgasm, frequency of orgasms, ratio of orgasms per instances of intercourse, etc. While almost half of the surveyed women said that they always had orgasms when they masturbated, only 9 percent reported always having an orgasm through sexual intercourse (Imamura, Unno, and Ishimaru 1990:662). The researchers found that although most women know how to have an orgasm and feel capable of having a fulfilling sex life, many remain unsatisfied by sexual intercourse with their male partners. As the responsibility is placed on the male partners' shoulders, the authors conclude that even in contemporary Japan women are afraid of being considered "unfeminine" if they explicitly show interest in sexual satisfaction (Imamura, Unno, and Ishimaru 1990:676–677).

The *More Report* is one of very few recent sex surveys that include questions on homosexual practices. While 42 percent of the surveyed women have a positive attitude toward homosexuality *(dōseiai)* in general, as opposed to 36 percent who describe their attitude as negative, only 8 percent report that they themselves have had homosexual experiences (Imamura, Unno, and Ishimaru 1990:671). The trend of dissociating sex from marriage among youth is also reflected in the sexual behavior of adult women. In contrast to the earlier survey results, roughly 80 percent of women between the ages of thirteen and sixty-one had sexual partners at the time of the survey, although only 22 percent of them were married (Imamura, Unno, and Ishimaru 1990:657). The majority had their first sexual experience between the ages of sixteen and twenty-two, while 7.5 percent had their first experience between the ages of thirteen and fifteen (Imamura, Unno, and Ishimaru 1990:656). While more than 70 percent of respondents shared the opinion that love *(aijō)* is necessary for having sex, half of them had had "sex without love" at least once (Imamura, Unno, and Ishimaru 1990:669).

The mass production of social scientific data on sexual behavior and attitudes, of course, bears its own problems. There is no reason to share a naïve faith in the validity of questionnaires, interviews, and statistical tables with its pioneers, Yamamoto Senji in Japan, Magnus Hirschfeld in Germany, Richard von Krafft-Ebing in Austria, or Alfred Kinsey in the United States. The proliferation since 1948 of the Kinsey Reports and other Kinsey-type inquiries in the United States may be, as Roy Porter (1994:2) speculated, an indicator of either an ardent New World faith in science (or sex) or a greater Old World prudery. Surveys on sexual behavior of ever more people in Japan, in any case, are firmly embedded in a culture of an abundance of social scientific surveys, as the impressive annually published collections of public opinion surveys attest.[16]

When the studies are comparative—like the studies carried out by, for example, the NHK (Nihon hōsō shuppan kyōkai 1986) and Eric D. Widmer, Judith Treas, and Robert Newcomb (1998)—the problems of this kind of data only multiply. As noted above, both research teams found a huge difference between attitudes toward premarital sex among youth in Northern and Western European countries at one end of the extreme and Japanese youth at the other end. One might speculate that Japanese respondents might feel pressed to conform in their response to conservative expectations about sexual experience, whereas European youth would conform to a permissive and sexually adventurous ideal there, thus widening the gap between the two groups.

Regardless of these potential pitfalls, from a historical perspective, two characteristics set these surveys apart from their early-twentieth-century versions, and one characteristic is shared by both types of investigations. For one thing, the creation of social scientific data on sex—once the task of self-appointed sexologists who were marginal to the academy, flirted with mass media, but for the most part clashed with the state and its agencies—has come to rest firmly in the hands of government institutions and media conglomerates. By asking some questions over and over again while omitting others, these surveys and the publication of their results contribute to the frequent reaffirmation of normative notions of (acceptable and desirable) sexual practice. The question of the ways in which the perception of social, political, and economic realities are molded by the very surveys that supposedly represent them has yet to be examined.

In contrast to the military surgeons and police officers who first began to systematically investigate the sexual practices of specific groups within Japanese society in the late nineteenth century, these present-day accountants of sexual behavior seem less overtly intrusive. However, they are similarly firm about the creation of a sexual normalcy and normativity that is now circulating, not within the comparatively closed elite of guardians of the nation-state, but on public display. The intimacy of sexuality—perhaps always merely imagined—has been turned into a long list of criteria against which one can measure oneself and others. Undoubtedly, the creation, administration, and management of normative sexuality continue to be negotiated in a highly heterogeneous forum of officials, media, sex experts, educators, and ordinary Japanese women and men. To talk about sex, even the language of percentages and tables suggests, means to talk about society—its social (and sexual and gendered) order, its power relations, and its potential for change. Even in today's public arena of newspaper reports, magazine articles, and late-night radio and television shows, sex and sexuality remain enfolded in a rhetoric of liberation, disclosure, and containment. These public debates reproduce a normativity that centers on heterosexuality and, through it, a gendered order of sexual matters and society.

Notes

1. A 1928 amendment by emergency imperial decree made the law's provisions much harsher by including the ability to impose the death penalty, and a 1941 revision broadened its scope to include preventive arrest. The law was rescinded in October 1945.

2. The claim that the middle and upper classes were morally and intellectually superior, and that therefore their reproduction was especially desirable, echoed the claims of Francis Galton (1822–1911), the founder of eugenics.

CHAPTER I

1. For more detailed analyses of early ideas of eugenics and "racial improvement," see Matsubara 1997, Otsubo and Bartholomew 1998, Morris-Suzuki 1998, Otsubo 1999, and Robertson 2001.

2. Nagai's book contained an evolutionist history of humankind, a physiological account of sumo wrestlers' bodies, and a physiological and hygienic analysis of the position of the Japanese population in the "competition of the races" *(minzoku kyōsō)*.

3. This supposed physical inferiority also was noticed at the same time by Western authors. In 1896 an English ethnologist wrote, "Compared with an average Chinese, the 'Manchus' or the Koreans, they [the Japanese] are a weak folk, who undoubtedly possess endurance but are physically weak with moderate muscle development, a weak chest and a noticeable tendency towards anemia which, however, can be led back to the diet of rice, fish, and vegetables." On the other hand, the author estimated the intellectual capability of the Japanese

to be comparable to that of inhabitants of progressive European countries (see Chamberlain 1912).

4. For an analysis of the complicated history of the cultural meanings of blood and its relationship to eugenics and genetics, see Robertson 2002.

5. The concern for control was reflected in what Carol Gluck has called the "Meiji ideology" (Gluck 1985) and in Tetsuo Najita's notion of regulation as opposed to eradication of conflicts (Najita 1983:16). It also considerably shaped discussions on the transformation of entire scientific disciplines (S. Tanaka 1993:15).

6. In the mid-1870s, the Home Department had 600,000 yen at its disposal, 200,000 of which were allocated to the Bureau of Hygiene. At the beginning of the 1880s, Nagayo Sensai attempted to increase the budget by introducing a tax on pharmaceutical products (Tsurumi 1937:303, 312). The Bureau of Hygiene existed until 1938, when the Ministry for Health and Welfare was founded, which comprised the former Bureau of Social Affairs and the Bureau of Hygiene in the Home Department. The establishment of the Ministry of Health and Welfare was first recommended by administrators in the Army Ministry, who had become increasingly concerned about the deteriorating physical qualities of male recruits. The new ministry consisted of five units: bureaus for physical strength, hygiene, society, and labor, and a council for insurance (Kameyama 1997 [1984]:134).

7. Gotō Shinpei published three such volumes, one for boys, one for youth, and one for adults, as "a present to the nation" (1926:3).

8. The Chōheirei was renamed Heiekihō (Military Service Law) in 1927 (Katō Y. 1996:4).

9. Yamagata Aritomo was the main force behind the introduction of conscription and one of the main engineers of the Imperial Army, which was originally modeled after the French army. After Germany defeated France in 1871, Yamagata focused on the German military as a model for the Japanese army. The structure of the Imperial Navy was based on that of the British navy, which was the most powerful in the world at the time. Yamagata served as Japan's prime minister twice, from 1889 to 1891 and from 1898 to 1900, and as justice minister from 1892 to 1893. In 1894 and 1895 he served as the commander of the First Army during the Sino-Japanese war.

10. For the development of recruitment rates between 1916 and 1945, see Katō Y. 1996:66 and Drea 1998:229, footnote 8.

11. Following an order by the Ministry of Education, "achievements in learning" (gakuryoku kentei) were tested in addition to the evaluation of the conscripts' character. However, the results of these tests were not used to determine recruitment (Katō Y. 1996:159).

12. Edward Drea (1998:86) has suggested that to be deprived of a son may not have been disadvantageous to the family's survival in all cases. Because families received a death benefit proportional to rank, some may have thought it beneficial to the family's survival if their son did not return home.

13. Mori Rintarō was the head of the Military Academy, the Army Medical Academy, and the Military Medicine Division of the Army Department in the colonial administration of Taiwan. He also served as the chair of the Medical De-

partment in the Army Ministry and as the director of the Association for Military Medicine (Rikugun Gun'i Gakkai), which was founded in 1884 (Maruyama 1984:viii).

14. Katarzyna Cwiertka (1999:118–140) has described the introduction into the Imperial Army and Navy of Western food that was considered healthier and more nutritious.

15. Ieda Sakichi referred to the following surveys on venereal disease patients in 1936: the 1912 survey of 789 patients in regional hospitals, the 1920 survey of 11,329 venereal disease–infected soldiers in all of Japan, the 1933 survey of 144 venereal disease–infected soldiers from the prefecture Kanagawa, and the 1935 survey of 324 soldiers (Ieda 1936:30–31). These surveys were also discussed in sexological journals (e.g., *Sei no Kenkyū* 1919b).

16. Until the beginning of World War I, Salvarsan and other drugs were mostly imported from Germany. When German-Japanese relations began to deteriorate after the outbreak of the war, Japanese scholars of pharmaceutics at the Imperial University of Tokyo, the hospital of the Manchurian Railway Company, and a few other institutions began to research the possibilities for producing a similar drug in Japan. After satisfactory experiments in animals, the drug was used on hospitalized patients of syphilis. However, in 1915, a representative of the Research Institute for Infectious Diseases warned that an overdose of the drug could be fatal and that researchers were still trying to figure out the right dose for successful treatment (*Yomiuri Shinbun* 1915b).

17. In 1905, German dermatologists Erich Hoffmann and F. Schaudinn discovered the syphilis pathogen. The author of the 1956 *World History of Sexuality (Weltgeschichte der Sexualität)* described the astounding healing rate with Salvarsan: "I still remember how the otherwise so skeptical Albert Neisser, who has in the meantime become the director of the University Clinic for Dermatology and Venereal Disease in Berlin, introduced an athlete to his students who had the words 'love, suffer, forget' tattooed on his chest. 'Look, gentlemen,' explained Neisser, '[T]hat was the motto of this patient, and now it has proven true. "Love"—that was love, "suffer"—that was the clap, and "forget"—that is Salvarsan.'" (Morus 1956:312).

18. Military physicians collected data on a great number of other factors as well. Among these were the professional background of diseased soldiers, their marital status, region of origin, and their place of service. They made international comparisons with European military organizations, comparisons with rates of venereal diseases among prostitutes, and comparisons of different kinds of venereal diseases (KRB 1927).

19. According to historian Louis Allen's findings (1984:596), a sergeant earned about 30 yen a month in 1945, a private first class 10.50 yen. Overseas, a private first class earned 7.80 yen in ten days.

20. Referring to the military sexual slavery of mostly Korean and Chinese girls and women between the ages of eleven and twenty-four, the Women's International War Crimes Tribunal on Japan's Military Sexual Slavery, held in Tokyo 7–12 December 2000, pronounced the emperor of Japan guilty of crimes against humanity. In Japan, the Asia-Japan Women's Resource Center under the leadership of Matsui Yayori and the Center for Research and Documentation on

Japan's War Responsibility are committed mainly to research on elements of the war in East Asia that haunt Japan to this day. For analyses in English, see Ustinia Dolgopol and Snehal Paranjape (1994); George Hicks (1995); Il-myōn Kim (1989); and Watanabe Kazuko (1994).

21. The Council for Former Army Comfort Women Hotline No. 110 (Jūgun Ianfu 110-ban Iinkai) was formed in 1991 in order to interview former comfort women and members of the Imperial Army about comfort stations established during World War II. As it was difficult to identify and contact people, the group established a phone hotline, number 110, and later published the recorded calls as a book (Yamasaki 1992).

22. After 1939, the German Wehrmacht designated certain brothels for military personnel under the "Order for the Protection of German Defense Power" ("Verordnung zum Schutz der deutschen Wehrkraft") and forced women primarily from Poland and Russia into sexual enslavement (Paul 1994:103–114). Even women who were not forced into prostitution by the German military authorities but had sexual relations with German military personnel were closely observed and studied (Hartmann 1946). According to the Medical Department of the United States Army, Wehrmacht brothels in Sicily were taken over by the United States occupation forces when they landed there in 1942 (see Paul 1994: 155, footnote 13). Similarly, in August 1945, the Japanese Home Department ordered regional police officials throughout the country to prepare special and exclusive "comfort facilities" for the occupation army (Dower 1999:124–125).

23. The comfort stations were officially reserved for soldiers. However, according to the testimonies of some former comfort women, in the evenings civilians paid to visit the enslaved women as well (Jūgun ianfu 110-ban henshū iinkai 1992:76–77).

24. It is not clear how many comfort stations existed on the Japanese "mainland." Hayashi Hiroshi (1993) noted that there were none on the mainland, but former members of the Imperial Army testified that there were indeed comfort stations there (Jūgun ianfu 110-ban henshū iinkai 1992:74).

25. Quoted in Yamazaki 1999 [1972]:69. *Karayuki-san* were Japanese women who went overseas to work in brothels that generally were for non-Japanese locals or foreign indentured laborers. Like other prostitutes at the time, they left Japan to escape a life of severe poverty or were sold by their parents, often under false pretexts. They usually are differentiated from the much debated comfort women, most of whom were not Japanese and were forced to perform sexual labor for Japanese soldiers in various occupied countries in Asia during Japan's imperialist expansion.

26. The Wassermann reaction, a method to detect antibodies in the blood of people infected with syphilis, was developed by the bacteriologist and serologist August Paul von Wassermann in 1906. Although only 70 percent of those infected react positively, it is still the best method to test for syphilis today.

27. In the reports of the Bureau of Hygiene, "infectious diseases" and "syphilis" were listed as two different categories. Here the results of the investigation are interesting mostly as an indication of the spread of syphilis (Naimushō eiseikyoku 18931894:198; 1897:39; 1900:41; 1910:41; 1930:54).

28. Joseph E. de Becker was born in London and went to Japan in 1887 and

stayed more than thirty years. By his own account, he spoke Japanese like a native (De Becker 1917:10). He was the legal advisor to the Tokyo and Yokohama Foreign Board of Trade and stood counsel for important foreign banks in Japan. Among other books on Japan's legal system, he published *The Annotated Civil Code of Japan* (London: Butterworth; Yokohama: Kelly & Walsh, 1909–1910) and *Commentary on the Commercial Code of Japan* (London: Butterworth, 1913).

CHAPTER 2

1. Markus Wawerzonnek (1984:20), an author familiar with the bibliometrical extent of the related literature, estimates that more than 10,000 monographs and articles related to sexuality were published in Germany between 1886 and 1933.

2. For a detailed analysis of Fujikawa Yū's career as a medical historian, see Matsumura, Hirono, and Matsubara 1998; Fujikawa H. 1982; Fujikawa Yū sensei kankōkai 1988.

3. Yoshida was a prominent pedagogue who soon after his statement in the newspaper reached the peak of his career as a professor at the Tōkyō Joshi Kōtō Shihan Gakkō, a teachers' college for those training to teach at girls' schools, which later became Ochanomizu University. He taught at the Tōkyō Joshi Kōtō Shihan Gakkō and from 1916 to 1934 at the Imperial University of Tokyo. Today, he is remembered mostly for introducing German "social pedagogy" *(Sozialpädagogik)* into Japan (Takemura H. 1991:49).

4. William Johnston has found that these convictions led one physician in 1889 to imply that a genetic relation existed between tuberculosis and syphilis, suggesting that children of syphilitic parents often grew up to contract tuberculosis. Other physicians administered Salvarsan, the first effective remedy for syphilis, to their tubercular patients (Johnston 1995:192, 215).

5. Shimoda gave the title of the book as *Science and Morals (Kagaku to dōtoku)* and noted that he was acquainted with the author, but he did not mention the author's name or whether the book was Japanese or written in a Euro-American language (Shimoda 1908c:5).

6. For examples of these articles, see one of the leading pedagogical journals that was published under the following titles: *Dai Nippon Kyōiku Gakkai Zasshi* (1883–1897), *Kyōiku Kōhō* (1897–1907), *Teikyoku Kyōiku* (1909–1944), and *Dai Nippon Kyōiku* (1944–1945); see also Robertson 2001.

7. The "crime of anal penetration" *(keikanzai)*, which called for a punishment of ninety days' work in a penitentiary, was briefly introduced during the early Meiji period. A new penal code came into force in January 1882 that in effect legalized consensual anal intercourse between adult males. The term "anal penetration" dropped out of the penal code entirely; instead, male-male and male-female anal intercourse now fell under the broader category of "obscenity crimes" *(waisetsuzai)* or "obscene acts" *(waisetsu no shogyō)*, which also included adultery, mistreatment of minors, rape, and pimping of minors (Iwaya 1902:268; see also Pflugfelder 1999:168–169). Gregory Pflugfelder (1999:163) has suggested that Japanese lawmakers felt that absolving male perpetra-

tors under the age of sixteen from criminal liability for their actions provided sufficient consideration of their status as minors.

8. Similar descriptions can be found in German sexological writings. See, for example, Hirschfeld 1926:81, 250.

9. From the recorded notes of the memoirs of a village nurse who organized a meeting of married couples to talk about family planning, it seems that some parents solved the problem of how to have sex in a bedroom they shared with their children by hitting their children on the head until they could be sure that they were sleeping soundly (Oba Miyoshi, quoted in Huston 1992:158).

10. A declared critic of naturalist literature, Mori Ōgai had subscribed to dominant tastes for some time, which came through in his themes and writing style (Hijiya–Kirschnereit 1981:101). His text *Vita Sexualis* was later recommended frequently by contributors to sexological journals and other publications that dealt with sexual issues (Aoki S. 1934), as discussed in chapter 3.

11. In 1905, three years after the founding of the German Society for the Prevention of Venereal Disease in Berlin (Haeberle 1992:11), Doi Keizō founded the Japanese Society for the Prevention of Venereal Disease or Nihon Seibyō Yobō Kyōkai (Nihon kagakushi gakkai 1972:443).

12. Japanese scientists and intellectuals had been drawn to Europe and America in increasing numbers, and by the beginning of the twentieth century every high school student learned German or English. Doctors, lawyers, government officials, and engineers in particular became accustomed to both English and German. As of 1912, the eight upper schools with approximately 800 students each were organized into three faculties, for law and literature, for technical sciences and agriculture, and for medicine. In the first and third faculties, nine hours of German and four hours of English were taught, with somewhat less taught in the second. Both contemporary Japanese and German authors considered the influences of the German language, medicine, and sciences to be dominant in Japan (Fujisawa 1912:19; Witte 1918:67).

13. Other strategies of linking sexology in Japan to international trends in the field were reports on sexology overseas and publications of Western sexologists in Japanese translation. Most of the sexological journals, many women's journals, and other magazines reported on the progress of sexual reform, sexological research, and other sexual issues in Western countries (see, e.g., Fukuomo 1911; Fujikawa Y. 1916, 1922; *Fujo Shinbun* 1923; *Hentai Shinri* 1921; Ida 1922; Katō K. 1927; Kawatani 1928; Ōma 1936; *Seikagaku Kenkyū* 1936; Tonda 1936; Yasuda T. 1936). In addition, *Purity* published an article by German hygienist Alfred Blaschko in translation (Burashuko 1914). *Sexological Research (Seikagaku Kenkyū)* printed articles by leading German sexologist Iwan Bloch (Buroho 1920), by Max Hodann on Magnus Hirschfeld's impressions of his visit to Japan (Hodan 1936; Ode 1936), and on Wilhelm Reise's concerns about the crises of sex (Reise 1936); the *Women's Newspaper (Fujo Shinbun)* printed Ellen Key's ideas about motherhood (Kei 1918); and *Popular Medicine* ran a series of articles by Mary Stopes about children's sex education (Sutopusu 1924, 1925a–b).

14. Thomas W. Laqueur (2003) has described the complicated history of

both Tissot's book and the cultural meanings of masturbation in the Western world.

15. Beard attributed the causes of neurasthenia to "overpressure of the higher nerve centers," claiming that it was a pathology peculiar to the American continent and unique to the American lifestyle (see Rabinbach 1990:153). For a detailed analysis of the discourse of neurasthenia in Europe and the United States, see Anson Rabinbach (1990:146–178). Hugo Shapiro (1990) has expertly traced the history of neurasthenia in China, where Japanese and European concepts of the pathology superseded more traditional notions of energy loss.

16. Shimoda also propagated the roles of mothers and fathers according to the theories of German pedagogue and social reformer Johann Heinrich Pestalozzi (Shimoda 1904a:320–322).

17. A broad range of magazines and journals began to deal with sex education, including *Women's Review (Fujin Kōron)* (Ichikawa 1919); *Women's Newspaper (Fujo Shinbun* 1923, 1930; Nagai 1919b–g, 1920a–d); *Popular Medicine (Tsūzoku Igaku)* (Iijima 1932); *Perverse Psyche (Hentai Shinri)* (Inoue 1923); *Purity (Kakusei* 1932; Misumi 1920); and *Sexological Research (Seikagaku Kenkyū)* (Kurotaki 1936; Nii 1936).

CHAPTER 3

1. By the 1920s, the Western book with the most Japanese translations was Darwin's *On the Origin of Species.* For an overview of the reception of Darwinism in Japan, see Shimao 1981; Suzuki Z. 1983:22–31. Parts of Yamamoto's translation of Havelock Ellis's work were published between 1926 and 1932. Yamamoto also published shorter excerpts of Ellis's work in *Birth Control Review* and *Sex and Society (Sei to Shakai).*

2. Among the 350 respondents were 20 women (Yamamoto Senji 1921g: 325). Yamamoto never mentioned the women in publications of the survey's results and systematically and statistically analyzed only the results from male students and, later, other men. One reason for this may have been that the audiences at his lectures were overwhelmingly male. When women came they attended in small numbers; one lecture was attended by one woman and a hundred men (Yamamoto Senji 1921g:322). Yamamoto did, however, lecture on both male and female sexuality (Yamamoto Senji 1921g:321) and also wrote articles exclusively on sex education for girls and women (i.e., Yamamoto Senji 1924a–b, 1926b).

3. *Outlook* was founded in 1918 and modeled after Theodore Roosevelt's weekly of the same name; it contained mostly articles on current issues. Okuma contributed at least one or two articles to each issue in which he commented critically on current issues (Idditti 1940:394–395).

4. Yamamoto wrote two articles on the sex education of women (1924a, 1924b), but only after World War II were girls' and women's sex lives surveyed to the same extent as boys' and men's. Acknowledging Yamamoto and Yasuda's pioneering role in "scientific" sex research, Asayama Shin'ichi published the first survey of both sexes in 1949. Concerned about the consequences of the war

on the sexual morale of youth, Saotome Kenichi, Arai Ichirō, Watanabe Tetsurō (Saotome at el. 1953), and soon quite a few others followed suit in the early 1950s. A host of large-scale surveys, to which I shall turn in the epilogue, followed in the 1970s, 1980s, and 1990s.

5. For example, Yasuda translated Sigmund Freud's *Studien zur Hysterie und Vorlesungen zur Einführung in die Psychoanalyse* in 1931 as *Seishin bunseki nyūmon*. He also was one of Yamamoto's closest allies in the birth control movement and became its leader after Yamamoto's death in 1929.

6. For similar remarks on the connection between social class and sexual morality, see, for example, Yoshida K. 1916; Abe 1918, 1927b; Honma 1918a–b, 1924; Ishige 1943a–e. Carol Gluck has noted that according to Japanese agrarian ideologists, urban life was marked by various "social diseases" *(shakai no yamai)* or "large city fevers" *(tokainetsu),* which endangered the moral integrity of young people from the countryside (Gluck 1985:161). The editors of the *Journal of the Sociological Society* also frequently expressed their "desire to awaken a sense of duty among the upper class" (see Ambaras 1998:10).

7. For those who had had sexual intercourse, questions included the time of year that their first intercourse had taken place; whether the respondent was "active," "neutral," or "passive"; whether special conditions (e.g., alcohol or peer pressure) had influenced the encounter; the age, occupation, and social status of the partner (i.e., unmarried, married, or prostitute); and whether respondents had noticed changes in their sex life or behavior and attitude toward the other sex following the first sexual intercourse. Those respondents who had not yet had sexual intercourse were asked why. The possible answers were that they had no particular reason; because the thought of sex disgusted them; for religious or ethical reasons; for aesthetic reasons; as a gift to their beloved; for hygenic reasons; to avoid venereal diseases; or due to lack of economic resources required to start a family (Yamamoto Senji 1924c:215).

8. In this example, the strangers' gender remains unclear. Here, as in Yamamoto's other writings, the possibility of same-sex encounters is neither explicitly mentioned nor explicitly excluded, but it is ignored as a topic necessitating a discussion in their own right.

9. Quite a few of the survey's questions dealt with first sexual feelings, deliberate ejaculation, and masturbation. Yamamoto and Yasuda asked whether respondents had experienced ejaculation during sleep *(musei);* when it had happened for the first time; whether they observed any regularities and whether they saw a connection between the frequency of ejaculation during sleep and the season, moon phase, or day of the week; and whether they observed peculiarities in their emotional condition or state of health prior to the ejaculation or on the following day. They also were asked to describe the dreams they had afterward and were encouraged to describe their experiences of ejaculation in instances of impatience or surprise, e.g., due to an exam or when they had just caught the train. The next set of questions concerned masturbation *(jii).* Questions included their age at the time they first masturbated; whether they asked somebody about the meaning of masturbation or whether they knew themselves; when and how they masturbated; how long and how often they masturbated; how they reacted when

they first heard about the supposedly harmful consequences of masturbation; how they would describe their health and emotional state; and whether they had ever lived in a group setting, e.g., in the military or in a dormitory. If they answered yes to the last question, they also were asked to describe what type of group it was and whether that lifestyle had had an impact on their sex life (Yamamoto Senji 1924c:212–214).

10. In Germany, Hirschfeld had begun examinations of the sexual behavior of young men in 1903 (Haeberle 1992:11). A quarter-century later, Alfred C. Kinsey, honored as the founder of empirical sex research in the United States, came to similar conclusions in *Sexual Behavior in the Human Male* (1948) and *Sexual Behavior in the Human Female* (1953).

11. *Jii* was a translation of the German *Ipsation* (derived from the Latin word *ipse* for "self"). Hirschfeld had introduced *Ipsation* in his writings for similar reasons (Hirschfeld 1926:248–249). Other Japanese sexologists who specifically researched autoerotic practices also used the German word *Onanie (onanii)*, probably for the same reasons (see, e.g., Kitano 1920, 1921).

12. In his numerous books, Iwan Bloch identified himself as "Spezialarzt für Sexualleiden" (special physician for sexual maladies). In 1919, *Das Sexualleben unserer Zeit* appeared in its twelfth edition, and 70,000 copies had been sold (Bloch 1919 [1906]: prologue). Sawada Junjirō also used the word *seigaku;* Miyatake Gaikotsu and Kurigayawa Hakuson more often used *seiyokugaku*, while Nagai Sen tended to speak of *seikagaku* (see Oshikane 1977:7–10).

13. As Theodore M. Porter (1986:27–30) has shown, the gathering of population statistics was motivated by the hope of improving living conditions and solving social problems. It reflected a search for reforms and the conviction that the statistics would deliver explanations for diseases, death, and crime. Yamamoto brought his views of the theory and practice of science with him when he returned to Kyoto and began to lecture and do research on human sexuality.

14. This was true not only for Japanese sociologists but also for their American colleagues. The founding fathers of American sociology also formulated their view of the world and their purpose in it in terms of "social reforms" before making sociology an academic subject. In their opinion, the science of society should be primarily an instrument of social practice, and social practice should be directed at the conscious solution of social problems (Bauman 1995:107).

15. For a detailed critique of the government's influence on personnel decisions and the involvement of university professors in party politics, see Yoshino 1927, 1928.

16. At the beginning of the twentieth century, Katō Hiroyuki, one of the cofounders of the Meiji Six Society (Meirokusha), retreated from his original ideas of justice and freedom. Around the turn of the century, Katō ceased to promote a social Darwinist concept of social evolution and the survival of the fittest and instead began to favor the notion of a social model that placed emphasis on social harmony. Katō adopted the idea of the state as a "social organism" and modified it so that it referred to a concept of society that supported the status quo. The welfare of society was equivalent to the welfare of the state. Patriotism

corresponded with loyalty to the emperor. If the state was a social organism, the emperor was at its heart and had to be protected as the most important organ of this organism (see Kawamura N. 1990:67).

17. Kagawa Toyohiko's engagement for the poor inspired biographers to examine his life and work even during his lifetime. See, e.g., Carola D. Barth (1936); Robert Schildgen (1988); Karl-Heinz Schell (1994).

18. The Labor Farmer Party was dedicated to achieving social equality by parliamentary means. In December 1926, Ōyama Ikuo became party leader. Under the guidance of the Communist Party of Japan, it served as a legal front for the far Left. The Labor Farmer Party was dissolved in 1928. Despite increasing doubts within the Left about the value of a new party, Ōyama and Kawakami Hajime founded a second party of the same name in November 1929 (see Hunter 1984:180–181).

19. Journals and magazines such as *Hentai Shinri* and even regional newspapers in both Japan proper and the colonies, such as *Yorozu Chōhō, Kōchi Shinbun, Tokushima Nichinichi Shinbun, Tokuyama Nippō, Hokuriku Taimusu,* and *Niigata Shinbun* noted the increasing number of journals and books dealing with sexual issues (*Seiron* 1927).

20. Subscriptions were offered for three months (1 yen, 20 sen), six months (2 yen, 20 sen), and one year (4 yen, 30 sen) (*Sei* November 1927:84). Erotic tales also were common in other journals and magazines, such as *Criminology (Hanzai Kagaku)* and *Sex Research (Sei no Kenkyū)*. See, e.g., Mitamura Engyō (1921); Miyagawa Hirō (1930a–f, 1931a–b).

21. Japan's first modern census, from 1920, spurred population studies on actual Japanese data. Among the countries Yokoyama compared with Japan were Russia, several European countries, the United States, and several South American countries (Yokoyama M. 1920:51–52).

22. The *Rational Sex Series* was published infrequently in Boston from 1907 on. It included works on sex education, such as "Sex Instruction for Women" (1919), "What Every Boy Should Know" (1924), and "What Every Young Woman Should Know" (1924), as well as translations of German-language treatises on sexology, psychoanalysis, and dream interpretation.

23. The issues of September and October 1920 are printed with the line "all articles of this journal are prohibited from reproduction" on the cover.

24. After World War II, Ōta served as a counselor for sexual problems (Ōta T. 1954a) and wrote articles for popular magazines. In *Marital Life (Fūfu Seikatsu),* for example, he described new American techniques for the enlargement of breasts in an article entitled "Beautiful Breasts are a Married Lady's Greatest Weapon," suggesting that these techniques would also soon become available in Japan (Ōta T. 1954b).

25. Advice columns had become common, especially in women's magazines and daily newspapers. Yamada Waka, for example, answered the questions of readers in the column "Advice for Women" ("Josei sōdan") in the *Tōkyō Asahi Shinbun* (see Yamada 1989 [1983]).

26. With a broadcast time of sixteen hours per day and a monthly fee of 75 sen for a subscription, radio enjoyed a rapid rise in the number of its listeners, from 343,000 in 1926 to over 1,000,000 in 1933, and drove the print media to

lower their prices and invent new marketing strategies (*Present Day Japan* 1934). As Sano Sumiyo from the Nihon Hōsō Kyōkai (NHK) told me, most sound documents from this time were destroyed during World War II. NHK program notes reveal, however, that Yamamoto Senji, Nagai Hisomu, and several other professors from universities in Tokyo, Nara, Kagoshima, Osaka, and Kyoto spoke on the radio about sex education, birth control, and eugenics. In 1928, Yamamoto spoke on a total of nineteen occasions on Radio Osaka to tens of thousands of listeners. Similarly, Nagai Hisomu spoke a total of thirteen times between 10 May 1927 and 26 July 1927 on "Heredity and Eugenics" and on 11 July 1929 on "Love from a Biological Perspective." Similar themes were broadcast from other radio stations in Okayama, Kyoto, Hiroshima, Kōchi, Matsue, Kumamoto, Fukuoka, Nagoya, Kanazawa, and Sendai (Nogami 1932; Nihon hōsō kyōkai Kansai shibu 1932; *Present Day Japan* 1926, 1934).

CHAPTER 4

1. According to Camille Limoges' analysis of public controversies, each "world of relevance" or group involved in a controversy has much latitude to construct in its own way both the various entities that inhabit the controversy and the relationship between those entities (Limoges 1993:420).

2. The director of the Research Society on the Population Question in Japan announced in 1934 that Japan's birth rate was twice as high as Europe's and its death rate 50 percent higher. The situation in the colonies was even more extreme, with a natural popular increase of 19.4 per 1,000 in Korea and 19.5 per 1,000 in Formosa. In 1933, the total population of the Japanese empire had reached 92 million (Shimomura 1934:58).

3. Emigration hardly eased the population problem in Japan proper. By 1934, only about 600,000 Japanese lived abroad, while there were 300,000 immigrants from Korea alone in Japan (Shimomura 1934:58).

4. Fujikawa Yū did not reveal his source, and the number may in fact stem from the first half of the 1910s rather than from 1919. Takayasu Itsuko provided the number of criminal convictions of abortion providers between 1905 and 1955. Her data show about 600 convictions per year during the years 1910–1914 and a sharply decreased rate thereafter, e.g., 545 in 1915, 387 in 1919, 170 in 1929, and 188 in 1939 (see Hardacre 1997:50).

5. Other homicide categories were "killing by someone else," "murder premeditated and with specific motives," "killing a direct relative or an in-law," and "incitement to murder" (Nihon teikoku shihōshō 1925:362–387).

6. Similarly, zoologist Ishikawa Chiyomatsu expressed his doubts about the steady population growth that was feared by birth control activists. He reminded them that in Germany as well, World War I had served as a "counterbalance" (Ishikawa 1928). For a characterization of Ishikawa Chiyomatsu's career, see Bartholomew (1989:59, 75, 261).

7. The *Tōkyō Asahi Shinbun* received tens of thousands of letters daily. A selection from the column "Advice for Women" ("Josei sōdan") was first published in 1983 as the eighth volume of *Famous Works on Modern Women's Problems (Kindai fujin mondai meicho zenshū)*. Readers' questions were categorized

into housing, women's problems, love, law, economics, and marriage (Yamada 1989 [1983]).

8. Abe was referring here to Oda Nobunaga (1534–1582) and Toyotomi Hideyoshi (1535–1598).

9. On the central role of Margaret Sanger in the American birth control movement and her international crusade, see Gordon (1983).

10. Among others, Nagai Hisomu expressed this concern. He noted that the civilization of a culture went hand in hand with its degeneration. Degeneration in turn resulted in ever-later marriages, which meant that middle- and upper-class men and women in particular were wasting valuable reproductive years. Nagai identified the ideal age for having children as being between twenty-four and twenty-five for men and between seventeen and eighteen for women (*Manchōhō* 1916).

11. By 1917, 170,000 copies of this text had been printed in the United States. The version that appeared in 1920 was already the tenth edition. Until World War I, Sanger had close ties to the Left, but thereafter she increasingly turned to middle- and upper-class women and to the medical profession. In the 1920 edition, the passages "birth control as a means in the class struggle," "recommendation of abortions" as a means of birth control, and other radical passages had been removed. The text, which Yamamoto translated in 1922, was the toned-down version from 1920 (Ogino M. 1994:83).

12. Kutsumi and her husband Mitamura were involved in the organization of communist cells in Hokkaidō, for which Kutsumi was eventually incarcerated and tortured (Kutsumi in Hane 1988:157).

13. The application form required information on the physical condition of the entire family (assuming that the couple already had five children). Husband and wife had to provide information on their occupation, age, and physical condition and the number and sex of their siblings. They were asked to provide the date of their wedding, the current number of family members, and their monthly income. In the rubric on children, they had to list the sex and age of all children including, if applicable, the age at which they had died. A major part of the application form was reserved for the applicant's reasons for wanting to practice birth control (*Sanji Chōsetsu Hyōron* April 1925: advertisement section).

14. The foundation of the Harmonization Society in 1919 under Home Minister Tokonami Takejirō was an attempt to co-opt major sections of the labor movement in the hope of countering its growing strength. The society had regionally organized branches in factories controlled by a central coordinating organization, but its mediation in disputes was rarely successful. Despite its shortcomings, the society conducted extensive and valuable research into labor and social problems, fostered educational work, and had some influence on government policy in such developments as the growth of labor exchanges (Hunter 1984:106–107).

15. These authors were apparently referring to Genesis 38:8–10: "Then Judah said to Onan, 'Lie with your brother's wife and fulfill your duty to her as a brother-in-law to produce offspring for your brother.' But Onan knew that the offspring would not be his; so whenever he lay with his brother's wife, he spilled his semen on the ground to keep from producing offspring for his brother."

16. For a discussion of competing theories in Japan, see Julie Rousseau (1998:197–213).

17. Up to the present day and despite the legalization of the pill in 1999, condoms continue to be the most commonly used contraceptive in Japan (Inoue and Ehara 1995:69). For an overview of the recent debate before the lifting of the ban on the pill, see Marumoto (1995), and Maruyama, Raphael, and Djerassi (1996). Only in 1974 did the Ministry of Health and Welfare approve of the intrauterine device, even though IUDs had been in use in other countries for a decade or more (Norgren 1998).

CHAPTER 5

1. The Meiji Civil Code introduced the prohibition of the publication of nude images in 1899. In 1900 the authorities began to amend regulations for publications that violated customs and morals (rather than the political order). Enacted in March 1900, the Peace Police Law consolidated and supplemented existing law-and-order legislation. Initially, "anti-government" groups referred mostly to the nascent labor movement, but the law also included a ban on political activity by soldiers, police, priests, women, and minors (Article 5). The Peace Police Law was modified in 1922 and 1926. Its significance decreased with the enactment of the Peace Preservation Law of 1925, but it was not abolished until October 1945 (Hunter 1984:166). Richard H. Mitchell (1973) has discussed the creation of the Peace Preservation Law in detail.

2. The Peace Preservation Law also was applied to other groups. Among them were the new religions, which were denounced as "pseudo-religions" or "quackery" and accused of open hedonism. Although most religions supported family ideology, the public tended to believe the wildest stories and was convinced that charismatic leaders seduced their female followers (Garon 1986: 293–298).

3. Censorship legislation during the late nineteenth and the first half of the twentieth century has been examined by James L. Huffman 1984; Gregory Kasza 1988:61–65; and Jay Rubin 1984:43–69. On present-day debates about pornography, see Peter Herzog (1993:64–68).

4. Yamamoto had close ties to the Communist Party but was never a member. Nonetheless, memorial festivals for his death—March 8 in Tokyo and March 15 in Kyoto—incited communist protest demonstrations. The Communist Party honored him with a posthumous membership after World War II (Beckmann and Okubo 1969:173).

5. An announcement of this twenty-page special section in the March 1935 edition of the magazine *Women's Review* can be found in *Central Review* (*Chūō Kōron* March 1935). Jennifer Robertson (1999) has analyzed the scandalization of lesbian "love suicides" in contemporary media.

6. My calculation is based on data provided in Naimushō keihokyoku 1981 (316–334, 255–267) and 1986 (1:151–178, 2:213–348). For detailed lists of censored newspapers, magazines, and books from the Meiji, Taishō, and Shōwa eras, see Naimushō keihokyoku (1976a–b, 1977a–b, 1981, 1986) and Akama (1927).

7. Whereas some Japanese intellectuals consciously differentiated between *jinshu* (race, biological) and *minzoku* (ethnic nation, biological and cultural), others used the two terms interchangeably (Doak 1997; Robertson 2001). Nagai Hisomu, for instance, seemed to have seen the German *Volk,* the Japanese *minzoku,* and the English "race" as equivalents (Otsubo and Bartholomew 1998:547). Koya Yoshio and the other authors of *Racial Biological Research* used *minzoku, jinshu,* and *jinrui* interchangeably and alternately translated these words as *Volk* and *Rasse (Minzoku Seibutsugaku Kenkyū—Rassenbiologische Untersuchungen).* Hiratsuka Raichō first promoted a sterilization law in 1917 for the sake of "racial improvement," which she referred to as *shuzoku kairyō* (Hiratsuka 1983 [1916]:335).

8. As Sumiko Otsubo and James Bartholomew (1998) have pointed out, Nagai took over eugenic institutionalization efforts left unfinished by others. Hiratsuka Raichō had made an initial attempt at eugenic legislation and led an unsuccessful campaign to enact a marriage restriction law. The incorporation of eugenic ideas in the curriculum of higher education had been advocated first by Naruse Jinzō. Yamanouchi Shigeo had established the first eugenic association, the Greater Japan Eugenics Society.

9. An abridged English version of Fujime's article appeared in *Gender and Japanese History* (Fujime, "One Midwife's Life," 1999).

10. Nagai remained unsuccessful until the end of the Second World War, but in 1949 the National Institute of Genetics was founded (Morris-Suzuki 1998).

11. These articles were printed in the journal *Racial Biological Research (Minzoku Seibutsugaku Kenkyū—Rassenbiologische Untersuchungen)* in volume 1 of 1936, volume 5 of 1938, and volume 7 of 1939; see also Koya and Takabatake 1939.

12. Matsubara Yōko (1998, 2000) and Sumiko Otsubo (1999) provide a detailed discussion of the attempts by Nagai and other eugenicists to establish eugenic legislation.

13. For the complete text of the National Eugenics Law, see Tiana Norgren 2001:140–145.

14. However, the reproductive rate was almost three times as high in 1941 as in 1940—it rose from 3.9 per 1,000 to 9.2 per 1,000—and it peaked at 14 per 1,000 in 1942. In 1943 it fell sharply, to 7.1, and it decreased drastically thereafter, reaching minus 22.9 in 1945 (BSOPM 1957:11).

15. In the health records of the army and navy, "hysteria" was listed as one of several mental diseases afflicting enlisted men (e.g., Kaigunshō 1909; Rikugunshō 1917).

16. "*Rēben*" resembles the German word for "life" *(Leben).* For a great variety and number of advertisements for hormonal extracts, see the advertisement sections of *Nihon oyobi Nihonjin* 1 May 1922; *Fujokai* May 1928; *Fujin no Tomo* November 1929, March 1935; *Tsūzoku Igaku* January 1927, November 1929, February 1932, January 1939, October 1940; *Josan no Tomo* November 1941). Tokkapin alone was advertised in print media as diverse as *Japan and the Japanese, Popular Medicine,* and *Present Day Japan.*

17. Neurasthenia was frequently discussed in Japanese popular medical journals (see, e.g., Nagahama 1925a–b; Andō 1930; Fujinami 1932; Matsumoto

1937; Sugimoto 1937) as well as in publications in other countries (see, e.g., Neuman 1974, 1975; Mosse 1996:84–85; Porter and Hall 1995:77, 214; Shapiro 1999).

18. *Women's Club* was one of the largest women's magazines in the interwar period. It started with a circulation of 40,000 copies in October 1920. By the beginning of the 1930s, circulation had reached half a million copies and thus took a share of almost 50 percent of the market for all women's magazines (Maeda 1993 [1973]:219).

19. For a detailed discussion of the contents of this encyclopedia and the ways in which it reflected attempts to create and define the "normal woman," see Frühstück forthcoming.

20. Takeuchi Shigeyo's role as eugenicist and one of only a few female participants in the Racial Hygiene Study Group has been highlighted by Sumiko Otsubo (1999).

21. This connection was also frequently made in newspaper reports on the development of the physical constitution of male and female youth. See, e.g., *Chūō Shinbun* (1913); *Yomiuri Shinbun* 1915a; *Hōchi Shinbun* (1916a–b).

22. A complete translation of the law can be found in Norgren 2001: 145–155.

23. About the ideal man, readers of this encyclopedia learned only that he had to be able to provide for the household (Date 1951b:28).

24. In the mid-1960s, Koya argued against the legalization of the contraceptive pill by pointing out that there was no need to hurry to legalize a method of birth control that might have side effects, especially when abortion was legal and other kinds of birth control were available. In fact, the Family Planning Federation of Japan, over which he presided, opposed the legalization of the pill, as did other interest groups, including the Japanese Family Planning Association, the Japanese Association of Obstetricians and Gynecologists, the Japanese Midwives Association, the LDP's Women's Bureau, and a designated abortion providers' group (Norgren 1998:83).

25. As Matsubara Yōko's research attests, eugenic thinking and practice among physicians who performed sterilizations and abortions as well as among potential parents who agreed to them have been firmly established ever since the late 1950s. In her recent research, Matsubara has found an unspoken agreement between physicians and potential parents that a child with disabilities would be undesirable because of the degree of discrimination it would suffer in Japan (conversation with Matsubara Yōko, July 1999).

26. A complete translation of the law can be found in Norgren 2001: 155–158.

27. When Nagai Hisomu died in 1956, obituaries also carefully refrained from referring to his wartime entanglement in racial hygiene politics (Fukuda 1957; Koike Shige 1957; Wakabayashi 1957). In Japan, Takagi Masashi (1989, 1991, 1993) was one of the first scholars to investigate Nagai's role in prewar and wartime Japanese eugenic policies.

28. For more biographical notes on Yamamoto Sugi, see also Akagawa 1999:282.

29. In the introduction to his report, Asayama (1949) acknowledged Yama-

moto's pioneering role in sex research. For "masturbation" he used *jii*, a term Yamamoto had introduced to emphasize the normalcy of the practice. Most other postwar sex researchers, however, unknowingly returned to the more accusatory language of the late nineteenth and early twentieth centuries. Only in the 1960s was the English term "masturbation" adopted.

30. For Okada, the crucial question for assessing the degree of sexual knowledge was whether children knew where they came from. According to the result of his study, only 20 percent knew the answer; 39.8 percent gave a wrong answer, and the rest had no idea. Equally worrisome to Okada was that the primary source of sexual knowledge was friends (20 percent), followed by family members (18 percent), books (15 percent), teachers (6 percent), and the students' own imaginations (6 percent).

31. The group's sample consisted of 452 third-year urban high school students from three different schools (96 boys and 125 girls) and 231 middle school graduates from rural areas (81 boys and 150 girls) (Saotome et el. 1953).

EPILOGUE

1. Between April 1998 (when Viagra was approved in the United States) and January 1999 (when it was approved in Japan) alone, hundreds of newspapers and magazines reported on the drug. Articles and article series appeared in media as diverse as the news magazine *Aera,* the business magazine *Nikkei Bijinesu,* popular science and health magazines such as *Nikkei Saiensu* and *Kurashi to Kenkō,* the women's magazine *Fujin Kōron,* liberal magazines such as *Shūkan Kinyōbi,* and right-wing papers such as *Sankei Shinbun* and *Shokun!*

2. In the United States, physicians differentiate between physical and nonphysical causes of impotence. Diabetes, medication for high blood pressure, hardening of the arteries leading to the penis, and the effects of prostate surgery rank highest among the most common physical causes, while depression is considered the number-one psychological cause (Leavy 1998).

3. Concerns about estrogen contamination resulting from widespread use of the pill seem misplaced, given that the urine of a woman in her fortieth week of pregnancy contains 10,000 times as much estrogen as that of a woman taking the pill (Kitamura K. 1999:44).

4. Medical doctor Leonore Tiefer (1994:365) has noted that definitions and norms for erections are absent from the medical literature. She concludes that the assumption that everyone knows what a "normal" erection is is central to the universalization and reification that supports both the medicalization of male sexuality and phallocentrism.

5. In her discussion of the debates over the legalization of the low-dose contraceptive pill, Tiana Norgren (1998) showed that mainstream women's groups as well as family planning organizations were rather ambivalent about the approval of the low-dose contraceptive pill. She persuasively argued that this ambivalence is to be attributed to the legacy of the aggressive pronatal policy of the 1920s, 1930s, and especially the 1940s, Japanese drug scandals of the 1960s, and concerns about side effects, among other factors.

6. In his analysis of the cultural context of condom use in present-day Japan, Samuel Coleman mentioned four factors for its widespread acceptance: easy use that does not require a medical examination or adjustment; successful marketing strategies; availability through grocery stores, pharmacies, vending machines, supermarkets, mail order, and home delivery; and a lack of reliable alternatives (Coleman 1981:29).

7. My analysis of the "rhetoric of reform" regarding the social welfare system for the elderly revealed that the Japanese administration reacted to the aging of society with a massive propagation of a common feeling of solidarity for the welfare of the community. Instead of the government investing in the establishment of affordable professional care institutions and a significant reform of existing homes for the elderly, this development means that women are more or less left alone with the problems and difficulties of caring for older people in their homes (Frühstück 2002).

8. When deciding whether or not to have a(nother) child, women typically consider the cost of having and raising a child, the size of their housing, the psychological and physical burdens, and the possibilities of harmonizing the duties of child-rearing with their own interests and work (Inoue und Ehara 1995:5). Due to the pathetically low contribution of their male partners to both childcare (Ishii-Kuntz 1994) and household chores (Imada 1997:5), these duties generally rest entirely on women's shoulders. For a broader analysis of women's roles in education, the household, work, and politics, see my article on gender inequity in present-day Japan (Frühstück 1999).

9. According to the 1990 *More Report (Moa ripōto NOW)* on sexual behavior and attitudes of women, 4.8 percent of 2,000 women surveyed between the ages of thirteen and sixty-one use the high-dose pill; 11 percent do not use any contraceptive whatsoever. The report notes that 60.3 percent have had at least one abortion, and 24.8 percent have had two (Imamura, Unno, and Ishimaru 1990:670).

10. In the July 1999 newsletter of the Ministry of Education, *The Education Ministry's Work (Monbushō no Hataraki)*, the ministry reported that its sex education guidelines of 1986, *Guidance on Sexual Matters within Student Guidance (Seitō shidō ni okeru sei ni kan suru shidō)*, had been replaced by new and significantly altered guidelines. In 1999, the ministry published a new 105-page document in which for the first time sex education is recommended for children from kindergarten through high school. The discussion of "concrete examples" such as respect for the other sex and "compensated dating" is encouraged (http://en.tokyo-shoseki.co.jp/kyouikukai/k9907/knews1.htm).

11. Since the 1970s, private organizations have attempted to develop a more diverse sexual pedagogy and to offer advice on sexual problems and have been engaged in the thorough, integrative study of sexuality. Most visibly, the Council for Education and Research on "Humans and Sex/Sexuality" ('Ningen to Sei' Kyōiku Kenkyū Kyōgikai), founded in 1982, criticized the kind of sex education the Ministry of Education had been promoting and demanded its reexamination according to the guidelines quoted in the above epigraph. Questioning the official guidelines for sex education that promote a "healthy, desirable, correct"

sexual behavior, sexual pedagogue Yamamoto Naogeki (Yamamoto Senji's son) demanded a fruitful combination of "sexual human rights" with "scientific sex education" (Hatta 2000).

12. AIDS, more than any other sexually transmitted disease, is another crucial issue in sex education in Japanese secondary schools. Instruction about HIV and AIDS often is designed to represent AIDS as the disease of others, whether these others are homosexuals or Japanese women who have casual relationships with foreigners (Kawahara 1996:157–158). This approach only reflects public debates about the causes of HIV that have leaned toward blaming foreigners and homosexuals and that have contributed significantly to discriminatory attitudes toward people with AIDS. After years of neglecting the disease after it was first reported in the *New York Times* in 1981, the chair of a government commission charged with formulating AIDS policy declared that the syndrome was now a danger for "people living ordinary lives," and proclaimed 1987 Japan's "AIDS Year One" (Treat 1994:651–652).

13. Sample sizes are still growing. In June 2001, the internet corporation Infopuranto created a questionnaire on sexual behavior and satisfaction within marriage under the guidance of a university professor from Chōfu Gakuen College. The questionnaire was sent out via email to 72,000 men and women. The results were published in the *Asahi Shinbun*.

14. In the study presented by Eric D. Widmer, Judith Treas, and Robert Newcomb (1998), data from a standardized questionnaire collected in twenty-four countries from large and nationally representative samples were used and cluster analysis was applied for the first time in a cross-national paper on sexual attitudes.

15. The women in the *More Report* were further categorized as 255 students, 133 housekeepers, 1,292 white-collar workers, 30 self-employed workers, 257 housewives, and 20 undefined (Imamura, Unno, and Ishimaru 1990: 656). A second volume of the *More Report,* this one on men, came out a few years after the first.

16. The prime minister's office collects all large-scale (about 1,000 respondents and above) public opinion surveys on a wide range of social, political, and economic issues, from opinions on Article 9 of the constitution to views on premarital sex, and publishes them annually as the *Yearbook of Public Opinion Surveys (Seron chōsa nenkan).*

Bibliography

SOURCES IN JAPANESE

Abe Isoo. 1911a. "Kōshō seido to shakai no fūgi" (The prostitution system and social customs). *Kakusei* 1(1):23–29.

———. 1911b. "Jindō mondai toshite kōshō seido o ronzu" (Discussing the prostitution system as humanitarian problem). *Kakusei* 1(2):93–97.

———. 1911c. "Kōshō seido to shakai no fūgi" (The prostitution system and social customs). *Kakusei* 1(4):219–222.

———. 1913. "Augusuto Beberu" (August Bebel). *Taiyō* 19(16):154–163.

———. 1915. "Teisō mondai ni tsuite" (On the chastity problem). *Kakusei* 5(7):3–5.

———. 1916. "Jiyū ren'ai o ronzu" (Discussing free love). *Kakusei* 6(12):4–7.

———. 1918. "Kaikyūteki dōtoku to byōdōteki dōtoku" (Class-specific morals and egalitarian morals). *Kakusei* 8(5):6–8.

———. 1919a. "Nani ga sore hodo fudōtoku ka" (What is so immoral?). *Fujin Kōron* 5(8):41–44.

———. 1919b. "Kodomo no ue ni" (About children). *Fujin Kōron* 5(9):41–43.

———. 1922. "Danjo kyōgaku to danjo kōsai" (Coeducation and the intercourse of the sexes). *Kakusei* 12(6):7–10.

———. 1923. "Ren'ai to kekkon" (Love and marriage). *Kakusei* 13(6):1–3.

———. 1924a. "Seiyoku to teisō kannen no kindaiteki kattō to sono kyūsai" (The modern conflict between sexual desire and chastity and its solution). *Hentai Shinri* 14(5):668–672.

———. 1924b. "Karyūbyō chōsa kikan no kyūmu" (Urgent duties of the organization for the survey of venereal diseases). *Kakusei* 14(4):1–3.

———. 1925. "Sanji seigen wa fudōtoku de nai" (Birth control is not immoral). *Sanji Seigen Hyōron* 1:1–2.

————. 1926a. "Shakai mondai toshite no ninshin chōsetsu" (Birth control as social problem). *Tsūzoku Igaku* 4(6):3–5.

————. 1926b. "Shippai seru shokumin seisaku" (The failing colonial policies). *Sei to Shakai* 14:2–5.

————. 1927a. "Ningen seikatsu no heiwa wa ninshin chōsetsu no jikkō de aru" (The peace of human life lies in the realization of birth control). *Tsūzoku Igaku* 5(7):2–4.

————. 1927b. "Gendai no teisōkan" (The current view of chastity). *Kakusei* 17(6):1–3.

————. 1929. "Kanzen naru sanji seigen no shudan to hōhō" (Means and methods of perfect birth control). *Tsūzoku Igaku* 7(9):43–46.

————. 1932. "Dōtokukan to keizaikan" (Views of morals and views of economy). *Kakusei* 22(2):1–4.

————. 1936. "Katei ni okeru teisō kyōiku" (Chastity education at home). *Kakusei* 26(12):1–3.

————. 1942. "Jinkō mondai to danjo mondai" (The population problem and the gender problem). *Kakusei* 32(3):3–5.

————. 1944. "Sōkon seido no teishō" (Advocacy of early marriage). *Kakusei* 34(7):1–3.

Adachi Yasuo. 1930. "Jogakusei no seiteki henka to seiseki no yūretsu" (Sexual changes in female pupils and the quality of their grades). *Tsūzoku Igaku* 8(4):95–97.

Akagawa Manabu. 1999. *Sekushuariti no rekishi shakaigaku* (Historical sociology of sexuality). Tokyo: Keisō shobō.

Akama Moritaka. 1927. *Kinshi honshomoku* (Catalogue of forbidden books). Kyoto: Bunkō shoten.

Akamatsu Keisuke. 1993. *Sonraku kyōdōtai to seiteki kihan* (Village communities and sexual norms). Tokyo: Genshosha.

Akamatsu Keisuke, Ueno Chizuko, and Ōtsuki Takahiro. 1995. *Waidan* (Filthy talk). Tokyo: Gendai shobo.

Akatsu Nobumasa. 1927. "Naze? Sono yō ni kakusu no desu" (Why hide in this manner?). *Seiron* 1(4):62–65.

Amemiya Yasuhiro. 1928. "Gendai seikatsu ni awareru bunmeibyō no ohanashi" (A story of diseases of civilization that occur in contemporary life). *Tsūzoku Igaku* 6(8):9–11.

Andō Kiyoyuki. 1930. "Jidoku rangyō kara kyokudo no shinkei suijaku" (From masturbatory misconduct to the worst neurasthenia). *Tsūzoku Igaku* 8(12): 128–130.

Anzai Sadako. 1953. *Yasen kangofu* (Field nurse). Tokyo: Fuji shobōsha.

Aoki Hisao. 1954. "Kikonsha no sanbun no ichi wa jūdatsu chōsetsu o shite iru: Mada jikkō shite inai hito wa donna hōhō o erandara yoi ka" (One-third of married people use contraceptives: Which method should those use who do not yet use contraceptives?) *Fūfu Seikatsu* 17(14):238–241.

Aoki Seizaburō. 1934. "Iseikan to seikyōiku" (Views of the other sex and sex education). *Tsūzoku Igaku* 11(1):2–5.

Arai Hyōgo, ed. 1934. *Kango to ryōhō: Katei iten* (Household medical encyclopedia for nursing and healing methods). Tokyo: Dai Nihon yūbenkai Kōdansha.

Araki Kiichirō. 1931. *Katei iten* (Household medical encyclopedia). Tokyo: Ōsaka mainichi shinbunsha and Tōkyō mainichi shinbunsha.

Arioka Jirō. 1990. "Kazoku no yōsei de nyūsho chōkika mo" (The possible extensions of institutionalization because of family needs). *Asahi Shinbun* 30 March, 4.

Asayama Shin'ichi. 1949. *Sei no kiroku. Sengo Nihonjin no seikōdō o kagaku-teki ni chōsa shita shiryō ni motozuku* (Documented sexuality: Based on scientifically acquired material on the sex lives of the Japanese after the war). Osaka: Rokugatsusha.

Burashuko, A. [Blaschko, Alfred]. 1914. "Eiseijō yori kōshō seido o ronzu" (Discussing the prostitution system from the viewpoint of hygiene). *Kakusei* 4(3):5–11.

Buroho, Iwan [Bloch, Iwan]. 1920. "Shinmarusasushugi no kenkyū" (Neomalthusian research). *Sei no Kenkyū* 2(1):2–9.

Chiba Shunji. 1993. "Minoue sōdan" (Advice). *Kokubungaku Kaishaku to Kyōsai no Kenkyū* 38(6):114.

Chichibu Jinijirō. 1952. *Kekkon hōten: Kanzen naru shinkon fūfu no seikōhō* (Marriage treasure book: Perfect sexual intercourse methods for newlyweds). Tokyo: Sōbunsha.

Chūma Okimaru. 1921. "Giin no karyūbyōsha kekkon seigen ni tsuite no tōron" (The parliamentary debate on marriage restrictions for persons with venereal diseases). *Josei Dōmei* 6(3):38–46.

Chūō Kōron. 1912. "Chūgaku teido no danjo gakusei ni seiyoku ni kan suru chishiki o atau to no kahi" (Reasons for and against sex education for middle school students). *Chūō Kōron* 27(1):179–213.

Chūō Shinbun. 1913. "Nihonjin no shinchō ga dandan takaku naru" (The Japanese become taller). *Chūō Shinbun* 14 August.

———. 1914. "Zenkoku kenkō chōsa" (National health survey). *Chūō Shinbun* 5 January.

Dai Nihon Kyōiku Zasshi. 1888. "Gakkō eisei" (School hygiene). *Dai Nihon Kyōiku Zasshi* 110:917–923.

Date Gen. 1951a. "Shojo-hen" (Girls' part). In *Musume to tsuma to haha no eisei hyakka zenshū* (Hygiene encyclopedia for daughters, wives, and mothers), ed. Shufu to seikatsu-sha, 10–27. Tokyo: Shufu to seikatsu-sha.

———. 1951b. "Kekkon-hen" (Part on marriage). In *Musume to tsuma to haha no eisei hyakka zenshū* (Hygiene encyclopedia for daughters, wives, and mothers), ed. Shufu to seikatsu-sha, 28–43. Tokyo: Shufu to seikatsu-sha.

Doi Keizō. 1934. "Seibyō no kigen to mannen" (Origin and dissemination of venereal disease). *Kakusei* 24(8):16–19.

Erisu, Haberokku [Ellis, Havelock]. 1925. "Hermann Rohleder no hininhō no kanōsei" (Possibilities of Hermann Rohleder's contraception method). *Hentai Shinri* 16(6):26–27.

Fūfu Seikatsu. 1954. "Igaku tokushū: Otto no 99% ga shiranai tsuma kankaku no kyūsho" (Medicine special: The key spot for a wife's feeling that 99% of husbands do not know). *Fūfu Seikatsu* 17(14):23–49.

Fujii Matsuichi. 1958. "Abe Isoo." In *Nihon rekishi daijiten* (Encyclopedia of Japanese history), ed. Kawade Takao, 153–154. Tokyo: Kawade shobō shinsha.

Fujikawa Hideo, ed. 1982. *Fujikawa Yū chosakushū* (Collected works of Fujikawa Yū). Kyoto: Shibunkyaku shuppan.

Fujikawa Yū. 1900. "Gakureki jidō no shikijō ni tsuite" (The sexual instinct in educated children). *Jidō Kenkyū* 2:454–460.

———. 1905. "Honshi no shui" (The aims of this journal). *Jinsei* 1(1):1.

———. 1907a. "Shikijō no kyōiku" (Education about sexual desire). *Jidō Kenkyū* 10(10):20–22.

———. 1907b. "Shikijō no kyōiku" (Education about sexual desire). *Jidō Kenkyū* 10(11):24–26.

———. 1908a. "Seiyoku kyōiku mondai" (The problem of sex education). *Chūō Kōron* 23(10):26–37.

———. 1908b. "Seiyoku kyōiku mondai" (The problem of sex education). *Yomiuri Shinbun* 30 October, 5.

———. 1912. "Baidoku no rekishi" (History of syphilis). *Chūō Kōron* 27(7): 91–102.

———. 1915. "Shakai eiseiron" (Theories of social hygiene). *Chūō Kōron* 30(8):145–152.

———. 1916. "Seiyō igaku to tōyō igaku" (Western medicine and Eastern medicine). *Chūō Kōron* 31(8):61–70.

———. 1919a. "Saikin no gakusetsu" (New scientific theories). *Hentai Shinri* 4(7):74–81.

———. 1919b. "Furyōshōnen mondai" (The problem of juvenile delinquency). *Kakusei* 9(6):12–14.

———. 1919c. "Shinakereba naranu hinin to shite wa naranu hinin" (Contraception that must be done and contraception that must not be done). *Fujin Kōron* 5(8):44–49.

———. 1919d. "Nihon fujin no biten toshite teisō no kontei" (Chastity as the basis of Japanese women's virtue). *Fujin Kōron* 5(9):36–39.

———. 1922. "Seiyokugaku no kenkyū" (Research in sexology). *Jinsei—Der Mensch* 9(5):162–164.

———. 1923. "Seiyoku no seishinka" (Psychologized sexual desire). *Hentai Shinri* 12(1):157–158.

———. 1924. "Seiyoku no mondai" (The sexual problem). *Chūō Kōron* 38(8): 51–62.

———. 1928. "Fujin zasshi to seiyoku mondai" (Women's magazines and the sexual problem). *Chūō Kōron* 43(6):77–80.

Fujikawa Yū sensei kankōkai, ed. 1988. *Fujikawa Yū sensei* (Professor Fujikawa Yū). Tokyo: Daikūsha.

Fujime Yuki. 1986. "Senkanki Nihon no sanji chōsetsu undō to sono shisō" (The birth control movement and its thought during interwar Japan). *Rekishi Hyōron* 430:79–100.

———. 1993. "Aru sanba no kiseki: Shibahara Urako to sanji chōsetsu" (Biography of a certain midwife: Shibahara Urako and birth control). *Nihonshi Kenkyū* 366:90–112.

——. 1999. *Sei no rekishigaku: Kōshō seido, dataizai taisei kara Baishun bō-shihō, Yūsei hogohō taisei e* (The historiography of sexuality: Shifting systems from licensed prostitution and criminalized abortion to the Prostitution Prevention Law and the Eugenic Protection Law). Tokyo: Fuji shuppan.

Fujinami Shunji. 1932. "Seiteki shinkei suijaku to seiyoku shōgai" (Sexual neurasthenia and sexual impairments). *Tsūzoku Igaku* 10(5):127–129.

Fujino Yutaka. 1993. *Nihon fashizumu to iryō* (Fascism and medicine in Japan). Tokyo: Iwanami shoten.

——. 1996. "Nihon fashizumu to byōsha shōgaisha" (Japanese fascism and the sick and handicapped). *Kikan: Sensō Sekinin Kenkyū* 12: 48–55.

——. 1998. "Nihon fashizumu to seibyō" (Japanese fascism and venereal diseases). *Kikan: Sensō Sekinin Kenkyū* 22: 54–61.

——, ed. 1999. *'Yūsei Undō' kaisetsu, sōmokuji, sakuin* (*Eugenics Movement*: Commentary, table of contents, and index). Tokyo: Fuji shuppan.

Fujitani T. 1994. "Kindai Nihon ni okeru kenryoku no tekunorojii" (Power and technology in modern Japan). *Shisō* 845:163–176.

Fujo Shinbun. 1911. "Dōsei no ai" (Same-sex love). *Fujo Shinbun* 11 August, 7.

——. 1912. "Dōsei no ai no kenkyū" (Research on same-sex love). *Fujo Shinbun* 11 August, 4.

——. 1923. "Seikyōiku no hon no igi" (The importance of books on sex education). *Fujo Shinbun* 1 July, 1.

——. 1930. "Seikyōiku no jiki to hōhō" (Time and method of sex education). *Fujo Shinbun* 29 June, 5–6.

Fukuda Kunizō. 1957. "Nagai sensei no fūkaku" (Profile of Professor Nagai). *Nihon Iji Shinpō* 1726:74.

Fukuomo Kansha. 1911. "Seiyoku mondai ni kan suru chojutsu" (Works concerning sexual issues). *Shinkōron* 26(9):7–10.

Furukawa Makoto. 1993. "Ren'ai to seiyoku no daisan teikoku" (The third reich of love and sexual desire). *Gendai Shisō* 21(7):110–145.

Furukawa Tetsushi. 1972. "Inoue Tetsujirō." In *Dainihon hyakka jiten. Encyclopedia Japonica*, ed. Saga Tetsuo, 250. Tokyo: Shōgakkan.

Furuya Toyako. 1922. "Dōseiai no joshi kyōikujō ni okeru shinigi" (The new significance of homosexuality in girls' education). *Fujin Kōron* 7(8): 24–29.

Fuse Nobuyoshi. 1923. "Hentai seiyoku to jūtaku mondai" (Sexual perversions and housing problems). *Kakusei* 13(2):20.

Gendai. 1998. "Ureshi hazukashi Baiagura" (Viagra, delightful and embarrassing). *Gendai* 32(10):206–214.

——. 1999. "Seiseikatsu no chiei to gijutsu" (Wisdom and techniques in your sex life). *Gendai* 33(1):163–175.

Gendai seikagaku kenkyūkai, ed. 1981. *Shinhan sekai seiikagaku: Sei no dēta bukku* (New edition on world medical sexology: Databook of sex). Tokyo: Bigakukan.

Gotō Shinpei. 1926. *Kōmin dokuhon: Shōnen no kan* (Citizens' reader: Volume for boys). Tokyo: Hakubunkan.

———. 1978 (1889). *Kokka eisei genri* (Principles of national hygiene). Tokyo: Sōzō shuppan.

Habuto Eiji. 1919. "Seiteki haji to shoyū no kannen" (Views on sexual shame and possession). *Fujin Kōron* 5(9):48–50.

———. 1921. "Seiteki hanmon kaiketsusho" (Solutions to sexual anguish). *Seiyoku to Jinsei* 2(3):35–36.

———. 1928a. "Seishōsetsu miiro no koi" (Three-colored sex in sex novels). *Seiron* 2(2):89–100.

———. 1928b. "Fujin no kaihō undō to seiteki seikatsu no hensen" (The women's liberation movement and the transition of sexual life). *Tsūzoku Igaku* 6(2):71–73.

Habuto Eiji and Sawada Junjirō. 1915. *Hentai seiyokuron* (Perverse sexual desire). Tokyo: Sunyōdō.

Hasegawa Nyozekan. 1922. "Sei no seikatsu ni okeru gendaijin no hanshō" (Reflections of contemporaries in sexual life). *Fujin Kōron* 7(7):9–19.

Hashizume Masuo. 1954. "Katsuyaku suru wagina to katsuyaku shinai wagina" (Active and passive vaginas). *Fūfu Seikatsu* 17(14):32–36.

Hatta Nobutaka. 2000. "Seikyōikusha Yamamoto Naogeki" (Sex educator Yamamoto Naogeki). *Asahi Shinbun* 17 July.

Hayakawa Jirō. 1936. "Chūsei ni okeru ren'ai oyobi kekkon" (Love and marriage in the Middle Ages). *Seikagaku Kenkyū* 1(5):15–25.

Hayasaka Chōichirō. 1930. "Enmu to seiyoku" (Erotic dreams and sexual desire). *Hanzai Kagaku* 1(4):42–49.

Hayashi Hiroshi. 1993. "Rikugun no ianjo kanri no ichisokumen: 'Eisei sakku' kōfu shiryō o tegakari ni" (One aspect of the management of the army's comfort stations: Clues to the delivery of "condoms"). *Kikan: Sensō Sekinin Kenkyū Sōkangō:* 12–19.

Hayashi Tadahiko. 1980. *Kasutori jidai* (Kasutori era). Tokyo: Asahi sonorama.

Hayashi Utako. 1936. "Junketsu mondai to josei no sekinin" (The issue of purity and women's responsibility). *Kakusei* 26(12):7–8.

Hentai Seiyoku. 1924a. "Joshi no danseika no genin ni kan suru shinchiken" (New insights about the causes of masculinization in women). *Hentai Seiyoku* 5(1):1–7.

———. 1924b. "Joshi no dōseiai to hanzai" (Female homosexuality and crime). *Hentai Seiyoku* 5(1):200–209.

———. 1924c. "Seiyoku kōshin to hisuterii" (The increase of sexual desire and hysteria). *Hentai Seiyoku* 5(6):239–247.

———. 1925a. "Yokujō to seiteki fūzoku no bunran" (Sexual desire and the destruction of sexual morals). *Hentai Seiyoku* 6(1):1–2.

———. 1925b. "Seishokuron" (On reproduction). *Hentai Seiyoku* 6(1):35–39.

Hentai Shinri. 1921. "Sei no kenkyū no ryūkō" (The fashion of sex research). *Hentai Shinri* 8(1):24.

Hinata Daigishi Fujin. 1911. "Fujin shakai to geishōgi mondai" (Women in society and the prostitution problem). *Kakusei* 1(3):40–43.

Hiratsuka Raichō, ed. 1983 (1916). *Hiratsuka Raichō chosakushū* (Collected works of Hiratsuka Raichō). Tokyo: Ōgetsu shoten.

Hirota Motokichi. 1919. *Shinkei suijaku ni tsuite* (About neurasthenia). Kyoto: Kakubundō shobō.

Hōchi Shinbun. 1916a. "Shinchō wa nobite jūryō ga heru" (Height increases, weight decreases). *Hōchi Shinbun* 14 June.

———. 1916b. "Wakai onna no sei ga takaku naru" (Young women become taller). *Hōchi Shinbun* 6 July.

Hodan, Makusu (Hodann, Max). 1936. "Magunusu Hirushuferuto kyōju no tsuioku" (Professor Magnus Hirschfeld's memories). *Seikagaku Kenkyū* 1(4):64–68.

Honda Misao. 1931. "Fujin kōza: Ninshin chōsetsu mondai ni tsuite" (Women's course: On the issue of birth control). In *Radio-Text*, ed. Nihon hōsō kyōkai Kansai shibu, 32–38. Osaka: Nihon hōsō shuppan kyōkai Kansai shisha.

Honma Hisao. 1918a. "Seiteki dōtoku no hakai" (The destruction of sexual morals). *Fujo Shinbun* 24 May, 3.

———. 1918b. "Seiteki dōtoku no hakai" (The destruction of sexual morals). *Fujo Shinbun* 20 July, 3.

———. 1924. "Shinseiteki dōtoku ni tsuite" (On the new sexual morals). *Fujo Shinbun* 24 February, 4–6.

Hosoi Wakizō. 1996 (1925). *Jokō aishi* (The sad history of factory women). Tokyo: Iwanami shoten.

Ichikawa Gensaburō. 1919. "Susunde seikyōiku no jissai o ronzu" (Voluntarily discussing the reality of sex education). *Fujin Kōron* 5(9):14–20.

———. 1936. "Sei no kyōiku no hitsuyō" (The necessity of sex education). *Seikagaku Kenkyū* 1(1):52–54.

Ida Hideaki. 1922. "Saishin kagaku no ue ni kizukaretaru jōshiki" (Common sense built upon recent science). *Nihon oyobi Nihonjin* 20 September, 835: 299–311.

Ieda Sakichi. 1936. "Seichishiki to seidōtoku no kanyō" (Fostering sexual knowledge and morals). *Kakusei* 26(3):30–31.

———. 1939. "Seinenkō no seibyō to risonjō mondai" (Venereal disease in factory workers and the problem of girls who migrated from the villages). *Kakusei* 29(3):17–19.

Iijima Miyasu. 1932. "Shijo ni tai suru seikyōiku wa naze ni subeki ka?" (Why shall we sexually educate children?). *Tsūzoku Igaku* 10(5):153–156.

Iizuka Kōji, ed. 1968. *Nihon no guntai* (The Japanese military). Tokyo: Hyōron-sha.

Imai Seiichi, ed. 1962. *Shinsai ni yuragu* (Shattered by the earthquake). Tokyo: Chikuma shobō.

Imai Tsuneo. 1906. *Katei oyobi kyōiku* (Family and education). Tokyo: Tōkaidō.

Imamura Naomi, Unno Yūki, and Ishimaru Kumiko, eds. 1990. *Moa ripōto NOW* (More report now). Tokyo: Shūeisha.

Inagaki Suematsu. 1908. "Seiyoku mondai to kongō kyōiku" (The sexual problem and coeducation). *Yomiuri Shinbun* 10 September, 5.

Inamura Ryūichi. 1925. "Nōson jinkō mondai" (The population problem in the peasantry). *Sanji Chōsetsu Hyōron* 5:24–28.

Inoue Teruko and Ehara Yumiko, eds. 1995. *Josei no dēta bukku* (Women's databook). Tokyo: Yūhikaku.

Inoue Tetsujirō. 1923. "Seiyoku kyōiku mondai" (The problem of education about sexual desire). *Hentai Shinri* 12(1):157.

Ishige Haruo. 1943a. "Ippu ippuron to junketsu 1" (Monogamy and purity 1). *Kakusei* 33(1):16–19.

———. 1943b. "Ippu ippuron to junketsu 2" (Monogamy and purity 2). *Kakusei* 33(2):18–20.

———. 1943c. "Ippu ippuron to junketsu 3" (Monogamy and purity 3). *Kakusei* 33(4):11–13.

———. 1943d. "Ippu ippuron to junketsu 4" (Monogamy and purity 4). *Kakusei* 33(5):13–15.

———. 1943e. "Ippu ippuron to junketsu 5" (Monogamy and purity 5). *Kakusei* 33(8):12–14.

Ishikawa Chiyomatsu. 1911. "Seiyoku ni kan suru atarashiki kansatsu" (New insights into sexual desire). *Shinkōron* 26(9):17–21.

———. 1928. "Sanji seigen wa hon ni hitsuyō ka" (Is birth control really necessary?). *Seiron* 2(1):6–9.

Ishikawa Hiroyoshi, Saitō Shigeo, and Wagatsuma Hiroshi, eds. 1984. *Nihonjin no sei* (Sexuality of the Japanese). Tokyo: Kabushikigaisha bungei shunju.

Ishizaki Nobuko. 1992. "Seishoku no jiyū to sanji chōsetsu undō: Hiratsuka Raichō to Yamamoto Senji" (Reproductive freedom and the birth control movement: Hiratsuka Raichō and Yamamoto Senji). *Rekishi Hyōron* 503: 92–107.

Itō Keiichi. 1969. *Heitai-tachi no rikugunshi* (The soldiers' army history). Tokyo: Banchō shobō.

Iwanaga Shinji. 1994. "Taishō-ki no eisei chōsa: Naimushō eiseikyoku 'Nōson hoken eisei jōtai jittai chōsa' ni kan suru joronteki kōsatsu" (Hygiene surveys of the Taishō era. Bureau of Hygiene in the Home Department: Introductory remarks on the "Survey on the condition of health and hygiene among the rural population"). In *Kindai Nihon shakai chōsashi 3* (The history of social research in modern Japan 3), ed. Kawai Takao, 79–118, Tokyo: Keiō tsūshin.

Iwaya Sueo. 1902. "Nan sho k'" (Pedophilia in Japan). *Jahrbuch für sexuelle Zwischenstufen* 4:265–271.

Jiji Shinpō. 1914. "Gakudō no shintai kensa" (Physical exam of pupils). *Jiji Shinpō* 6 January.

Josei Dōmei. 1921. "Karyūbyōsha ni tai suru kekkon seigen narabi ni rikon seikyū ni kan suru seigensho" (Petition for the restriction of marriage and divorce of persons with venereal diseases). *Josei Dōmei* 1(1):4–8.

Jūgun ianfu 110-ban henshū iinkai. 1992. *Jūgun ianfu 110-ban* (Former army comfort women's hotline number 110). Tokyo: Jūgun ianfu 110-ban henshū iinkai.

Kagawa Toyohiko. 1925. "Beikoku no sanji chōsetsu renmei senden bira" (The propaganda bill of the American Birth Control League). *Sanji Chōsetsu Hyōron* 8:33–37.

——. 1926. "Seiyoku mondai yori mitaru kōshō" (Public prostitution as sexual problem). *Kakusei* 16(3):7–13.

——. 1936. "Haishō undō no konpon seishin" (The basic spirit of the abolition movement). *Kakusei* 26(1):7–10.

——. 1937. "Seiseikatsu no shukusei" (The extinction of sexual life). *Kakusei* 27(2):5–11.

Kaigunshō. 1897. *Kaigunshō Meiji nijūkyū nendo nenpō* (Annual report of the Navy Ministry for the year Meiji 29). Tokyo: Kaigunshō.

——. 1906. *Kaigunshō Meiji sanjūhachi nendo nenpō* (Annual report of the Navy Ministry for the year Meiji 38). Tokyo: Kaigunshō.

——. 1907. *Kaigunshō Meiji sanjūkyū nendo nenpō* (Annual report of the Navy Ministry for the year Meiji 39). Tokyo: Kaigunshō.

——. 1909. *Kaigunshō Meiji yonjūichi nendo nenpō* (Annual report of the Navy Ministry for the year Meiji 41). Tokyo: Kaigunshō.

Kaigunshō imukyoku. 1900. *Nisshin senyaku kaigun eiseishi* (Hygiene history of the Sino-Japanese war). Tokyo: Kaigunshō imukyoku.

Kaji Tokijirō. 1926a. "Seiyoku no jiyū to seigen" (Freedom and control of sexual desire). *Tsūzoku Igaku* 4(6):85–88.

——. 1926b. "Seiyoku no jiyū to seigen" (Freedom and control of sexual desire). *Sei to Shakai* 14:10–17.

Kakusei. 1932. "Sei no himitsu o kakusazu ni oshieyo!" (Unveil the secret of sexuality!). *Kakusei* 22(7):26.

Kameyama Michiko. 1997 (1984). *Kindai Nihon no kango-shi II: Sensō to kango* (The history of nursing in modern Japan 2: War and nursing). Tokyo: Domesu shuppan.

Kami Shōichirō. 1977. *Gekidōki no kodomo* (Children during shocking times). In *Nihon kodomo no rekishi 6* (A history of Japanese children 6), ed. 'Nihon Kodomo no Rekishi' henshū iinkai. Tokyo: Dai ippō shuppan.

Kanda Hyōzō. 1925. "BC o musan fujin no shoyū e" (Birth control into the hands of proletarian women). *Sanji Chōsetsu Hyōron* 6:47–49.

Kaneko Eiju et al. 1955. "Rinshō sōdan no igaku" (Advice from clinical medicine). *Fūfu Seikatsu* 2:67–94.

Kanzaki Suzushi. 1954a. "Kodomo no aru fūfu no pēji: Kodomo o kuimono ni suru na" (Page for couples with children: Do not victimize children). *Fūfu Seikatsu* 15(6):154–155.

——. 1954b. ""Kodomo no aru fūfu no pēji: Hahaoya o komaraseru sei ni kan suru kodomo no shitsumon" (Children's questions about sex that trouble mothers). *Fūfu Seikatsu* 17(14):70–71.

——. 1955. "Kodomo no aru fūfu no pēji: Shishunki no mon: Shōnenki no seikyōiku wa kōshite" (Page for couples with children: The gate to puberty: Instruction on sex education during puberty). *Fūfu Seikatsu* 16(11):130–131.

Kariya Haruo. 1993. *Edo no seibyō* (Venereal diseases in the Edo period). Tokyo: Sanichi shobō.

Katayama K. 1911. "Inshu to seiyoku" (Alcohol and sexual desire). *Shinkōron* 26(9):25–28.

Katō Jirō. 1911. "Dantai seikatsu no kōjō to honnōyoku" (Instincts and the improvement of life in groups). *Shinkōron* 26(9):28–31.

Katō Koyume. 1927. "Sekai hentai seiyoku shofu" (World bibliography on perverse sexual desire). *Hentai Shiryō* 2(8):49–51.

Katō Tokiya. 1925a. "Igakujō yori mitaru sanji chōsetsu no hanashi" (Birth control viewed from a medical perspective). *Sanji Chōsetsu Hyōron* 1:19–23.

——. 1925b. "Sanji seigenhō no jissaiteki kachi ni tsuite" (About the real value of birth control). *Sanji Chōsetsu Hyōron* 4:46–47.

Katō Yōko. 1996. *Chōheisei to kindai Nihon, 1868–1945* (The conscription system and modern Japan, 1868–1945). Tokyo: Yoshikawa kobunkan.

Katsura Jinzō. 1926. "Sanji chōsetsu undō no jissai hōmen" (A realistic side of the birth control movement). *Sei to Shakai* 14:59–62.

Kawai Hayao. 1997. " 'Enjō kōsai' to iu mūbumento" (The "compensated dating" movement). *Sekai* March, 137–148.

Kawai Takao, ed. 1989. *Kindai Nihon shakai chōsashi 1* (The history of social research in modern Japan 1). Tokyo: Keiō tsūshin.

——. 1991. *Kindai Nihon shakai chōsashi 2* (The history of social research in modern Japan 2). Tokyo: Keiō tsūshin.

——. 1994. *Kindai Nihon shakai chōsashi 3* (The history of social research in modern Japan 3). Tokyo: Keiō tsūshin.

Kawamura Kunimitsu. 1996. *Sekushuariti no kindai* (Modern sexuality). (Kōdansha sensho mechie 86). Tokyo: Kōdansha.

Kawatani Masao. 1928. "Kaigai seiron nyūsu" (Overseas news on sex theories). *Seiron* 2(2):39–41.

Kei, Eren [Key, Ellen]. 1918. "Bosei no sonchō" (Respect for motherhood). *Fujo Shinbun* 28 June, 4.

Kimura Ryōko. 1992. "Fujin zasshi no jōhō kūkan to josei taishū dokushasō no seiritsu" (The information space of women's magazines and the emergence of a female mass readership). *Shisō* 812:231–252.

Kindai josei bunka-shi kenkyūkai. 2001. *Sensō to josei zasshi, 1931-nen–1945-nen* (War and women's magazines, 1931–1945). Tokyo: Domesu shuppan.

Kitamura Hitoshi. 1933. "Hentai seiyoku to hanzaisō no dashin" (An examination of perverse sexuality and crime forms). *Tsūzoku Igaku* 11(1):37–40.

Kitano Hiromi. 1919. "Sei no mondai: sei to seikatsu, kenkyū no rekishi" (Sexual issues: Sex and life, research history). *Sei no Kenkyū* 1(1):1–4.

——. 1920. "Onanii no kenkyū" (Research on masturbation). *Sei no Kenkyū* 2(2):47–54.

——. 1921. "Onanii ni kan suru tōkei" (Statistics on masturbation). *Sei no Kenkyū* 3(1):16–19.

Kiyokawa Ikuko. 1991. "Riterashī no fukyū to 'sōtei kyōiku chōsa'. Riterashī no fukyū to shakai chōsa 1" (Literacy and the "educational surveys of young men" 1). In *Kindai Nihon shakai chōsashi 2* (The history of social research in modern Japan 2), ed. Kawai Takao, 3–42. Tokyo: Keiō tsūshin.

Koide Mitsuji. 1932. *Shinhen joshi kōmin kyōkasho* (New edition: Textbook for civic education for girls). Tokyo: Meibundō.

Koide Shun. 1936. "Hirschfeld hakushi no Nihon inshōki" (Dr. Hirschfeld's impressions of Japan). *Seikagaku Kenkyū* 1(2):107–113.

Koike Shige. 1957. "Nagai Hisomu hakushi no fu o kiite" (Obituary for Dr. Nagai Hisomu). *Nihon Iji Shinpō* 1726:73.

Koike Shirō. 1925. "Mazushiki hito e no sanji chōsetsu" (Birth control for the poor). *Sanji Chōsetsu Hyōron* 4:11–13.

Koiwa [Itsu?]. 1925. "Sanji seigen to musan kaikyū" (Birth control and the proletariat). *Sanji Chōsetsu Hyōron* 2:9–11.

Kojima Munekichi. 1942. *Rikugun naimu zensho jō* (Compendium to the internal affairs of the army 1). Tokyo: Muyōdō.

Kōseishō imukyoku, ed. 1955. *Isei hachijūnenshi* (An eighty-year history of the medical system). Tokyo: Insatsukyoku chōyōkai.

———. 1976. *Isei hyakunenshi* (A one-hundred-year history of the medical system). Tokyo: Honsha eigyōsho.

KRB [Kurume Rikugun Byōin]. 1927. *Rikugun ni okeru karyūbyō: Heichihō ni okeru karyūbyō man'en no jōkyō* (Venereal disease in the army: The condition of the dissemination of venereal diseases according to regions). Tokyo: Rikugunshō.

Kurotaki Shigeyoshi. 1936. "Seikyōiku no shomondai" (Various problems of sex education). *Seikagaku Kenkyū* 1(7):55–66.

Kurozumi Hisashi. 1925a. "Mottomo osorubeki seibyō no jiryō to yōsei" (Care of and recovery from the most serious venereal diseases). *Tsūzoku Igaku* 3(6):57–59.

———. 1925b. "Mottomo osorubeki seibyō no jiryō to sono yōjō" (Care of and recovery from the most terrible venereal diseases). *Tsūzoku Igaku* 3(7):69–70.

———. 1925c. "Mottomo osorubeki seibyō no jiryō to sono yōjō" (Care of and recovery from the most terrible venereal diseases). *Tsūzoku Igaku* 3(9):82–84.

Kurushima Takehiko. 1899. *Nichiyō hyakka zensho dai yonjūhen: Kokumin hikkei rikugun ippan* (Everyday use encyclopedia 40: Indespensable army handbook for the people). Tokyo: Hyakubunkan.

Kutsumi Fusako. 1925. "Naze ni wareware wa hantai shita ka!" (Why we were against it!). *Sanji Chōsetsu Hyōron* 4:53.

Kuwatani Sadaichi. 1911. "Senritsu subeki joseikan no tentō seiyoku" (The despicable inverted sexual desire among women). *Shinkōron* 26(9):35–42.

Maeda Ai. 1993 (1973). "Kindai dokusha no seiritsu" (The formation of a modern readership). Tokyo: Iwanami shoten.

Manchōhō. 1916. "Ningen o ōku fuyasaneba naranu" (People must multiply tremendously). *Manchōhō* 1 December, n.p.

Marumoto Yuriko. 1995. "Ososuginai ka, Nihon no piru kaikin" (Isn't it too late for the legalization of the pill in Japan?). *Hon no Mado* 6, 14–17.

Maruyama Hiroshi. 1984. *Mori Ōgai to eiseigaku* (Mori Ōgai and hygiene). Tokyo: Keisō shobō.

Masaki Jinsaburō. 1927 (1922). *Shinrigaku ka kyōtei* (Unauthorized manual of psychology). N.p.

Masuda Hōson. 1924. *Jidō shakai-shi* (A social history of children). Tokyo: Kōseikyaku shuppan.

Matsubara Yōko. 1993. "Meiji matsuki ni okeru seikyōiku ronsō. Fujikawa Yū

chūshin ni" (The dispute on sex education at the end of the Meiji era: Focusing on Fujikawa Yū). *Ningen Bunka Kenkyū Nenpō* 17:231–239.

———. 1997. "'Bunka kokka' no yūseihō" (The eugenic law in "cultured
states"), *Gendai Shisō* 25(4):821.

———. 2000. "Nihon: Sengo no yūsei hogohō to iu na no danshūhō" (Japan:
The sterilization law named Postwar Eugenic Protection Law). In Yonemoto
Shōhei, Matsubara Yōko, Nudeshima Jirō, and Ichinokawa Yasutaka, *Yūseigaku no ningen shakai: Seimeikagaku no seiki wa doko e mukau no ka* (Eugenics in human society: In which direction does the century of life sciences
turn?), 170–236. Tokyo: Kōdansha.

Matsumoto Shizuo. 1937. "Seishin suijaku to shuin (onanī)" (Neurasthenia and
masturbation). *Tsūzoku Igaku* 15(3):98– 100.

Matsuura Ushitarō. 1912. "Eiseijō yori shōgi o hitsuyō to suru ya" (Are prostitutes necessary from the standpoint of hygiene?). *Kakusei* 2(4):10–19.

———. 1926a. "Seiyoku mondai no konponteki kaiketsu" (Basic solutions to
the sexual problem). *Tsūzoku Igaku* 4(11):45–46.

———. 1926b. "Seiyoku mondai no konponteki kaiketsu" (Basic solutions to
the sexual problem). *Fujo Shinbun* 31 October, 4–5.

———. 1927. "Sei no eisei" (Sexual hygiene). *Kakusei* 17(1):4–5.

———. 1928. "Eisei to dōtoku" (Hygiene and morals). *Kakusei* 18(3):23–27.

———. 1929. "Teisō oyobi seibyō to kōshō no mondai" (Chastity, venereal disease, and the prostitution problem). *Tsūzoku Igaku* 7(2):31–35.

Minami Hiroshi, ed. 1965. *Taishō bunka* (Taishō culture). Tokyo: Keisō shobo.

Minami Ryō. 1908a. "Seiyoku mondai o shitei ni oshifuru no rigai 1" (Advantages and disadvantages of sex education for children 1). *Yomiuri Shinbun* 16
September, 5.

———. 1908b. "Seiyoku mondai o shitei ni oshifuru no rigai 2" (Advantages
and disadvantages of sex education for children 2). *Yomiuri Shinbun* 19 September, 5.

———. 1908c. "Seiyoku mondai o shitei ni oshifuru no rigai 3" (Advantages
and disadvantages of sex education for children 3). *Yomiuri Shinbun* 22 September, 5.

———. 1908d. "Seiyoku mondai o shitei ni oshifuru no rigai 4" (Advantages
and disadvantages of sex education for children 4). *Yomiuri Shinbun* 23 September, 5.

Mishima Tsūryō. 1906. "Gakkō seito no shikijō mondai" (Sexual issues among
pupils). *Jika Zasshi* 70, 95–104.

Misumi Tamō. 1920. "Danjo no seiteki kyōiku" (The sexual education of man
and woman). *Kakusei* 10(9):30–31.

Mitamura Engyō. 1921. "Edo jidai no seiyoku kyōiku" (Sex education in the
Edo period). *Sei no Kenkyū* 3(4):97–103.

Mitamura Shirō. 1925. "Ikanaru baai ni hinin o mitomerubeki ka?" (In which
cases must we recognize contraception?). *Sanji Chōsetsu Hyōron* 4:50–51.

Miwata Motomichi. 1921. "Ai to jiyū to makoto" (Love, freedom, and truth).
Kakusei 11(12):29–30.

Miyagawa Hirō. 1930a. "Edo jidai no seiteki hanzai" (Sex crimes of the Edo period). *Hanzai Kagaku* 1(1):53– 61.

————. 1930b. "Edo jidai no seiteki hanzai sono futatsu" (Sex crimes of the Edo period 2). *Hanzai Kagaku* 1(2):27–31.

————. 1930c. "Edo jidai no seiteki hanzai no mitsu" (Sex crimes of the Edo period 3). *Hanzai Kagaku* 1(3):48–59.

————. 1930d. "Edo jidai no seiteki hanzai no yotsu" (Sex crimes of the Edo period 4). *Hanzai Kagaku* 1(4):64–73.

————. 1930e. "Edo jidai no seiteki hanzai no mutsu" (Sex crimes of the Edo period 6). *Hanzai Kagaku* 1(6):59–68.

————. 1930f. "Edo jidai no seiteki hanzai no nanatsu" (Sex crimes of the Edo period 7). *Hanzai Kagaku* 1(7):27–36.

————. 1931a. "Edo jidai no seiteki hanzai no yatsu" (Sex crimes of the Edo period 8). *Hanzai Kagaku* 2(1):59–68.

————. 1931b. "Edo jidai no seiteki hanzai no kokonotsu" (Sex crimes of the Edo period 9). *Hanzai Kagaku* 2(2):63–72.

Miyako Shinbun. 1917. "Tōkyō no kodomo wa chihō no kodomo yori hijō ni yowai" (Tokyo's children are much weaker than children in the regions). *Miyako Shinbun* 5 November.

Miyamoto Shintarō, ed. 1965. *Fujin Kōron no gojūnen* (Fifty years of *Fujin Kōron*). Tokyo: Chūō kōronsha.

Miyatake Gaikotsu [Miyatake Tobone]. 1906a. "Fushinsei naru rataiga" (Unholy nude). *Kokkei Shinbun* 113:341.

————. 1906b. "Shinsei naru rataiga" (Holy nude). *Kokkei Shinbun* 113:342.

Mori Ōgai [Mori Rintarō]. 1992 (1909). *Wita sekusuarisu* (Vita sexualis). Tokyo: Shinchōsha.

Mori Rintarō [Mori Ōgai]. 1889. *Rikugun eisei kyōtei* (Army hygiene manual). Tokyo: Rikugun igakkō. Reprinted 1989 in *Ōgai zenshū dai nijūhachikan* (Ōgai's collected works, volume 28), ed. Midorikawa Takashi, 305–375. Tokyo: Iwanami shoten.

————. 1891a. "Kōshū eisei ryakusetsu" (An outline of public hygiene). Reprinted 1979 in *Ōgai zenshū dai jūichikan* (Ōgai's collected works, volume 11), ed. Ishikawa Atsushi, 317–331. Tokyo: Iwanami shoten.

————. 1891b. *Eiseigaku dai'i* (Great principles of hygienics). Reprinted 1989 in *Ōgai zenshū dai sanjūkan* (Ōgai's collected works, volume 30), ed. Midorikawa Takashi, 156–187. Tokyo: Iwanami shoten.

Mukō Gunji. 1908a. "Seiyoku mondai o shitei ni oshifuru no rigai 1" (Advantages and disadvantages of sex education for children 1). *Yomiuri Shinbun* 1 September, 5.

————. 1908b. "Seiyoku mondai o shitei ni oshifuru no rigai 2" (Advantages and disadvantages of sex education for children 2). *Yomiuri Shinbun* 3 September, 5.

————. 1908c. "Seiyoku mondai o shitei ni oshifuru no rigai 3" (Advantages and disadvantages of sex education for children 3). *Yomiuri Shinbun* 3 September, 5.

————. 1908d. "Naho seiyoku mondai to shitei to ni tsuite 1" (On the sexual problem and children 1). *Yomiuri Shinbun* 6 September, 5.

————. 1908e. "Naho seiyoku mondai to shitei to ni tsuite 2" (On the sexual problem and children 2). *Yomiuri Shinbun* 8 September, 5.

Murakami Osaku. 1926. "Seibyō yobō hōan o hyōsu" (Criticizing the petition for the prevention of venereal diseases). *Kakusei* 16(7):6–7.

Muta Kazue. 1992. "Senryaku toshite no onna: Meiji Taishō no 'onna no gensetsu' o megutte" (Woman as strategy: On the "discourse of women" in the Meiji and Taishō eras). *Shisō* 812:211–230.

———. 1996. *Senryaku toshite no kazoku: Kindai Nihon no kokumin kokka keisei to josei* (Family as strategy: The formation of the Japanese modern nation-state and women). Tokyo: Shinyōsha.

Nagahama Shigeru. 1925a. "Jidoku no heigai to seishokki: Shōgai no konji ryōhō" (The harmful effects of masturbation and the sexual organs: Methods of healing the harm). *Tsūzoku Igaku* 3(8):25–27.

———. 1925b. "Jidoku no heigai to seishokki: Shōgai no konji ryōhō" (The harmful effects of masturbation and the sexual organs: Methods of healing the harm). *Tsūzoku Igaku* 3(11):70–72.

Nagai Hisomu [Nagai Sen]. 1916. *Jinseiron* (On humankind). Tokyo: Jitsugyō no Nihonsha.

———. 1919a. "Bāsu kontororu o kontororu seyo!" (Control birth control!). *Fujin Kōron* 5(8):50–52.

———. 1919b. "Shōnen danjo to seiteki seikatsu" (The sex lives of boys and girls). *Kakusei* 9(11):25–28.

———. 1919c. "Seinen danjo no seiteki seikatsu 1" (The sex lives of boys and girls 1). *Fujo Shinbun* 30 October, 4.

———. 1919d. "Seinen danjo no seiteki seikatsu 2" (The sex lives of boys and girls 2). *Fujo Shinbun* 7 December, 4.

———. 1919e. "Seinen danjo no seiteki seikatsu 3" (The sex lives of boys and girls 3). *Fujo Shinbun* 14 December, 4.

———. 1919f. "Seinen danjo no seiteki seikatsu 4" (The sex lives of boys and girls 4). *Fujo Shinbun* 21 December, 4.

———. 1919g. "Seinen danjo no seiteki seikatsu 5" (The sex lives of boys and girls 5). *Fujo Shinbun* 28 December, 3.

———. 1920a. "Seinen danjo no seiteki seikatsu 6" (The sex lives of boys and girls 6). *Fujo Shinbun* 18 January, 4.

———. 1920b. "Seinen danjo no seiteki seikatsu 7" (The sex lives of boys and girls 7). *Fujo Shinbun* 25 January, 4.

———. 1920c. "Seinen danjo no seiteki seikatsu 8" (The sex lives of boys and girls 8). *Fujo Shinbun* 1 February, 4.

———. 1920d. "Seinen danjo no seiteki seikatsu 9" (The sex lives of boys and girls 9). *Fujo Shinbun* 8 February, 4.

———. 1954. "Reiniku itchi no fūfu no aijō" (A married couple's love that unites body and soul). *Fūfu Seikatsu* 15(6):23–25.

Nagamine Shigetoshi. 2001. *Modan toshi no dokusho kūkan* (Reading space in modern cities). Tokyo: Nihon editā sukūru shuppanbu.

Nagashiro Rōkaku. 1911. "Seiyoku kankaku no shinka to ren'ai no shinsei" (The progress of sexual sense and the sacredness of love). *Shinkōron* 26(9): 61–63.

Naikaku sōri daijin kanbō kōhōshitsu. 1983. *Zenkoku yoron chōsa no genkyō* (The current status of nationwide opinion surveys). Tokyo: Ōkurashō.

Naimushō eiseikyoku. 1893–1894. *Eiseikyoku nenpō* (Annual report of the bureau of hygiene). Tokyo: Naimushō eiseikyoku.

———. 1895. *Eiseikyoku nenpō* (Annual report of the bureau of hygiene). Tokyo: Naimushō eiseikyoku.

———. 1897. *Eiseikyoku nenpō* (Annual report of the bureau of hygiene). Tokyo: Naimushō eiseikyoku.

———. 1900. *Eiseikyoku nenpō* (Annual report of the bureau of hygiene). Tokyo: Naimushō eiseikyoku.

———. 1907. *The sanitary institutions of Japan.* Tokyo: Naimushō eiseikyoku.

———. 1910. *Eiseikyoku nenpō* (Annual report of the bureau of hygiene). Tokyo: Naimushō eiseikyoku.

———. 1930. *Eiseikyoku nenpō* (Annual report of the bureau of hygiene). Tokyo: Naimushō eiseikyoku.

Naimushō keihokyoku. 1976a. *Hakkinbon kankei shiryō shūsei daiichi: Kinshi tankōbon mokuroku Meiji 21–Shōwa 9* (Collection of material on censored books 1: Index of censored books Meiji 21–Shōwa 9). Tokyo: Kohokusha.

———. 1976b. *Hakkinbon kankei shiryō shūsei daini: Kinshi tankōbon mokuroku Shōwa 10–Shōwa 16* (Collection of material on censored books 2: Index of censored books Shōwa 10–Shōwa 16). Tokyo: Kohokusha.

———. 1977a. *Hakkinbon kankei shiryō shūsei daisan: Kinshi tankōbon mokuroku Shōwa 16–Shōwa 19* (Collection of material on censored books 3: Index of censored books Shōwa 16–Shōwa 19). Tokyo: Kohokusha.

———. 1977b. *Hakkinbon kankei shiryō shūsei daiyon: Tankōbon shobun nisshi Shōwa 16–Shōwa 17* (Collection of material on censored books 4: Index of censored books Shōwa 16–Shōwa 17). Tokyo: Kohokusha.

———. 1981. *Shōwa gonen-chū ni okeru shuppan keisatsu gaikan* (Outline of the publication police 1930). Tokyo: Ryūin shoten.

———. 1986. *Shuppan keisatsu kankei shiryō shūsei 1920–1931* (Collection of material on the publication police 1920–1931). 8 volumes. Tokyo: Fuji shuppan.

Naka Arata. 1977. *Fukoku kyōhei-ka no kodomo* (Children during the time of rich nation, strong army). In *Nihon kodomo no rekishi 5* (A history of Japanese children 5), ed. 'Nihon Kodomo no Rekishi' henshū iinkai. Tokyo: Dai ippō shuppan.

Nihon hōsō kyōkai Kansai shibu, ed. 1932. "Katei kyōiku kōza" (Family education course). In *Radio-Text,* 12–17 September. Osaka: Nihon hōsō shuppan kyōkai Kansai shisha.

Nihon hōsō shuppan kyōkai, ed. 1986. *Nihon no wakamono: Sono ishiki to kōdō* (Japan's youth: Their consciousness and behavior). Tokyo: Nihon hōsō kyōkai.

Nihon kagakushi gakkai, ed. 1972. *Nihon kagaku gijutsushi taikei 24kan* (Outline of the history of Japanese science and technology 24). Tokyo: Daiippōki shuppan kabushikigaisha.

Nihon kingendaishi jiten henshū iinkai, ed. 1978. *Nihon kingendaishi jiten* (Encyclopedia of modern and present-day Japanese history). Tokyo: Tōyō keizai shinpōsha.

Nihon seikyōiku kyōkai, ed. 1975. *Seishōnen no seikōdō: Wagakuni no kōkō-*

sei, daigakusei ni kan suru chōsa hōkoku (Sexual behavior of youth: Report on Japanese high school and university students). Tokyo: Shōgakkan.

———. 1983. *Seishōnen no seikōdō: Wagakuni no kōkōsei, daigakusei ni kan-suru chōsa bunseki* (Sexual behavior of youth: Survey analysis of Japanese high school and university students). Tokyo: Shōgakukan.

———. 1990. *'Seikyōiku shin shidō yōkō' no shushi* (The contents of the "new curriculum guidelines for sex education"). Tokyo: Nihon seikyōiku kyōkai.

Nihon teikoku shihōshō, ed. 1925. *Nihon teikoku shihōshō dai49keiji tōkei nenpō. Taishō 14* (Annual report of criminality statistics of the Japanese empire's Ministry of Justice 49: Taishō 14). Tokyo: Nihon teikoku shihōshō.

Nihon tōkei kyōkai. 1951. *Nihon tōkei nenkan* (Japan statistical yearbook). Tokyo: Nihon tōkei kyōkai.

Nii Itaru. 1936. "Seiteki muchi no higeki" (The trajedy of the lack of sexual knowledge). *Seikagaku Kenkyū* 1(9):38–58.

Nishigaito Masaru. 1993. *Seikyōiku wa ima* (Sex education today). Tokyo: Iwa-nami shoten.

Nogami Toshio. 1932. "Seinen no shinri to seikyōiku" (The psyche of youth and sex education). In *Radio-Text,* ed. Nihon hōsō kyōkai Kansai shibu, 245–325. Osaka: Nihon hōsō shuppan kyōkai Kansai shisha.

Odagiri Akinori. 1979a. "Kaisetsu"" (Commentary). In *Yamamoto Senji zen-shū. Daiikkan: Jinsei seibutsugaku, seikagaku* (Collected works of Yama-moto Senji. Volume 1: Human biology, sexual science), ed. Sasaki Toshiji and Odagiri Akinori, 565–582. Tokyo: Sekibunsha.

———. 1979b. "Kaisetsu" (Commentary). In *Yamamoto Senji zenshū. Daini-kan: Seikyōiku* (Collected works of Yamamoto Senji. Volume 2: Sex educa-tion), ed. Sasaki Toshiji and Odagiri Akinori, 507–520. Tokyo: Sekibunsha.

Odajima Shōkichi. 1943 (1938). *Kaigun eiseigaku* (Hygienics in the navy). Tokyo: Yamato Bunsha Shuppanbu.

Ode Shun. 1936. "Hirschfeld hakushi no Nihon inshōki" (Notes on Dr. Hirsch-feld's impressions of Japan). *Seikagaku Kenkyū* 1(2):107–113.

Ogi Shinzō, Kumakura Isao, and Ueno Chizuko, eds. 1990. *Nihon kindai shisō taikei 23. Fūzoku sei* (Thought in modern Japan 23: Customs, morals, and sexuality). Tokyo: Iwanami shoten.

———. 1994. *Seishoku no seijigaku* (The politics of reproduction). Tokyo: De-gawa shuppansha.

Ogino Miho. 1994. *Seishoku no seijigaku: Feminizumu to basu kontorōru* (The politics of reproduction: Feminism and birth control). Tokyo: Yamakawa shuppansha.

Ogino Miho, Tanabe Reiko, and Himeoka Toshiko, eds. 1990. *Seido toshite no onna. Sei san kazoku no hikaku shakaishi* (Woman as system: Comparative social history of sexuality, birth, and family). Tokyo: Heibonsha.

Oguma Eiji. 1995. *Tanitsu minzoku shinwa no kigen* (The origin of the myth of homogeneity). Tokyo: Kabushikigaisha Shinyōsha.

Oguri Sadao. 1926. "Shakai kairyō jitsuron. Ninshin seigen no hitsuyō oyobi sono jikkōhō" (Concrete discussion of societal improvement. The necessity of birth control and the methods of its realization). *Tsūzoku Igaku* 4(9): 13–15.

Okamoto Kazuhiko. 1982. "Seiyō bunmei no ryūnyū to dentōteki kyōdōtai no hōkai" (The importation of Western civilization and the destruction of traditional communities). *Gendai Seikyōiku Kenkyū* 6:118–126.

———. 1983a. "Taishū no gaku toshite no seikagaku no tenkai" (The development of sexology as the science of the masses). *Gendai Seikyōiku Kenkyū* 14: 108–118.

———. 1983b. "Yunyū seikagaku kara Nihon no seikagaku e" (From imported to Japanese sexology). *Gendai Seikyōiku Kenkyū* 2:118–127.

Okuda Sōtarō. 1925. "Kōbe ni okeru sanji seigen undō no rekishi" (The history of the birth control movement in Kōbe). *Sanji Chōsetsu Hyōron* 2:25–27.

Ōma Tomoshigekazu. 1936. "Ren'ai kekkon oyobi sei ni kan suru ryōsho no suisen" (Recommendation of good books on love-marriage and sex/sexuality). *Seikagaku Kenkyū* 1(5):60–63.

Ōmura Chōei. 1886. "Heishiki teisō no hitsuyō ni kansuru" (On the necessity of military-style exercise). *Dai Nippon Kyōiku Zasshi* 27:49–67.

Ōsaka Asahi Shinbun. 1922. "Jōriku yurusareru Sangā fujin jinmon genshitsu hoshō kensa no ato" (After the questioning Mrs. Sanger was allowed to land in Japan). *Ōsaka Asahi Shinbun* 11 March.

Oshikane Atsushi. 1977. *Ishi no seikagaku* (Doctors' sexology). Tokyo: Gakken shoin.

Ōshima Tatsuo and Toyama Toshiki. 1998. "Baiagura ni muragaru chūkōnen" (Middle-aged and older men swarming around Viagra). *Aera* 7 September, 11(35):10–13.

Ōta Fumio [Ōta Tenrei]. 1936. "Seishun seikatsu no chōsa" (Survey on the life of youth). *Seikagaku Kenkyū* 1(7):100–102.

Ōta Tenrei [Ōta Fumio]. 1954a. "Ringu no shōgai de wa nai" (It is not the failure of the ring). *Fūfu Seikatsu* 15(6):203–204.

———. 1954b. "Utsukushī nyūbō wa okusama no saidai no bukki" (Beautiful breasts are a married lady's greatest weapon). *Fūfu Seikatsu* 15(6):182–190.

———. 1954c. "Kuritorisu no kankaku no kyōjaku wa hito ni yotte dō chigau ka?" (How does the intensity of clitoris feeling differ individually?). *Fūfu Seikatsu* 17(14):28–31.

———. 1955. "Fūfu seikatsu jūnen o hete mo otto to itchisenu tsuma no chikan mo, kō sureba naoru" (Even when ten years of marital life have gone by the slowness of a wife who has not united with her husband can be healed like this). *Fūfu Seikatsu* 16(11):87–88.

———. 1976. *Nihon sanji chōsetsu hyakunenshi* (One-hundred-year history of birth control in Japan). Tokyo: Shuppan kagaku sōgō kenkyūsho.

———. 1980. *Datai kinshi to yūsei hogohō* (The prohibition of abortion and the Eugenic Protection Law). Tokyo: Keieisha kagaku kyōkai.

Raichō [Hiratsuka Raichō]. 1918. "Bosei hogo mondai ni tsuite—futatabi Yosano Akikoshi ni yokosu" (On the issue of the protection of motherhood—again to Yosano Akiko). *Fujin Kōron* 3(8):40–52.

Raise, Wiruherumu [Reise, Wilhelm]. 1936. "Sei no kiki" (Crisis of sex/sexuality). *Seikagaku Kenkyū* 1(5):73–78.

Rikugunshō. 1876. *Rikugunshō daiichi nenpō* (First annual report of the Army Ministry). Tokyo: Rikugunshō.

———. 1879. *Rikugunshō daisan nenpō* (Third annual report of the Army Ministry). Tokyo: Rikugunshō.

———. 1894. *Rikugunshō dainanakai tōkei nenpō* (Seventh annual statistical report of the Army Ministry). Tokyo: Rikugunshō.

———. 1897. *Dai Nippon teikoku Rikugunshō daijūkai tōkei nenpō* (Tenth annual statistical report of the Army Ministry of the Greater Japanese Empire). Tokyo: Rikugunshō.

———. 1917. *Taishō rokunen Rikugunshō tōkei nenpō* (Annual statistical report of the Army Ministry of the year Taishō 6). Tokyo: Rikugunshō.

Saitō Hikaru. 1993. "Nijū nendai Nihon yūseigaku no ikkyokumen" (One aspect of Japanese eugenics in the 1920s). *Gendai Shisō* 21(7):128–158.

Saitō Miho. 2001. "Josei zasshi ni miru yūsei shisō no fukyū ni tsuite" (On the dissemination of eugenic thought in women's magazines). In *Sensō to josei zasshi 1931nen–1945nen* (War and women's magazines, 1931–1945), ed. Kindai josei bunka-shi kenkyūkai, 104–125. Tokyo: Domesu shuppan.

Sakai Kanekiyo. 1924a. "Seiteki joseikan" (A sexual view of women). *Tsūzoku Igaku* 2(11):42–44.

———. 1924b. "Seiteki joseikan" (A sexual view of women). *Tsūzoku Igaku* 2(12):41–44.

———. 1925a. "Seiteki joseikan" (A sexual view of women). *Tsūzoku Igaku* 3(1):41–44.

———. 1925b. "Seiteki joseikan" (A sexual view of women). *Tsūzoku Igaku* 3(2):43–45.

———. 1925c. "Seiteki joseikan" (A sexual view of women). *Tsūzoku Igaku* 3(4):41–42.

———. 1925d. "Seiteki joseikan" (A sexual view of women). *Tsūzoku Igaku* 3(5):49–51.

———. 1925e. "Seiteki joseikan" (A sexual view of women). *Tsūzoku Igaku* 3(6):45–47.

———. 1925f. "Danjo seiteki tokuchō no kōsatsu" (Inquiry into the sexual characteristics of men and women). *Tsūzoku Igaku* 3(9):63–66.

———. 1925g. "Danjo seiteki tokuchō no kōsatsu" (Inquiry into the sexual characteristics of men and women). *Tsūzoku Igaku* 3(10):55–57.

———. 1926a. "Danjo seiteki tokuchō no kōsatsu" (Inquiry into the sexual characteristics of men and women). *Tsūzoku Igaku* 4(3):73–76.

———. 1926b. "Danjo seiteki tokuchō no kōsatsu" (Inquiry into the sexual characteristics of men and women). *Tsūzoku Igaku* 4(4):92–94.

———. 1926c. "Danjo seiteki tokuchō no kōsatsu" (Inquiry into the sexual characteristics of men and women). *Tsūzoku Igaku* 4(5):64–66.

———. 1926d. "Danjo seiteki tokuchō no kōsatsu" (Inquiry into the sexual characteristics of men and women). *Tsūzoku Igaku* 4(6):70–72.

———. 1926e. "Danjo seiteki tokuchō no kōsatsu" (Inquiry into the sexual characteristics of men and women). *Tsūzoku Igaku* 4(9):80–82.

———. 1926f. "Danjo seiteki tokuchō no kōsatsu" (Inquiry into the sexual characteristics of men and women). *Tsūzoku Igaku* 4(9):96–98.

———. 1926g. "Danjo seiteki tokuchō no kōsatsu" (Inquiry into the sexual characteristics of men and women). *Tsūzoku Igaku* 4(10):99–102.

Sanji Chōsetsu Hyōron. 1925a. "Wareware no shuchō" (Our assertions). *Sanji Seigen Hyōron* 1:1.

———. 1925b. "Kensetsuteki sanji chōsetsu oyobi jinshu kaizen kyōkai: Sono kai ni dare ga hairubeki mono ka" (Association of Constructive Birth Control and Race Improvement: Who must join this association?). *Sanji Chōsetsu Hyōron* 1:6, 10.

———. 1925c. "Seibyō yobōyaku to sanji seigen" (Birth control and medicine for the prevention of venereal diseases). *Sanji Chōsetsu Hyōron* 1:29–30.

———. 1925d. "Henshū kōki" (Publishing postscript). *Sanji Chōsetsu Hyōron* 3:40.

———. 1925e. "Jutai chōsetsu sōdansho monshasū kenbetsuhyō" (Graph, by prefecture, of advice seekers at offices for contraception advice). *Sanji Chōsetsu Hyōron* 4:41.

Saotome Kenichi et al. 1953. "Sei ni kan suru chōsa seiseki" (Documentation of a survey about sex). *Eisei Tōkei* 6(8):30–33.

Sasaki Toshiji. 1979. "Kaisetsu" (Commentary). In *Yamamoto Senji zenshū. Daisankan: Sanji Chōsetsu Hyōron, Sei to Shakai* (Collected works of Yamamoto Senji. Volume 3: *Birth Control Review, Sex and Society*), ed. Sasaki Toshiji and Odagiri Akinori, 687–706. Tokyo: Sekibunsha.

Sawada Shirōsaku. 1936. "Josei to tabū" (Women and taboo). *Seikagaku Kenkyū* 1(1):38–43.

Sei no Kenkyū. 1919a. "Sei no mondai" (The sexual problem). *Sei no Kenkyū* 1(1):1–4.

———. 1919b. "Taishō shichinendo ni okeru jinkō shōgi yūkyaku taishōhyō" (Number of prostitutes and clients in the population in the year Taishō 7). *Sei no Kenkyū* 3(3):n.p.

———. 1919c. "Seiteki hanmon sōdansho kaisetsu" (Founding of an advice office for sexual anguish). *Sei no Kenkyū* 3(3):n.p.

Sei to Shakai. 1923. "Sei to shakai" (Sex and society). *Hentai Seiyoku* 3:93–96.

———. 1926a. "Sanji chōsetsu ze ka hi ka" (Birth control right or wrong). *Sei to Shakai* 11:39–45.

———. 1926b. "Sanji chōsetsu ze ka hi ka" (Birth control right or wrong). *Sei to Shakai* 12:36–40.

———. 1926c. "Nihon sansei undō no atarashii ichi chūshin" (One new focus of Japan's birth control movement). *Sei to Shakai* 12:50–53.

Seikagaku Kenkyū. 1936. "Ren'ai kekkon oyobi sei ni kan suru ryōsho no suisen" (Recommendation of good books on love-marriage and sex/sexuality). *Seikagaku Kenkyū* 1(5):60–63.

Seiron. 1927. "*Seiron* ni tai suru sehyō ippan" (General reputation of *Sexual Theory*). *Seiron* 1(4):52.

Senda Kako. 1978. *Jūgun ianfu* (Former army comfort women). Tokyo: Sanichi shobō.

Shimada Saburō. 1916. "Danjo kōsai mondai kenkyū no hitsuyō" (The necessity of research on the intercourse of man and woman). *Kakusei* 6(6):6–7.

Shimanaka Yūsaku. 1921. "Hatsubai kinshi no kōsatsu 1: Honshi zengō no hatsubai kinshi ni tsuite" (On the sale prohibition 1: On the prohibition to sell the last issue of this magazine). *Fujin Kōron* 6(7):1–8.

Shimazaki Seisuke. 1991. "Ōta Tenrei." In *Taishū bunka jiten* (Encyclopedia of mass culture), ed. Ishikawa Hiroyoshi et al., 96. Tokyo: Kobundō.

Shimizu Masaru. 1989. *Nihon no seigaku jishi* (The beginnings of Japanese sexology). Tokyo: Kawade shobō shinsho.

Shimoda Jirō. 1904a. *Joshi kyōiku* (Girls' education). Tokyo: Zenkōdō.

————. 1904b. "Joshi kyōiku no mokuteki ni tsuite" (On the goals of girls' education). *Fujo Shinbun* 1 February, 6.

————. 1908a. "Seiyoku mondai o shitei ni shirashimuru rigai 1" (Advantages and disadvantages of sex education for children 1). *Yomiuri Shinbun* 11 September, 5.

————. 1908b. "Seiyoku mondai o shitei ni oshifuru no rigai 2" (Advantages and disadvantages of sex education for children 2). *Yomiuri Shinbun* 12 September, 5.

————. 1908c. "Seiyoku mondai o shitei ni oshifuru no rigai 3" (Advantages and disadvantages of sex education for children 3). *Yomiuri Shinbun* 20 September, 5.

————. 1914. "Fujin no taikaku" (The physical condition of women). *Yomiuri Shinbun* 10 November, 7.

Shinozaki Nobuo. 1953. *Nihonjin no seiseikatsu* (The sex life of the Japanese). Tokyo: Bungei shuppan kabushikigaisha.

————. 1954a. "Seimondai kenkyūkai no pēji: Sōsetsu ni yosete" (Study Group for Sexual Problems page: Laying the foundation). *Fūfu Seikatsu* 15(6):168–169.

————. 1954b. "Kekkon mondai shirīzu: Donna katachi no fūfu kenka ga ichiban ōi ka?" (Marital problem series: What kind of marital quarrels are most frequent?). *Fūfu Seikatsu* 17(14):84–85.

Shinozaki Nobuo and Moriyama Yutaka. 1952. "Jūtai chōsetsu to jinkō chūzetsu" (Termination of pregnancy and control of conception). In *Katei ryōhō hyakka jiten* (Household medical encyclopedia), ed. Tōkyō denryoku kenkō hoken kumiai, 235–241. Tokyo: Tōkyō denryoku kenkō hoken kumiai.

Shūkan Asahi, ed. 1981. *Nedan no Meiji Taishō Shōwa fūzokushi* (Cultural history of prices during the Meiji, Taishō, and Shōwa eras). Tokyo: Asahi shinbunsha.

Sudō Rieko. 1925. "Seichishiki no kekkaku ga unda fūfu aibetsu no kanashimi" (Separated couple's sadness came from lack of sexual knowledge). *Tsūzoku Igaku* 3(7):65–67.

Sugimoto Seiji. 1937. "Seiteki shinkei suijakusha no seiyoku tōseihō" (Ways to control the sexual desire of neurasthenics). *Tsūzoku Igaku* 15(4):93–96.

Sugita Naogeki. 1924. "Seibyō to seishinbyō no kankei" (The relationship between venereal disease and mental illness). *Kakusei* 14(8):17–19.

Sugiura Kiyoshi. 1926. "Kagakujō yori mitaru sei no nazo" (The secret of sex/sexuality as seen from the viewpoint of science). *Tsūzoku Igaku* 4(12): 99–101.

Sugiyama Motojirō. 1925. "Nōson mondai to sanji seigen" (The farmer problem and birth control). *Sei to Shakai* 9:30–35.

Sugiyama Nakashi. 1928. "Gendai sesō ni arawareta sanji chōsetsu no riron to jissai" (Current theories versus the reality of birth control). *Tsūzoku Igaku* 6(9):1–6.

Sutopusu, Mari [Stopes, Mary C.]. 1924. "Kāsan! Boku dōshite umareta no ka?" (Mother! How was I born?). *Tsūzoku Igaku* 2(12):52–54.

————. 1925a. "Kāsan! Boku dōshite umareta no ka?" (Mother! How was I born?). *Tsūzoku Igaku* 3(1):53–55.

————. 1925b. "Kāsan! Boku dōshite umareta no ka?" (Mother! How was I born?). *Tsūzoku Igaku* 3(2):46–48.

Suzuki Yūko. 1993 (1997). *'Jūgun ianfu' mondai to seibōryoku* (The "comfort women" issue and sexual violence). Tokyo: Miraisha.

Suzuki Zenji. 1983. *Nihon no yūseigaku* (Japanese eugenics). Tokyo: Sankyo shuppan.

Suzuki Zenji, Matsubara Yōko, and Sakano Tetsu. 1995. "Yūseigakushi kenkyū no dōkō III: Amerika oyobi Nihon no yūseigaku ni kan suru rekishi kenkyū" (Tendencies in the research on eugenics 3: Historiography of eugenics in America and Japan). *Kagakushi Kenkyū* 34(194):97–106.

Tagawa Shinichi. 1928. "Rinbyō wa bunmeibyō da to iu wa kanashiki kotoba narazu ya. Rokunenkan no mansei rinshitsu kushin zenji no kokuhaku" (Isn't that a sad expression, "Gonorrhea is a disease of civilization"? Confessions on the six-year fight against chronic gonorrhea and its treatment). *Tsūzoku Igaku* 6(8):92–94.

Takagi Masashi. 1989. "'Taishō demokurashī' ni okeru 'yūseiron' no tenkai to kyōiku" (Education and the development of "eugenics theories" during the "Taishō democracy"). *Nagoya Daigaku Kyōiku Gakubu Kiyō* 36:167–178.

————. 1991. "1920–1930 nendai ni okeru yūseigakuteki nōryokukan: Nagai Hisomu oyobi Nihon minzoku eisei gakkai (kyōkai) no kenkai o chūshin ni" (The eugenic view of skills during the 1920s and 1930s: The views of Nagai Hisomu and the Japanese Society of Racial Hygiene). *Nagoya Daigaku Kyōiku Gakubu Kiyō* 38:161–171.

————. 1993. "Senzen Nihon ni okeru yūsei shisō no tenkai to nōryokukan kyōikukan" (The development of eugenic thought in prewar Japan and the view of capability and education). *Nagoya Daigaku Kyōiku Gakubu Kiyō* 40(1):41–52.

Takashima Beihō [Takashima Heisaburō]. 1898–1899. "Wagakuni ni okeru jidō kenkyū no hattatsu" (The development of pediatric research in our country). *Jidō Kenkyū* 1:53–63.

Takemura Hideki. 1991. "'Ogetsu shōgakkōgai sankō gakkō chōsa' to sangakkyū nikyōinsei: Nihon saishō no gakkō chōsa seiritsu ni kansuru chōsa shiteki kōsatsu" ("School survey of Ogetsu Elementary School and three other schools" and the system of three grades and two instructors: A historical overview of the formation of Japan's first school surveys). In *Kindai Nihon shakai chōsashi 2* (The history of social research in modern Japan 2), ed. Kawai Takao, 43–78. Tokyo: Keiō tsūshin.

Takemura Tamio. 1980. *Haishō undō* (The movement for the abolition of prostitution). Tokyo: Chūō kōron.

Takeuchi Haruhiko. 1989. "Meijiki kankō chōsa ni miru 'kankō' to kindai"

("Customs" and modernity viewed in the custom surveys of the Meiji era). In *Kindai Nihon shakai chōsashi 1* (The history of social research in modern Japan 1), ed. Kawai Takao, 33–60. Tokyo: Keiō tsūshin.

Takeuchi Shigeyo. 1934. "Kekkon eisei" (Hygiene of married couples). In *Kango to ryōhō: Katei iten* (Household medical encyclopedia for nursing and healing methods), ed. Arai Hyōgo, 395–405. Tokyo: Dai Nihon yūbenkai Kōdansha.

Tanaka Chiune. 1928. "Hentaikon" (Perverse marriage). *Seiron* 1(4):48–50.

Tanaka Kōichi. 1927. *Edo jidai no danjo kankei* (Gender relations during the Edo period). Osaka: Kindai bungeisha.

Taniguchi Zentarō. 1925. "Imin seisaku no 'gainenteki yūgi'" (The "conceptual play" of emigration policies). *Sanji Chōsetsu Hyōron* 6:42–46.

———. 1960. "Yamamoto Senji." In *Nihon rekishi daijiten* (Encyclopedia of Japanese history), ed. Kawade Takao, 257. Tokyo: Kawade shobō shinsha.

Tatsuyama Yoshiaki. 1908. "Seiyoku kyōiku mondai ni tsuite" (On the problem of sex education). *Kyōiku gakujutsukai* 18:266–272.

Tōkoku Shinbun. 1916. "Sōtei no kensa" (The examination of conscripts). *Tōkoku Shinbun* 25 April.

Tōkyō Asahi Shinbun. 1916. "Jogakusei no taikaku ga yoku natta" (The physical condition of girls has become better). *Tōkyō Asahi Shinbun* 28 May.

———. 1917. "Chōhei kensa kara mita: Gakusei to shokkō no taikaku" (The physical constitution of students and workers as viewed through the conscription examination). *Tōkyō Asahi Shinbun* 29 June.

———. 1922a. "Ryōken sashō o kyozetsu sareta Sangā fujin kataru" (Mrs. Sanger, who was denied an immigration visa, talks). *Tōkyō Asahi Shinbun* 20 February.

———. 1922b. "Kōkan o ataeru ai no Sangā fujin tachimachi fueta Nihon no tomodachi" (A Mrs. Sanger full of love has found many Japanese friends). *Tōkyō Asahi Shinbun* 7 March.

———. 1922c. "Sangā no kōen wa kinshi" (Sanger's lectures prohibited). *Tōkyō Asahi Shinbun* 10 March.

———. 1922d. "Joikai no sanji seigenron" (Theories on birth control at a meeting of female doctors). *Tōkyō Asahi Shinbun* 16 April.

Tōkyō Nichi Nichi Shinbun. 1913. "Doitsu shōnen no imawashii seiyoku" (The detestable sexual desire of German youth). *Tōkyō Nichi Nichi Shinbun* 12 November.

———. 1914. "Shinuru hito ga ooi" (Many people die). *Tōkyō Nichi Nichi Shinbun* 19 June.

Tonda Kō. 1936. "Saikin no Doitsu seikagaku bunken kara" (From recent German sexological literature). *Seikagaku Kenkyū* 1(7):79–81.

Tsuchida Kyōson. 1925. "Gokai sareta sanji chōsetsu" (Misunderstandings about birth control). *Sanji Chōsetsu Hyōron* 3:2–5.

———. 1926. "Shakai ni okeru seiseikatsu: Ninshiki no jiko giman" (Sexual life in society: Cognizance of self-deception). *Sei to Shakai* 14:6–9.

Tsuji Shinji. 1884. "Gakkō eiseihō" (Rules of school hygiene). *Dai Nihon Kyōiku Zasshi* 10:79–84.

Tsurumi Yūsuke, ed. 1937. *Gotō Shinpei dai ikkan* (Gotō Shinpei, volume 1). Tokyo: Gotō Shinpei hakuden hensankai.

Tsūzoku Igaku. 1924. "Seikyōiku no yakamashiki gendai ni minaoshite" (Revisiting the noise about sex education). *Tsūzoku Igaku* 2(12):49–51.

———. 1925. "Onna no tsumi ka? Otoko no tsumi ka?" (Women's crime? Men's crime?). *Tsūzoku Igaku* 4(6):64–66.

———. 1937a. "Fushigi na josei no nikutai. Seiseikatsu no kakumei. Ninshin no chōsetsu mo jiyū jizai" (The mysterious female body, the revolution of sexual life, free decision on birth control). *Tsūzoku Igaku* 15(3):10.

———. 1937b. "Hayakereba hayai hodo yoi: Kodomo e no seikyōiku" (The sooner the better: Sex education for children). *Tsūzoku Igaku* 15(7):63–64.

Ueda Toshihide. 1998. "'Funōraku' ga kiku mekanizumu" (The mechanism by which the "impotence" drug works). *Aera* 8 June, 11(22):77.

Ueno Chizuko. 1990. "Kaisetsu" (Commentary). In *Nihon kindai shisō taikei 23. Fūzoku sei* (Thought in modern Japan 23: Customs, morals, and sexuality), ed. Ogi Shinzō, Kumakura Isao, and Ueno Chizuko, 505–550. Tokyo: Iwanami shoten.

Unno Kōtoku. 1925a. "Shakai seisaku to sanji seigen" (Social policies and birth). *Sanji Chōsetsu Hyōron* 2:2–8.

———. 1925b. "Sanjiken no hinin" (The disapproval of the right to birth control). *Sei to Shakai* 9:16–19.

Wada Fumio. 1993. "Umeyo fuyaseyo kuni no tame" (Procreate and multiply for the nation). *Kokubungaku Kaishaku to Kyōsai no Kenkyū* 38(6):172.

Wakabayashi Tsutomu. 1957. "Nagai sensei no purofuiru" (Profile of professor Nagai). *Nihon Iji Shinpō* 1726:74.

Washiyama Yayoi [Yoshioka Yayoi]. 1908a. "Seiyoku no daiheigai 1" (Great vices of sexual desire 1). *Yomiuri Shinbun* 30 September, 5.

———. 1908b. "Seiyoku no daiheigai 2" (Great vices of sexual desire 2). *Yomiuri Shinbun* 1 October, 5.

Watanabe Katsumasa. 1978. *Shinbun shūroku Taishōshi* (A Taishō history based on a compilation of newspaper articles). Tokyo: Taishō shuppan.

Watanabe Yoshishige. 1886. "Seiketsuron" (On cleanliness). *Dai Nihon Kyōiku Zasshi* 46:32–35.

Watashitachi no rekishi o tsuzuru kai. 1987. *Fujin zasshi kara mita 1930 nendai* (The 1930s viewed from the perspective of women's magazines). Tokyo: Dōjidaisha.

Yamada Waka. 1915. "Ren'ai no jiyū to honnō" (Liberty of love and instinct). *Seitō* 5(10):72–78.

———. 1919a. "Kekkon to ren'ai 1" (Marriage and love 1). *Fujo Shinbun* 12 October, 4.

———. 1919b. "Kekkon to ren'ai 2" (Marriage and love 2). *Fujo Shinbun* 19 October, 4.

———. 1919c. "Kekkon to ren'ai 3" (Marriage and love 3). *Fujo Shinbun* 26 October, 4.

———. 1922. *Katei no shakaiteki igi* (The social significance of the family). Tokyo: Kindai bunmeisha.

————. 1989 (1983). *Josei sōdan* (Advice for women), ed. Yamada Waka. Tokyo: Tōkyō asahi shinbunsha.

Yamai Teruhiko and Kinoshita Hideaki. 1982. *Tōkyō rikugun yōnen gakkōshi* (History of the Tokyo Military Academy). Tokyo: Tōyōkai.

Yamakawa Kikue. 1925. "Shufu no mondai" (The housewife problem). *Sanji Chōsetsu Hyōron* 3:18–21.

Yamamoto Senji. 1921a. "Okoriyasuki gokai to sono keikai, oyobi sono ta no chūi"" (Common misunderstandings and how to avoid them, as well as other cautions). Reprinted 1979 in *Yamamoto Senji zenshū. Daiikkan: Jinsei seibutsugaku, seikagaku* (Collected works of Yamamoto Senji. Volume 1: Human biology, sexual science), ed. Sasaki Toshiji and Odagiri Akinori, 51–53. Tokyo: Sekibunsha.

————. 1921b. "Sumiyaka ni seikyōiku o hodokose"" (Urgently conduct sex education). Reprinted 1979 in *Yamamoto Senji zenshū. Dainikan: Seikyōiku* (Collected works of Yamamoto Senji. Volume 2: Sex education), ed. Sasaki Toshiji and Odagiri Akinori, 25–28. Tokyo: Sekibunsha.

————. 1921c. "Shokuji dōyō ni toriatsukahitai 'sei' kyōiku no mondai" (I would like to take up the problem of sex education just like talking about a meal). Reprinted 1979 in *Yamamoto Senji zenshū. Dainikan: Seikyōiku* (Collected works of Yamamoto Senji. Volume 2: Sex education), ed. Sasaki Toshiji and Odagiri Akinori, 19–24. Tokyo: Sekibunsha.

————. 1921d. "Seishun no kiki to junkagakuteki seikyōiku no teishō" (Lecture on the crisis of puberty and purely scientific sex education). Reprinted 1979 in *Yamamoto Senji zenshū. Dainikan: Seikyōiku* (Collected works of Yamamoto Senji. Volume 2: Sex education), ed. Sasaki Toshiji and Odagiri Akinori, 29–58. Tokyo: Sekibunsha.

————. 1921e. "Seikyōiku no mondai" (The problem of sex education). *Hentai Shinri* 8(2):174–175.

————. 1921f. "Jinsei seibutsugaku shoin" (Short introduction to human biology). Reprinted 1979 in *Yamamoto Senji zenshū. Daiikkan: Jinsei seibutsugaku, seikagaku* (Collected works of Yamamoto Senji. Volume 1: Human biology, sexual science), ed. Sasaki Toshiji and Odagiri Akinori, 47–140. Tokyo: Sekibunsha.

————. 1921g. "Seikyōiku" (Sex education). Reprinted 1979 in *Yamamoto Senji zenshū. Dainikan: Seikyōiku* (Collected works of Yamamoto Senji. Volume 2: Sex education), ed. Sasaki Toshiji and Odagiri Akinori, 125–389. Tokyo: Sekibunsha.

————. 1922a. "Seigaku no shimei to sono mokuteki" (Tasks and goals of sexology). Translation of Iwan Bloch, "Aufgaben und Ziele der Sexualwissenschaft" (1914). Reprinted 1979 in *Yamamoto Senji zenshū. Daiikkan: Jinsei seibutsugaku, seikagaku* (Collected works of Yamamoto Senji. Volume 1: Human biology, sexual science), ed. Sasaki Toshiji and Odagiri Akinori, 195–204. Tokyo: Sekibunsha.

————. 1922b. "Sengo Doitsu ni okeru seikenkyū" (Sex research in postwar Germany). Reprinted 1979 in *Yamamoto Senji zenshū. Daiikkan: Jinsei seibutsugaku, seikagaku* (Collected works of Yamamoto Senji. Volume 1: Hu-

man biology, sexual science), ed. Sasaki Toshiji and Odagiri Akinori, 291–
300. Tokyo: Sekibunsha.

———. 1922c. *Sangā joshi kazoku seigenhō hihan* (Critique of Sanger's family
limitation methods). Kyoto: Kyōto ishikai.

———. 1922d. "Seiteki inpeishugi no tame ni okiru heigai no ichirei: Hininhō
inpei no kekka" (One example of the harm caused by the secretive way in
which we deal with sexuality: The results of keeping methods of contraception secret). *Nihon oyobi Nihonjin* 20 September, 840:118–128.

———. 1923. "Nihonjin dangakusei no seiseikatsu no tōkeiteki chōsa" (Statistical survey on the sex life of Japan's male students). Reprinted 1979 in *Yamamoto Senji zenshū. Daiikkan: Jinsei seibutsugaku, seikagaku* (Collected
works of Yamamoto Senji. Volume 1: Human biology, sexual science), ed.
Sasaki Toshiji and Odagiri Akinori, 189–194. Tokyo: Sekibunsha.

———. 1924a. "Onna ni taishite seikyōiku 1" (Sex education for women 1).
Tsūzoku Igaku 2(9):31–33.

———. 1924b. "Onna ni taishite seikyōiku 2" (Sex education for women 2).
Tsūzoku Igaku 2(11):39–41.

———. 1924c. "Wakai otoko no seiseikatsu" (The sex lives of young men).
Reprinted 1979 in *Yamamoto Senji zenshū. Daiikkan: Jinsei seibutsugaku,
seikagaku* (Collected works of Yamamoto Senji. Volume 1: Human biology,
sexual science), ed. Sasaki Toshiji and Odagiri Akinori, 205–289. Tokyo:
Sekibunsha.

———. 1925a. "Kensetsuteki sanji chōsetsu to wa donna mono ka" (What is
constructive birth control?). *Sanji Chōsetsu Hyōron* 1:3–6.

———. 1925b. "Seikyōiku kōwa" (Lecture on sex education). *Sanji Chōsetsu
Hyōron* 1:31–36.

———. 1925c. "Kensetsuteki sanji chōsetsu to wa donna mono ka" (What is
constructive birth control?). *Sanji Chōsetsu Hyōron* 2:12–16.

———. 1925d. "Seikyōiku kōwa" (Lecture on sex education). *Sanji Chōsetsu
Hyōron* 2:34–39.

———. 1925e. "Seikyōiku kōwa" (Lecture on sex education). *Sanji Chōsetsu
Hyōron* 3:56–59.

———. 1925f. "Chōsetsuhō mondō" (Questions and answers on birth control).
Sanji Chōsetsu Hyōron 5:37–40.

———. 1925g. "Seikyōiku kōwa" (Lecture on sex education). *Sanji Chōsetsu
Hyōron* 5:51–57.

———. 1925h. "Chōsetsuhō mondō" (Questions and answers on birth control). *Sanji Chōsetsu Hyōron* 6:37–41.

———. 1925i. "Seikyōiku kōwa" (Lecture on sex education). *Sanji Chōsetsu
Hyōron* 6:50–56.

———. 1925j. "*Sanji Chōsetsu Hyōron* kara *Sei to Shakai* e (From *Birth Control Review* to *Sex and Society*). *Sei to Shakai* 9:2–15.

———. 1925k. "Seikyōiku kōwa" (Lecture on sex education). *Sei to Shakai*
9:54–64.

———. 1925l. "Seikyōiku kōwa" (Lecture on sex education). *Sei to Shakai*
10:60–67.

————. 1925m. "Seikyōiku kōwa" (Lecture on sex education). *Sei to Shakai* 11:62–67.

————. 1925n. "Seikyōiku kōwa" (Lecture on sex education). *Sei to Shakai* 13:52–57.

————. 1925o. "Seikyōiku kōwa" (Lecture on sex education). *Sei to Shakai* 14:83–101.

————. 1925p. "Seiji to seinen" (Politics and youth). Reprinted 1979 in *Yamamoto Senji zenshū. Daisankan: Sanji Chōsetsu Hyōron, Sei to Shakai* (Collected works of Yamamoto Senji. Volume 3: *Birth Control Review, Sex and Society*), ed. Sasaki Toshiji and Odagiri Akinori, 557–567. Tokyo: Sekibunsha.

————. 1926a. "Datai no tetteiteki bokumetsuaku" (Effective methods to eliminate abortion). *Tsūzoku Igaku* 4(6):15–18.

————. 1926b. "Onken na shojomaku no chishiki to ōbō na danshi no motometa dōtei" (Knowledge about the tender hymen and the virginity demanded by brutal men). *Tsūzoku Igaku* 4(9):13–16.

————. 1926c. "Seikyōiku kōwa" (Lecture on sex education). *Sei to Shakai* 14: 83–100.

————. 1926d. "Watakushi koto ni san" (Two or three things about me). *Sei to Shakai* 14:102–111.

————. 1927a. "Ninshin chōsetsu jikkō no shomondō" (Various questions and answers concerning the realization of birth control). *Tsūzoku Igaku* 5(3): 97–99.

————. 1927b. "Ninshin chōsetsu jikkō no shomondō" (Various questions and answers concerning the realization of birth control). *Tsūzoku Igaku* 5(5): 99–101.

————. 1927c. "Sanji seigen wa hitsuyō naru zangyaku no jindōka" (Birth control is the necessary humanization of atrocities). *Tsūzoku Igaku* 5(7): 31–34.

————. 1927d. "Ninshin chōsetsu jikkō no shomondō" (Various questions and answers concerning the realization of birth control). *Tsūzoku Igaku* 5(7): 97–99.

————. 1927e. "Sei to jinsei tōkei" (Sex/sexuality and human statistics). Reprinted 1979 in *Yamamoto Senji zenshū. Daiikkan: Jinsei seibutsugaku, seikagaku* (Collected works of Yamamoto Senji. Volume 1: Human biology, sexual science), ed. Sasaki Toshiji and Odagiri Akinori, 489–511. Tokyo: Sekibunsha.

————. 1928. "Tsūzoku seikyōiku no katei kōza" (Family course in popular sex education). *Tsūzoku Igaku* 6(11):73–76.

Yamamoto Senji, Yasuda Tokutarō, and Katsura Jinzō. 1925. "Gappyō" (Joint review). *Sanji Chōsetsu Hyōron* 7:38–43.

Yamamoto Senji, Aru ichi gakusei, and Yūki Shizuko. 1925. "Gappyō" (Joint review). *Sei to Shakai* 9:83–35.

Yamamoto Sugi. 1954. "Kekkon no kōfuku o sayū suru seiseikatsu" (The sex life that rocks marital happiness). *Fūfu Seikatsu* 15(6):231–233.

Yamasaki Hiromi. 1992. "'Jūgun ianfu 110-ban' kaisetsu no keika" (Report on the establishment of "Comfort women number 110"). In *Jūgun ianfu 110-*

ban: *Denwa no mukō kara rekishi no koe ga* (Former army comfort women number 110: Voices of history over the phone), ed. Jūgun ianfu 110-ban henshū iinkai, 11–16. Tokyo: Akashi shoten.

Yamauchi Kōji. 1998. "Wadai no kusuri ga zokuzoku jōriku" (The much talked about drug is pouring in). *Aera* 7 September, 11(35):14.

Yamauchi Shigeo. 1919. "Sei no kyōiku to shintai no boro" (Sex education and the weaknesses of the body). *Kakusei* 9(9):27–30.

Yasuda Ichirō. 1955. "Nihon ni okeru seikagaku no hattatsu" (The development of sexology in Japan). *Chūō Kōron* 70(12):280–285.

———. 1957. *Nihonjin no seiseikatsu* (The sex life of the Japanese). Tokyo: Kawade shobō.

Yasuda Satsuki. 1915. "Gokuchū no onna yori otoko ni" (From female prisoners to men). *Seitō* 5(6):33–45.

Yasuda Tokutarō. 1925. "Seiseikatsu no gōrika" (The rationalization of the sex life). *Sanji Chōsetsu Hyōron* 3:15–17.

———. 1935. "Dōseiai no rekishikan" (A historical view of homosexuality). *Chūō Kōron* 3, 146–152.

———. 1936. "Seikyōiku shiryōshū" (Collection of material on sex education). *Seikagaku Kenkyū* 1(2):42–63.

Yokoyama Masao. 1920. "Tōkeijō yori mitaru Nihon fujin no bunben nōritsu" (Statistics on the childbirth rate of Japanese women). *Sei* 1(5):50–52.

Yokoyama Tetsuo. 1929. "Seigaku no taika Habuto hakushi shinkei suijaku ni taoru" (The doyen of sexology dies from neurasthenia). *Tsūzoku Igaku* 7(10):1–4.

Yomiuri Shinbun. 1915a. "Musume no shinchō" (The height of girls). *Yomiuri Shinbun* 2 May.

———. 1915b. "606-gō wa yakunaku dekiru" (Number 606 can be translated). *Yomiuri Shinbun* 16 June.

———. 1915c. "Tōkyō no joji wa yowaku naru" (Girls in Tokyo become weaker). *Yomiuri Shinbun* 17 June.

———. 1917. "Chōhei kensa furihazu: Kihi wa sukunaku natta ga taikaku wa mada" (Deflecting the conscription examination: Evasion has decreased but physical condition is still unsatisfactory). *Yomiuri Shinbun* 30 July.

Yomiuri shinbun shakaibu, ed. 1984. *Seikyōiku no genjo* (The current state of sex education). Tokyo: Tairiku shobō.

Yoshida Fumio. 1927. "Minzoku eisei no keihatsu to gendai shakaisō" (Enlightenment about race hygiene and current social classes). *Tsūzoku Igaku* 5(2):8–10.

Yoshida Kumaji. 1908a. "Seiyoku mondai o shitei ni oshifuru no rigai 1" (Advantages and disadvantages of sex education for children 1). *Yomiuri Shinbun* 7 October, 5.

———. 1908b. "Seiyoku mondai o shitei ni oshifuru no rigai 2" (Advantages and disadvantages of sex education for children 2). *Yomiuri Shinbun* 8 October, 5.

———. 1908c. "Seiyoku mondai o shitei ni oshifuru no rigai 3" (Advantages and disadvantages of sex education for children 3). *Yomiuri Shinbun* 11 October, 5.

———. 1916. "Kyōiku aru fujin no teisōkan" (Views of chastity among educated women). *Kakusei* 6(11):8–10.

———. 1923. "Seikyōiku no mondai" (The problem of sex education). *Kakusei* 13(7):7–10.

Yoshida Sumitarō. 1925. "Binbōnin no kodakusan" (The many children of the poor). *Sanji Chōsetsu Hyōron* 2:31–33.

Yoshino Sakuzō. 1927. "Kyōju to seitōin to no ryōritsu furyōritsu" (Balancing professorship and party membership). *Chūō Kōron* 42(3):119–148.

———. 1928. "Shakai jihyō: Daigaku ni tai suru shisō danatsu" (Social critique: The suppression of thought at universities). *Chūō Kōron* 43(6):45–66.

Yubara Motoichi. 1908. "Seiyoku mondai o shitei ni oshiyuru rigai" (Advantages and disadvantages of sex education for children). *Yomiuri Shinbun* 26 September, 5.

Yutani Jirōshichi. 1932. "Seibyō no tōsei" (The control of venereal diseases). *Kakusei* 22(8):5–10.

SOURCES IN OTHER LANGUAGES

Allen, Louis. 1984. *Burma: The longest war, 1941–1945.* London: Dent.

Amaha, Eriko. 1998. "Potent potion: Japanese men will go a long way for Viagra." *Far Eastern Economic Review* 18 June, 56.

Ambaras, David. 1998. "Social knowledge, cultural capital, and the new middle class in Japan, 1895–1912." *Journal of Japanese Studies* 24(1):1–33.

Arai Shoichi. 1953. *The family planning movement in Japan.* Tokyo: Population Problems Research Council and *Mainichi Newspaper,* 19–44.

Arnold, David. 1993. *Colonizing the body: State medicine and epidemic disease in nineteenth-century India.* Berkeley: University of California Press.

Asahi Shinbun. 2001. "Japanese infertility spawns profits for overseas firms." *Asahi Shinbun* 29 June, 25.

Barshay, Andrew E. 1988. *State and the intellectual in imperial Japan: The public man in crisis.* Berkeley: University of California Press.

Barth, D. Carola. 1936. *Taten in Gottes Kraft. Toyohiko Kagawa: Sein Leben für Christus und Japan.* Heilbronn: Eugen Salzer Verlag.

Bartholomew, James R. 1978. "Japanese modernization and the imperial universities, 1876–1920." *Journal of Asian Studies* 37(2):251–271.

———. 1982. "Science, bureaucracy, and freedom in Meiji and Taishō Japan." In *Conflict in modern Japan,* ed. Tetsuo Najita and Victor Koschmann, 295–341. Princeton: Princeton University Press.

———. 1989. *The formation of science in Japan: Building a research tradition.* New Haven: Yale University Press.

———. 1997. "Science in twentieth-century Japan." In *Science in the twentieth century,* ed. John Krige and Dominique Pestre, 879–896. Australia: Harwood Academic Publishers.

Bauman, Zygmunt. 1995. *Ansichten der Postmoderne.* Hamburg: Argument Verlag.

Beard, George M. 1881. *American nervousness: Its causes and consequences.* New York: Putnam.

Beard, Mary R. 1953. *The force of women in Japanese history.* Washington, D.C.: Public Affairs Press.

Beckmann, George M., and Okubo Genji. 1969. *The Japanese communist party.* Stanford, Calif.: Stanford University Press.

Bernstein, Gail Lee. 1976. "Women in rural Japan." In *Women in changing Japan,* ed. Joyce Lebra et al., 25–50. Boulder, Colo.: Westview Press.

Birken, Lawrence. 1988. *Consuming desire: Sexual science and the emergence of a culture of abundance, 1871–1914.* Ithaca, N.Y.: Cornell University Press.

Bloch, Iwan. 1919 (1906). *Das Sexualleben unserer Zeit.* Berlin: Louis Marcus Verlagsbuchhandlung.

Bollinger, Richmod. 1994. *La donna é mobile: Das modan gāru als Erscheinung der modernen Stadtkultur.* Wiesbaden: Harrassowitz.

Bourdieu, Pierre. 1980. *Questions de sociologie.* Paris: Minuit.

Bowers, John Z. 1970. *Western medical pioneers in feudal Japan.* Baltimore: Johns Hopkins University Press.

Braisted, William Reynolds, trans. 1976. *Meiroku zasshi: Journal of the Japanese enlightenment.* Cambridge, Mass.: Harvard University Press.

Brandt, Allan M. 1987. *No magic bullet: A social history of venereal disease in the United States since 1880.* Oxford: Oxford University Press.

Braun, Karl. 1995. *Die Krankheit Onania: Körperangst und die Anfänge moderner Sexualität im 18. Jahrhundert.* Frankfurt am Main: Campus Verlag.

BSOPM [Bureau of Statistics, Office of the Prime Minister], ed. 1957. *Japan statistical yearbook—Nihon tōkei nenkan.* Tokyo: Nihon tōkei kyōkai.

———. 1980. *Japan statistical yearbook—Nihon tōkei nenkan.* Tokyo: Nihon tōkei kyōkai.

Bullough, Vern L. 1994a. *Science in the bedroom: A history of sex research.* New York: Basic Books.

———. 1994b. "The development of sexology in the USA in the early twentieth century." In *Sexual knowledge, sexual science: The history of attitudes to sexuality,* ed. Roy Porter and Mikulás Teich, 303–323. Cambridge: Cambridge University Press.

———. 1997. "American physicians and sex research and expertise, 1900–1990." *Journal of the History of Medicine* 52(2):236–253.

Burns, Susan. 1998. "Bodies and borders: Syphilis, prostitution, and the nation in Japan, 1860–1890." *U.S.–Japan Women's Journal,* English supplement 15:3–30.

Chamberlain, Alexander Francis. 1912. "The Japanese race." *Journal of Race Development* 3:176–187.

Chung, Chin Sung. 1997. "The origin and development of the military sexual slavery problem in imperial Japan." *positions: east asian cultures critique* 5(1):219–253.

Coleman, Samuel. 1981. "The cultural context of condom use in Japan." *Studies in Family Planning* 12(1):28–39.

———. 1983. *Family planning in Japanese society.* Princeton: Princeton University Press.

Conrad, Sebastian. 1999. *Auf der Suche nach der verlorenen Nation: Geschichts-*

schreibung in Westdeutschland und Japan, 1945–1960. Göttingen: Vandenhoeck & Ruprecht.

Cwiertka, Katarzyna. 1999. "The making of a modern culinary tradition in Japan." Ph.D. diss., Leiden University.

Davidson, Arnold I. 1987. "Sex and the emergence of sexuality." *Critical Inquiry* 14(1):16–48.

De Becker, J. E. 1905. *The nightless city or the history of the Yoshiwara Yukwaku*. Yokohama and London: n.p.

———. 1917. "Japan's people have no design on United States: Even if they wish to fight us, the difficulties would be insurmountable, says Briton who knows the Orient." *New York Times Magazine* 20 May, 10.

———. 1921. *The principles and practices of the civil code of Japan: A complete theoretical and practical exposition of the motifs of the Japanese civil code.* London: Butterworth & Co.

Dikötter, Frank. 1995. *Sex, culture and modernity in China: Medical science and the construction of sexual identities in the early Republican period.* London: Hurst & Co.

———, ed. 1997. *The construction of racial identities in China and Japan.* London: Hurst & Co.

Doak, Kevin M. 1997. "What is a nation and who belongs? National narratives and the ethnic imagination in twentieth-century Japan." *American Historical Review* 102(2):283–309.

Dolgopol, Ustinia, and Snehal Paranjape. 1994. *Comfort women: An unfinished ordeal.* Geneva: International Commission of Jurists.

Dower, John W. 1999. *Embracing defeat: Japan in the wake of World War II.* New York: W. W. Norton.

Drea, Edward J. 1998. *In the service of the emperor: Essays on the Imperial Japanese Army.* Lincoln: University of Nebraska Press.

Duus, Peter. 1982. "Liberal intellectuals and social conflict in Taishō Japan." In *Conflict in modern Japanese history,* ed. Tetsuo Najita and Victor Koschmann, 412–440. Princeton: Princeton University Press.

———. 1995. *The abacus and the sword: The Japanese penetration of Korea, 1895–1910.* Berkeley: University of California Press.

Eardley, I. 1998. "New oral therapies for the treatment of erectile dysfunction." *British Journal of Urology* 81:122–127.

Economist. 1997. "Bitter pill." *Economist* 1 November, 70–71.

Ellis, Havelock. 1906 (1905). *Sexual selection in man: Touch, smell, hearing, vision.* Philadelphia: F. A. Davis.

Engelstein, Laura. 1992. *The keys to happiness: Sex and the search for modernity in fin-de-siècle Russia.* Ithaca, N.Y.: Cornell University Press.

Enjoji Muenori. 1942. "Mutter und Kind in Japan." *Mitteilungen der Anthropologischen Gesellschaft in Wien* 72:350–358.

Eugenical News. 1925. "Eugenics in Japanese." *Eugenical News* 10(2):23.

Foucault, Michel. 1977 (1969). "What is an author?" In *Language, countermemory, practice: Selected essays and interviews,* ed. Donald F. Bouchard, 113–138. Ithaca, N.Y.: Cornell University Press.

————. 1990 (1978). *The history of sexuality. Volume 1: An introduction,* trans. Robert Hurley. New York: Vintage Books.

Freud, Sigmund. 1962 (1905). *Three essays on the theory of sexuality,* trans. and ed. James Strachey. New York: Basic Books.

Frühstück, Sabine. 1997. *Die Politik der Sexualwissenschaft: Zur Produktion und Popularisierung sexologischen Wissens in Japan 1908–1941.* Vienna: Institut für Japanologie.

————. 1998a. "The taming of sex: On the history of empirical sex research in Japan." Paper presented at the International Convention of Asian Scholars, Noordwijkershout, the Netherlands, 24–28 June.

————. 1998b. "Then science took over: Sex leisure and medicine at the beginning of the twentieth century." In *The culture of Japan as seen through its leisure,* ed. Sepp Linhart and Sabine Frühstück, 59–79. Albany: SUNY Press.

————. 1999. "Immer noch auf dem Weg zur Chancengleichheit? Zur Situation der Frau in Japan." *Zeitschrift für angewandte Sozialforschung* 21(1–2): 23–44.

————. 2000. "Managing the truth of sex in imperial Japan." *Journal of Asian Studies* 59(2):332–358.

————. 2002. "Rhetorics of reform: On the institutionalization and de-institutionalization of old age." In *Aging and social policy: A German-Japanese comparison,* ed. Ralph Lützeler and Harald Conrad, 299–351. Munich: Iudicium.

————. Forthcoming. "Die Macht des Wissens: Weibliche Sexualität und Gesundheit im modernen Japan." In *Körperlichkeit und Sexualität in Japan,* ed. Michiko Mae. Berlin: LIT-Verlag.

Fujikawa Yū. 1911. *Geschichte der Medizin in Japan: Kurzgefaßte Darstellung der Entwicklung der japanischen Medizin mit besonderer Berücksichtigung der Einführung der europäischen Heilkunde in Japan.* Tokyo: Kaiserlich japanisches Unterrichtsministerium.

Fujime Yuki. 1997. "Licensed prostitution system and the Prostitution Abolition Movement in modern Japan," trans. Kerry Ross. *positions: east asian cultures critique* 5(1):139–170.

————. 1999. "One midwife's life: Shibahara Urako, birth control, and early Shōwa reproductive activism." In *Gender and Japanese history 1: Religion and customs, the body and sexuality,* ed. Wakita Haruko, Anne Bouchy, and Ueno Chizuko, 297–326. Osaka: Osaka University Press.

Fujisawa Rennosuke. 1912. "Die deutsche Sprache in Japan." *Asien: Organ der deutsch-asiatischen Gesellschaft* 12(2):18–19.

Furukawa Makoto. 1994. "The changing nature of sexuality: The three codes framing homosexuality in modern Japan." *U.S.–Japan Women's Journal,* English supplement 7:98–127.

Fuwa Takeo. 1933. "Die Todesstrafe in Japan." *Monatsschrift für Kriminalpsychologie und Strafrechtsreform* 24:271–286.

Gallagher, Catherine, and Thomas Laqueur. 1987. "Introduction." In *The making of the modern body: Sexuality and society in the nineteenth century,* ed.

Catherine Gallagher and Thomas Laqueur, vii–xv. Berkeley: University of California Press.

Garon, Sheldon M. 1986. "State and religion in imperial Japan, 1912–1945." *Journal of Japanese Studies* 12(2):273–302.

———. 1993a. "Women's groups and the Japanese state: Contending approaches to political integration, 1890–1945." *Journal of Japanese Studies* 19(1):5–41.

———. 1993b. "The world's oldest debate? Prostitution and the state in imperial Japan, 1900–1945." *American Historical Review* 3:710–732.

———. 1994. "Rethinking modernization and modernity in Japanese history: A focus on state-society relations." *Journal of Asian Studies* 53(2):346–366.

———. 1997. *Molding Japanese minds: The state in everyday life.* Princeton: Princeton University Press.

Gevitz, Norman. 1992. "'But all these authors are foreigners': American literary nationalism and domestic medical guides." In *The popularization of medicine, 1650–1850,* ed. Roy Porter, 232–251. London: Routledge.

Gluck, Carol. 1985. *Japan's modern myths: Ideology in the late Meiji period.* Princeton: Princeton University Press.

Gordon, Linda. 1983. "The politics of birth control, 1920–1940: The impact of professionals." In *Women and health: The politics of sex in medicine,* ed. Elisabeth Fee, 151–175. New York: Baywood Publishing Company.

Hacking, Ian. 1999 (1986). "Making up people." In *The science studies reader,* ed. Mario Biagioli, 161–171. New York: Routledge.

Haeberle, Erwin J. 1992. "Die Entwicklung der Sexualwissenschaft in Stichworten." In *Sexualwissenschaft heute: Ein erster Überblick,* ed. Erwin J. Haeberle and Rolf Gindorf, 7–18. Düsseldorf: Deutsche Gesellschaft für sozialwissenschaftliche Sexualforschung.

Hane, Mikiso, trans. and ed. 1988. *Reflections on the way to the gallows: Rebel women in prewar Japan.* Berkeley: University of California Press.

Hara Junsuke. 1996. "Sexual consciousness and activities of Japanese youth: Defiance, settling down and the familialization of sexual matters." In *Sexuality and human bonding: Proceedings of the XII world congress of sexology,* ed. Matsumoto Seiichi, 77–80. Amsterdam: Elsevier.

Hardacre, Helen. 1997. *Marketing the menacing fetus in Japan.* Berkeley: University of California Press.

Harootunian, Harry D. 1974. "Introduction: A sense of ending and the problems of Taishō." In *Japan in crisis: Essays in Taishō democracy,* ed. Bernard S. Silberman and Harry D. Harootunian, 3–28. Princeton: Princeton University Press.

Hartmann, Grethe. 1946. *The girls they left behind: An investigation into the various aspects of the German troops' sexual relations with Danish subjects.* Copenhagen: Ejnar Munksgaard.

Hauser, Renate. 1994. "Krafft-Ebing's psychological understanding of sexual behaviour." In *Sexual knowledge, sexual science: The history of attitudes to sexuality,* ed. Roy Porter and Mikulás Teich, 210–230. Cambridge: Cambridge University Press.

Henderson, Charles W. 1998. "Japanese tourists head overseas to get Viagra." *Impotence & Male Health Weekly Plus* 22 June, 10.

————. 1999a. "Japan seen poised to allow Viagra sales next year." *Impotence & Male Health Weekly Plus* 11 January.

————. 1999b. "Viagra speeds contraceptive pill OK in Japan." *Impotence & Male Health Weekly Plus* 15 March.

Herzog, Peter J. 1993. *Japan's pseudo-democracy*. Sandgate: Japan Library.

Hicks, George. 1995. *The comfort women: Sex slaves of the Japanese imperial forces*. London: Souvenir Press.

Hijiya-Kirschnereit, Irmela. 1981. *Selbstentblößungsrituale: Zur Theorie und Geschichte der autobiographischen Gattung "Shishōsetsu" in der modernen japanischen Literatur*. Stuttgart: Franz Steiner Verlag.

Hilgartner, Stephen. 1990. "The dominant view of popularization: Conceptional problems, political uses." *Social Studies of Science* 20:519–539.

Hirakawa Sukehiro. 1989. "Japan's turn to the West." In *The Cambridge history of Japan*, volume 5, ed. Marius B. Jansen, 435–498. Cambridge: Cambridge University Press.

Hirschfeld, Magnus. 1926. *Geschlechtskunde auf Grund dreißigjähriger Forschung und Erfahrung 1*. Stuttgart: Julius Püttmann Verlagsbuchhandlung.

————. 1935 (1933). *Men and women: The world journey of a sexologist*, trans. O. P. Green. New York: G. P. Putnam's Sons.

Hollander, Dore. 1999. "The pill comes to Japan!" *Family Planning Perspectives* 31(4):159.

Hoston, Germaine A. 1992. "The state, modernity and the fate of liberalism in prewar Japan." *Journal of Asian Studies* 51(2):287–307.

Huffman, James L. 1984. "Freedom and the press in Meiji–Taishō Japan." *The Transactions of the Asiatic Society* 19:137–171.

Hunter, Janet E. 1984. *Concise dictionary of modern Japanese history*. Berkeley: University of California Press.

Huston, Perdita. 1992. *Motherhood by choice: Pioneers in women's health and family planning*. New York: Feminist Press.

Hygiene. 1911. *Hygiene: Offizielle Monatsschrift der internationalen Hygiene-Ausstellung Dresden 1911*. Dresden: Verlag der Internationalen Hygiene-Ausstellung Dresden.

Idditti, Smimasa. 1940. *The life of Marquis Shigenobu Okuma: A maker of new Japan*. Tokyo: Hokuseido Press.

Imada Sachiko. 1997. "Work and family life." *Japan Labor Bulletin* 36(8):4–8.

Ishii-Kuntz, Masako. 1994. "Paternal involvement and perception toward fathers' roles: A comparison between Japan and the United States." *Journal of Family Issues* 15(1):30–48.

Ishimoto Shidzue. 1935. *Facing two ways: The story of my life*. New York: Farrar and Rinehart.

Jannetta, Ann Bowman. 1987. *Epidemics and mortality in early modern Japan*. Princeton: Princeton University Press.

————. 1997. "From physician to bureaucrat: The case of Nagayo Sensai."

In *New directions in the study of Meiji Japan,* ed. Helen Hadacre, 151–160. Leiden: Brill.

Japan Times and Mail, ed. 1937. "Tomoda Goshi Kaisha, Ltd. Pioneer importers of medical supplies now engaged in exportation of pharmaceutical products to all parts of Asia." In *Japan in 1937,* ed. *Japan Times and Mail,* 136. Tokyo: *Japan Times and Mail.*

———. 1938. "Social welfare works: Creation of new ministry this year marks important step in Japan's benevolent enterprises." In *Japan in 1938,* ed. *Japan Times and Mail,* 153–159. Tokyo: *Japan Times and Mail.*

Johnson, Malia S. 1987. "Margaret Sanger and the birth control movement in Japan, 1921–1955." Ph.D. diss., University of Hawaii.

Johnston, William Donald. 1995. *The modern epidemic: A history of tuberculosis in Japan.* Cambridge, Mass.: Council of East Asian Studies, Harvard University.

Kasza, Gregory J. 1988. *The state and the mass media, 1918–1945.* Berkeley: University of California Press.

Katalog. 1911. *Katalog der von der kaiserlich japanischen Regierung ausgestellten Gegenstände.* Berlin: Rudolf Mosse.

Kato Toshinobu. 1978. "The development of family planning in Japan with industrial involvement." In *Population studies transition series,* volume 2, ed. ESCAP Population Division, 3–34. New York: United Nations.

Kawahara Yukari. 1996. "Politics, pedagogy, and sexuality: Sex education in Japanese secondary schools." Ph.D. diss., Yale University.

Kawamura Nozomu. 1990. "Sociology and socialism in the interwar period." In *Culture and identity: Japanese intellectuals during the interwar years,* ed. J. Thomas Rimer, 61–82. Princeton: Princeton University Press.

Kevles, Daniel J. 1985. *In the name of eugenics.* Berkeley: University of California Press.

Kim, Il-myŏn. 1989. "Die Wahrheit über japanische Armeebordelle." *Kagami* 3:5–58.

Kitamura Kunio. 1999. "The pill in Japan: Will approval ever come?" *Family Planning Perspectives* 31(1):44.

Kosaka Masaaki. 1958. *Japanese thought in the Meiji era,* trans. David Abosch. Tokyo: Pan-Pacific Press.

Koya Yoshio. 1957. "Family planning among Japanese on public relief." *Eugenics Quarterly* 4(1):17–23.

———. 1961. "Sterilization in Japan." *Eugenics Quarterly* 8(3):135–141.

Koya Y. and Takabatake T. 1939. "Beitrag zur Untersuchung des konstitutionellen Befindens der Schulkinder Japans." *Minzoku Eiseigaku Kenkyū—Rassenbiologische Untersuchungen* 7:123–137.

Kühl, Stefan. 1994. *The Nazi connection: Eugenics, American racism, and German national socialism.* Oxford: Oxford University Press.

Laqueur, Thomas W. 2003. *Solitary sex: A cultural history of masturbation.* New York: ZONE Books.

Latour, Bruno. 1987. *Science in action.* Cambridge, Mass.: Harvard University Press.

Leavy, Walther. 1998. "Brothers (and sisters) and the new sex pill." *Ebony* 53(9):154–156.

Lebzelter, Victor. 1926. "Konstitution und Rasse." In *Die Biologie der Person: Ein Handbuch der allgemeinen und speziellen Konstitutionslehre 1*, ed. Th. Brugsch and F. H. Lewy, 749–858. Berlin: Urban & Schwarzenberg.

Lefebvre, Henri. 1995 (1962). *Introduction to modernity*, trans. John Moore. New York: Verso.

Leuschner, Oskar. 1906. "Japan." In *Enzyklopädisches Handbuch für Erziehungskunde*, ed. Joseph Loos, 790–793. Vienna: A. Pichler, Pichlers Witwe & Sohn.

Limoges, Camille. 1993. "Expert knowledge and decision-making in controversy contexts." *Public Understanding of Science* 2:417–426.

Linhart, Sepp. 1974. "Das Entstehen eines modernen Lebensstils in Japan während der Taishō Periode (1912–1926)." *Saeculum* 25(1):115–127.

Lone, Stewart. 1994. *Japan's first modern war: Army and society in the conflict with China, 1894–95*. London: St. Martin's Press.

Low, Morris Fraser. 1989. "The butterfly and the frigate: Social studies of science in Japan." *Social Studies of Science* 19:313–342.

Mahaffy, George C. 1916. "Sexual neurasthenia." *Journal of the Kansas Medical Society* 16:323–326.

Marshall, Byron K. 1992. *Academic freedom and the Japanese imperial university, 1868–1939*. Berkeley: University of California Press.

Martin, Emily. 1999 (1990). "Toward an anthropology of immunology: The body as nation-state." In *The science studies reader*, ed. Mario Biagioli, 358–371. New York: Routledge.

Marui Eiji. 1980. "Public health and 'koshu-eisei': Speciality and universality of the modern Japanese public health." In *Public health: Proceedings of the fifth international symposium on comparative history of medicine—east and west*, ed. Ogawa Teizō, 99–107. Osaka: Taniguchi Foundation.

Maruyama Hiromi, James H. Raphael, and Carl Djerassi. 1996. "Why Japan ought to legalize the pill." *Nature* 379:579–580.

Mathias, Regine. 1995. "Vom 'Fräulein vom Amt' zur 'Office Lady'—weibliche Angestellte im Japan der Vorkriegszeit." In *Japanische Frauengeschichte(n)*, ed. Erich Pauer and Regine Mathias, 47–69. Marburg: Förderverein Marburger Japan-Reihe.

Matsubara Yōko. 1998. "The enactment of Japan's sterilization laws in the 1940s: A prelude to postwar eugenic policy." *Historia Scientiarum* 8(2):187–201.

Matsumura Noriaki, Hirono Yoshiyuki, and Matsubara Yōko. 1998. "Fujikawa Yū, pioneer of the history of medicine in Japan." *Historia Scientiarum* 8(2):157–171.

Mihalopoulos, Bill. 1993. "The making of prostitutes: The *karayuki-san*." *Bulletin of Concerned Asian Scholars* 25(1):41–56.

Mitchell, Richard H. 1973. "Japan's Peace Preservation Law of 1925: Its origins and significance." *Monumenta Nipponica* 28:317–345.

Mori Rintarō [Mori Ōgai]. 1885. *Die Organisation des japanischen Sanitätscorps einst und jetzt.* Reprinted 1989 in *Ōgai zenshū dai nijūhachikan* (Ōgai's collected works, volume 28), ed. Midorikawa Takashi, 3–15. Tokyo: Iwanami shoten.

———. 1886. *Japanische Soldatenkost vom Voit'schen Standpuncte.* Reprinted 1989 in *Ōgai zenshū dai nijūhachikan,* ed. Midorikawa Takashi, 16–33. Tokyo: Iwanami shoten.

———. 1886–1891. *Aus "Jahresbericht über die Leistungen und Fortschritte auf dem Gebiete des Militär-Sanitätswesens."* Reprinted 1989 in *Ōgai zenshū dai nijūhachikan,* ed. Midorikawa Takashi, 141–160. Tokyo: Iwanami shoten.

———. 1888. *Ethnographisch-hygienische Studie über Wohnhäuser in Japan.* Reprinted 1989 in *Ōgai zenshū dai nijūhachikan,* ed. Midorikawa Takashi, 103–122. Tokyo: Iwanami shoten.

———. 1891. *Zwei Jahre in Korea.* Reprinted 1989 in *Ōgai zenshū dai nijūhachikan,* ed. Midorikawa Takashi, 161–213. Tokyo: Iwanami shoten.

———. 1911. *Japan und seine Gesundheitspflege.* Tokyo: Rikugunsho, Imukyoku.

Morris-Suzuki, Tessa. 1998. "Debating racial science in wartime Japan." In *Beyond Joseph Needham: Science, technology, and medicine in East and Southeast Asia,* ed. Morris F. Low, 354–375. Chicago: University of Chicago Press.

Morus [Richard Lewinsohn]. 1956. *Eine Weltgeschichte der Sexualität.* Hamburg: Rowohlt Verlag.

Mosse, George L. 1996. *The image of man: The creation of modern masculinity.* Oxford: Oxford University Press.

Muramatsu Minoru. 1955. *Some facts about family planning in Japan.* Tokyo: *Mainichi Newspaper.*

———. 1960. "Family planning practice among the Japanese." *Eugenics Quarterly* 7(1):23–30.

Muzik, Michael. 1996. *Presse und Journalismus in Japan.* Yomiuri shinbun: *Die auflagenstärkste Zeitung der Welt.* Vienna: Böhlau Verlag.

Nagai Sen [Nagai Hisomu]. 1928a. "Die Körperkonstitution des Japaners." In *Die Biologie der Person: Ein Handbuch der allgemeinen und speziellen Konstitutionslehre 2,* ed. Th. Brugsch and F. H. Lewy, 425–509. Berlin: Urban & Schwarzenberg.

———. 1928b. "Individuum und Individualität in Japan." In *Die Biologie der Person: Ein Handbuch der allgemeinen und speziellen Konstitutionslehre 4,* ed. Th. Brugsch and F. H. Lewy, 773–798. Berlin: Urban & Schwarzenberg.

Najita, Tetsuo. 1983. "Introduction: A synchronous approach to the study of conflict in modern Japanese history." In *Conflict of modern Japanese history,* ed. Tetsuo Najita and Victor Koschmann. Princeton: Princeton University Press.

Nakatani Yoji. 1995. "Relationship of mental health legislation to the perception of insanity at the turn of the 20th century in Japan." Unpublished manuscript in author's possession.

Narita Ryūichi. 1995. "Women and views of women within the changing hygiene conditions of late ninteenth– and early twentieth–century Japan." *U.S.–Japan Women's Journal*, English supplement 8:64–86.

———. 1999. "Mobilized from within: Women and hygiene in modern Japan." In *Women and class in Japanese history*, ed. Hitomi Tonomura, Anne Walthall, and Wakita Haruko, 257–273. Ann Arbor: Center for Japanese Studies, University of Michigan.

Neubert, R. 1911. *Geissel des Lebens: Führer durch die Aufklärungsschau "Geschlechtskrankheiten."* Dresden: Verlag der Hygiene-Ausstellung Dresden 1911.

Neuman, R. P. 1974. "The sexual question and social democracy in imperial Germany." *Journal of Social History* 7(3):271–286.

———. 1975. "Masturbation, madness and the modern concepts of childhood and adolescence." *Journal of Social History* 8(3):1–27.

Newsweek. 1999. "Sensitive news." *Newsweek* 17 May, 133(20):6.

Nomura Masaichi. 1990. "Remodelling the Japanese body." *Senri Ethnological Studies* 27:259–276.

Norgren, Tiana. 1998. "Abortion before birth control: The interest group politics behind postwar Japanese reproduction policy." *Journal of Japanese Studies* 24(1):59–94.

———. 2001. *Abortion before birth control: The politics of reproduction in postwar Japan*. Princeton: Princeton University Press.

Nye, Robert A. 1991. "The history of sexuality in context: National sexological traditions." *Science in Context* 4(2):387–406.

Ochiai Emiko. 1999a. "The reproductive revolution at the end of the Tokugawa period." In *Women and class in Japanese history*, ed. Hitomi Tonomura, Anne Walthall, and Wakita Haruko, 187–215. Ann Arbor: Center for Japanese Studies, University of Michigan.

———. 1999b. "Modern Japan through the eyes of an old midwife: From an oral life history to social history." In *Gender and Japanese history 1: Religion and customs, the body and sexuality*, ed. Wakita Haruko, Anne Bouchy, and Ueno Chizuko, 235–295. Osaka: Osaka University Press.

Ogawa Naohiro and Robert D. Retherford. 1991. "Prospects of increased contraceptive pill use in Japan." *Studies in Family Planning* 22(6):378–383.

Ogino Kyūsaku. 1930. "Ovulationstermin und Konzeptionstermin." *Zentralblatt der Gynäkologie* 54(8):464–478.

Ortega y Gasset, José. 1985 (1929). *The revolt of the masses*, trans. Anthony Kerrigan, ed. Kenneth More, foreword by Saul Bellow. Notre Dame, Ind.: University of Notre Dame Press.

Osterhammel, Jürgen. 1999 (1995). *Colonialism: A theoretical overview*, trans. Shelley Frisch. Princeton: Markus Wiener Publishers.

Ōsugi Sakae. 1992 (1930). *The autobiography of Osugi Sakae*, trans. Byron Marshall. Berkeley: University of California Press.

Ōta Tenrei [Ōta Fumio]. 1934. "A study on the birth control with an intrauterine instrument." *Japanese Journal of Obstetrics and Gynecology* 17(3): 210–214.

Otsubo, Sumiko. 1999. "Feminist maternal eugenics in wartime Japan." *U.S.–Japan Women's Journal*, English supplement 17:39–76.

Otsubo, Sumiko, and James R. Bartholomew. 1998. "Eugenics in Japan: Some ironies of modernity, 1883–1945." *Science in Context* 11(3–4):545–565.

Oxford, Wayne H. 1973. *The speeches of Fukuzawa: A translation and critical study*. Tokyo: Hokuseido Press.

Paul, Christa. 1994. *Zwangsprostitution: Staatlich errichtete Bordelle im Nationalsozialismus*. Berlin: Edition Hentrich.

Pflugfelder, Gregory M. 1999. *Cartographies of desire: Male-male sexuality in Japanese discourse, 1600–1950*. Berkeley: University of California Press.

Porter, Roy. 1994. "Introduction." In *Sexual knowledge, sexual science: The history of attitudes to sexuality*, ed. Roy Porter and Mikulás Teich, 1–26. Cambridge: Cambridge University Press.

Porter, Roy, and Lesley Hall, ed. 1995. *The facts of life: The creation of sexual knowledge in Britain, 1650–1950*. New Haven: Yale University Press.

Porter, Theodore M. 1986. *The rise of statistical thinking, 1820–1900*. Princeton: Princeton University Press.

Present Day Japan. 1926. "Radio in Japan." *Present Day Japan* 2:45.

———. 1934. "Radio broadcasting in Japan. Stations, listeners-in, equipment, programs and hours." *Present Day Japan* 10:111–112.

Rabinbach, Anson. 1990. *The human motor: Energy, fatigue, and the origins of modernity*. Berkeley: University of California Press.

Reich, Wilhelm. 1974 (1936). *The sexual revolution: Toward a self-regulating character structure*, trans. Therese Pol. New York: Farrar, Straus and Giroux.

Ribbing, Seved. 1921 (1911). "Sexuelle Aufklärung, Pädagogik und Erziehung." In *Handbuch der Sexualwissenschaften mit besonderer Berücksichtigung der kulturgeschichtlichen Beziehungen*, ed. Albert Moll, 969–997. Leipzig: Verlag von F. C. W. Vogel.

Robertson, Jennifer. 1989. "Gender-bending in paradise: Doing 'female' and 'male' in Japan." *Genders* 5:188–207.

———. 1992. "The politics of androgyny in Japan: Sexuality and subversion in the theater and beyond." *American Ethnologist* 19(3):419–442.

———. 1998. *Takarazuka: Sexual politics and popular culture in modern Japan*. Berkeley: University of California Press.

———. 1999. "Dying to tell: Sexuality and suicide in imperial Japan." *Signs: Journal of Women in Culture and Society* 25(1):1–35.

———. 2001. "Japan's first cyborg? Miss Nippon, eugenics, and wartime technologies of beauty, body, and blood." *body & society* 7(1):1–34.

———. 2002. "Blood talks: Eugenic modernity and the creation of new Japanese." *History and Anthropology* 13(3):1–26.

Rodd, Laurel Rasplica. 1991. "Yosano Akiko and the Taishō debate over the 'new woman.'" In *Recreating Japanese women, 1600–1945*, ed. Gail Lee Bernstein, 175–198. Berkeley: University of California Press.

Roden, Donald. 1980. *Schooldays in imperial Japan: A study in the culture of a student elite*. Berkeley: University of California Press.

———. 1990. "Taishō culture and the problem of gender ambivalence." In

Culture and identity: Japanese intellectuals during the interwar years, ed. J. Thomas Rimer, 37–55. Princeton: Princeton University Press.

Rousseau, Julie M. 1998. "Enduring labors: The 'new midwife' and the modern culture of childbearing in early twentieth century Japan." Ph.D. diss., Columbia University.

Rubin, Gayle. 1975. "The traffic in women: Notes on the 'political economy' of sex." In *Toward an anthropology of women,* ed. Rayna Reiter, 157–210. New York: Monthly Review Press.

Rubin, Jay. 1984. *Injurious to public morals: Writers and the Meiji state.* Seattle: University of Washington Press.

Russett, Cynthia Eagle. 1989. *Sexual science.* Cambridge, Mass.: Harvard University Press.

Sanger, Margaret. 1929. "The civilizing force of birth control." In *Sex in civilization,* ed. V. F. Calverton and S. D. Schmalhausen, 525–537. New York: Macaulay Company.

SBHD [Sanitary Bureau of the Home Department]. 1929. *The annual report of the Sanitary Bureau of the Home Department of the Imperial Japanese Government for the 2nd year of Showa (1927).* Tokyo: Sanitary Bureau of the Home Department.

Scalapino, Robert A. 1967. *The Japanese communist movement, 1920–1966.* Berkeley: University of California Press.

Schell, Karl-Heinz. 1994. *Kagawa Toyohiko (1888–1960): Sein soziales und politisches Wirken.* München: Iudicium Verlag.

Schellstede, Sangmie Choi. 2000. *Comfort women speak: Testimony by sex slaves of the Japanese military.* New York: Holmes & Meier.

Schildgen, Robert. 1988. *Toyohiko Kagawa: Apostle of love and social justice.* Berkeley: Centenary Books.

Sebald, William J., trans. 1936. *The criminal code of Japan.* Kobe: Japan Chronicle Press.

Shapiro, Hugh. 1999. "The puzzle of spermatorrhea in republican China." *positions: east asian cultures critique* 6(3):551–596.

Sheets-Pyenson, Susan. 1985. "Popular science periodicals in Paris and London: The emergence of a low scientific culture, 1820–1875." *Annals of Science* 42:549–572.

Shimao Eikoh. 1981. "Darwinism in Japan." *Annals of Science* 38:93–102.

Shimomura Hiroshi. 1934. "The population of Japan." *Present-Day Nippon: Annual English Supplement to the Asahi Osaka and Tokyo,* 10:58.

Shinohara Miyohei, ed. 1967. *Personal consumption expenditures: Estimates of long-term economic statistics of Japan since 1868.* Tokyo: Toyo keizai shinposha.

Shinozaki Nobuo. 1978. "Basic guidelines for propagating family planning in business organizations." In *Population studies transition series,* volume 2, ed. ESCAP Population Division, 35–42. New York: United Nations.

Sievers, Sharon L. 1983. *Flowers in salt.* Stanford, Calif.: Stanford University Press.

Silverberg, Miriam. 1991. "The modern girl as militant." In *Recreating Japanese women, 1600–1945,* ed. Gail Lee Bernstein, 239–266. Berkeley: University of California Press.

———. 1992. "Constructing the Japanese ethnography of modernity." *Journal of Asian Studies* 51(1):30–54.

———. 1993. "Constructing a new cultural history of prewar Japan. In *Japan in the world,* ed. Masao Miyoshi and H. D. Harootunian, 115–143. Durham, N.C.: Duke University Press.

———. 1995. "Advertising every body: Images from the Japanese modern years." In *Choreographing history,* ed. Susan Leigh Foster, 129–148. Bloomington: Indiana University Press.

———. 1998. "The cafe waitress serving modern Japan." In *Mirror of modernity: Invented traditions of modern Japan,* ed. Stephen Vlastos. Berkeley: University of California Press.

Smith, Robert J., and Ella Lury Wiswell. 1982. *The women of Suyemura.* Chicago: University of Chicago Press.

Sone Hiromi. 1999. "Prostitution and public authority in early modern Japan." In *Women and class in Japanese history,* ed. Hitomi Tonomura, Anne Walthall, and Wakita Haruko, 169–185. Ann Arbor: Center for Japanese Studies, University of Michigan.

Soviak, Eugene. 1990. "Tsuchida Kyōson and the sociology of the masses." In *Culture and identity: Japanese intellectuals in the interwar years,* ed. J. Thomas Rimer, 83–98. Princeton: Princeton University Press.

Stead, Alfred. 1905. *Great Japan: A study of national efficiency.* London: John Lane.

Steger, Brigitte. 1994. "From impurity to hygiene: The role of midwives in the modernization of Japan." *Japan Forum* 6(2):175–187.

Stoler, Ann Laura. 1999 (1995). *Race and the education of desire: Foucault's History of sexuality and the colonial order of things.* Durham, N.C.: Duke University Press.

Tama Yasuko. 1994. "The logic of abortion: Japanese debates on the legitimacy of abortion as seen in post–World War II newspapers." *U.S.–Japan Women's Journal,* English supplement 7:3–30.

Tamanoi, Mariko Asano. 1998. *Under the shadow of nationalism.* Honolulu: University of Hawai'i Press.

Tanaka, Stefan. 1993. *Japan's orient: Rendering pasts into history.* Berkeley: University of California Press.

Tashiro Hiroko and Donald Macintyre. 1998. "Bring it to Japan, fast." *Time International* 15 June, 150(42):53.

Taylor, E. C. 1920. "Types of neurological and psychiatric cases common in the Navy." *United States Naval Medical Bulletin* 14(2):191–201.

Tiefer, Leonore. 1994. "The medicalization of impotence: Normalizing phallocentrism." *Gender & Society* 8(3):363–377.

Tipton, Elise K. 1997. "Ishimoto Shizue: The Margaret Sanger of Japan." *Women's History Review* 6(3):337–355.

Treat, John Whittier. 1994. "AIDS panic in Japan, or how to have a sabbatical in an epidemic." *positions: east asian cultures critique* 2(3):629–679.

Tsunoda, Ryusaku, W. Theodore de Bary, and Donald Keene, eds. 1964. *Sources of Japanese tradition*, volume 2. New York: Columbia University Press.

Uno, Kathleen S. 1991. "Japan." In *Children in historical and comparative perspective: An international handbook and research guide*, ed. Joseph M. Hawes and N. Ray Hiner, 389–419. New York: Greenwood Press.

———. 1999. *Passages to modernity: Motherhood, childhood, and social reform in early twentieth century Japan*. Honolulu: University of Hawai'i Press.

Watanabe Kazuko. 1994. "Militarism, colonialism, and the trafficking of women: 'Comfort women' forced into sexual labor for Japanese soldiers." *Bulletin for Concerned Asian Scholars* 26(4):3–17.

Watts, Jonathan. 1999. "When impotence leads contraception." *Lancet* 6 March, 353:819.

Wawerzonnek, Markus. 1984. *Implizite Sexualpädagogik in der Sexualwissenschaft 1886 bis 1939*. Cologne: Pahl Rugenstein Verlag.

Wettley, Annemarie, and W. Leibbrand. 1959. *Von der "Psychopathia sexualis" zur Sexualwissenschaft*. Stuttgart: Ferdinand Enke Verlag.

Widmer, Eric D., Judith Treas, and Robert Newcomb. 1998. "Attitudes toward nonmarital sex in 24 countries." *Journal of Sex Research* 35(4):349–358.

Witte, J. 1918. "Die Bedeutung der deutschen Geisteskultur für die ostasiatischen Völker und die deutschen Interessen." *Asien: Organ der deutsch-asiatischen Gesellschaft* 15(4):67–68.

Yamamoto Senji. 1921. "Milieu and background intellectual of my own." Reprinted 1979 in *Yamamoto Senji zenshū. Daiikkan: Jinsei seibutsugaku, seikagaku* (Collected works of Yamamoto Senji. Volume 1: Human biology, sexual science), ed. Sasaki Toshiji and Odagiri Akinori, 513–516. Tokyo: Sekibunsha.

Yamazaki Tomoko. 1999 (1972). *Sandakan brothel no. 8: An episode in the history of lower-class Japanese women*, trans. Karen Colligan-Taylor. New York: M. E. Sharpe.

Index

Abe Isoo, 13, 96, 97, 103–104, 109, 129–130; birth control movement and, 133, 134, 140, 150; censorship and, 159; eugenics and, 147–148

abortion: approval of contraceptive pill and, 190, 213n24; birth control movement and, 142–144, 150–151; feminist views on, 123; frequency of, in 1990s, 190; late marriage and, 149; postwar legislation and, 177; regulation of, 120–122, 127–128

abstinence, as means of birth control, 145

adolescents, sexual behavior of, 193–197

advertising: birth control and, 116–118, *117*, *145*, *146*; hormone products and, 169–172; in sexological journals, 109–115

advice columns, 111, 208n25, 209n7

AIDS prevention, 188, 190, 192, 216n12

Akimoto Seiji, 104, 145

Akiyama Yoshio, *101*, 103–104, 158

Allen, Louis, 201n19

Andō Kakuichi, 179

Androstin (Andorosuchin; hormone product), 170, *173*

Anzai Sadako, 17, 35–36, 38

Army Hygiene Council, 34–35

army medical inspector general *(rikugun gun'isōkan)*, 21–22, 28

Asayama Shin'ichi, 181–183, 205n4, 213n29

Association for Statistics (Tōkei Kyōkai), 21

Bartholomew, James, 9, 212n8

Beard, George M., 81

"biochemical race index," 22

birth control: advertising and, 116–118, *117*, *145*, *146*; approval of oral contraceptives and, 188–193; counseling centers and, 137–140; eugenics and, 134, 138, 140, 147–148; feminist views on, 123–128; leftist vs. bourgeois differences on, 134–136; legislation against, 118, 163; options for, 123, 125, 130, 131, 137, 142, 144–147; petitions for legalization of, 120, 150–151; shaping of movement for, 118–120, 130–144; *See also* abortion; condom use; eugenics; sterilization

Birth Control Review (Sanji Chōsetsu Hyōron) (journal), 83–85, 111, 140

birth rate: contraceptive pill approval and, 188, 191; negative growth of, as concern, 188, 191; population growth in 1930s and, 118–120, 123, 124, 209n2; as problem for women, 104, 122–128

Bismarck, Otto von, 22

Bloch, Iwan, 84, 93–94, 105, 106, 207n12

259

Compositor:	G&S Typesetters, Inc.
Text and display:	Sabon
Printer and binder:	Thomson-Shore